To

_____

From

_____

Date

_____

Spirit-Lifting Devotions for Grandmothers

ISBN-10: 0-8249-4506-9
ISBN-13: 978-0-8249-4506-0

Published by Guideposts
16 East 34th Street
New York, New York 10016
Guideposts.org

Distributed by Ideals Publications, a Guideposts company
2636 Elm Hill Pike, Suite 120
Nashville, TN 37214

Guideposts and *Ideals* are registered trademarks of Guideposts.

Acknowledgments
Every attempt has been made to credit the sources of copyrighted material used in this book. If any such acknowledgment has been inadvertently omitted or miscredited, receipt of such information would be appreciated.

A Note from the Editors
Guideposts, a nonprofit organization, touches millions of lives every day through products and services that inspire, encourage and uplift. Our magazines, books, prayer network and outreach programs help people connect their faith-filled values to their daily lives. To learn more, visit Guideposts.org or GuidepostsFoundation.org. For more information about *Daily Guideposts*, visit DailyGuideposts.org.

Unless otherwise noted, Scripture references are from The Holy Bible, New International Version®, NIV®. Copyright © 1973, 1978, 1984 by Biblica, Inc.™ Used by permission of Zondervan. All rights reserved worldwide. Other Scriptures are taken from The Holy Bible, King James Version (KJV). The New King James Version (NKJV). Copyright © 1982 by Thomas Nelson, Inc. Used by permission. The New American Standard Bible® (NASB), Copyright © 1960, 1962, 1963, 1968, 1971, 1972, 1973, 1975, 1977, 1995 by The Lockman Foundation. Used by permission. The Revised Standard Version Bible (RSV). Copyright 1952 [second edition 1971], Division of Christian Education of the National Council of the Churches of Christ in the United States of America. Used by permission. The Holy Bible, New Living Translation (NLT), copyright 1996, 2004. Used by permission of Tyndale House Publishers, Inc., Wheaton, Illinois. *The Living Bible* (TLB) © 1971. Used by permission of Tyndale House Publishers, Inc., Wheaton, Illinois 60189.

Cover design, Interior design and typeset by Thinkpen Design, Inc., www.thinkpendesign.com

Printed and bound in China

10 9 8 7 6 5 4 3 2 1

DAILY GUIDEPOSTS

365 SPIRIT-LIFTING DEVOTIONS FOR Grandmothers

Guideposts

INTRODUCTION

Remember the warmth and comfort of Grandma's hugs? The smell of the cookies you made together, flour up to your elbows, baking in the oven? Remember Grandma's prayers and words of wisdom that helped you through some of life's rough patches? And do you remember, or are you anticipating, the birth of your first grandchild, or a grandchild's stroll down the aisle toward a new life, or some other milestone in between?

Those memories—and God in them—are what *365 Spirit-Lifting Devotionals for Grandmothers* is all about. Each day these devotions bring you

- a Scripture to help you focus on God and His Word;
- glimpses of God in the real-life experiences of others;
- prayers to pray for yourself and your loved ones.

In addition to all that, your heart will be warmed, your soul encouraged, and your imagination stimulated about keeping up with the grandchildren, near and distant; changing relationships with adult children; leaving a spiritual legacy to your grandchildren, and so much more.

Whether you're already a grandmother, expect to become one, or are still making memories with your own grandmother, this collection will encourage your heart through glimpses of God in the joys, sorrows, challenges, and life lessons passed from generation to generation.

—LUCILE ALLEN

JANUARY 1

An old man's grandchildren are his crowning glory.
—PROVERBS 17:6 (TLB)

*M*y fiftieth year was a blockbuster. I went to Europe for the first time in my life, chaperoning twenty-six teenagers! And that summer I even water-skied behind my brother's speedboat on the Ohio River. But the most important thing that happened to me that year after I turned fifty was becoming a grandmother for the second time.

Hannah was born a month early with a head full of thick, shocking red hair. The first time I saw her she was still in the neonatal intensive care unit at the hospital, attached to all sorts of wires and monitors and sleeping in a heated bassinet. Her back seemed only a few inches wide as she snuggled into my hand. Her skinny little arms were punctuated with perfectly formed fingers that squeezed my little finger.

Holding and rocking my dainty, darling redheaded granddaughter in that hospital brought on such feelings of joy that during my two-day visit I practically begged my son, Hannah's dad, to let me go in instead of him during the few minutes each hour that one of us was allowed in the intensive care unit. Most of the time Michael gave in and stood outside looking through the thick windows of the nursery while I rocked and cuddled my precious grandchild.

As Hannah and I snuggled, I knew without a doubt that no matter what adventures I have, where I go or what I accomplish in my next fifty years, absolutely *nothing* can come close to the intense feelings and joy of being a mother—and a grandmother.

> *heavenly Father, I thank You for the beautiful*
> *grandchildren who renew my life with joy.*
> —PATRICIA LORENZ

All Scripture is inspired by God and is profitable
for teaching. —2 TIMOTHY 3:16 (NASB)

I was stuck in a hospital bed, recuperating from surgery. The previous patient, a little girl, had left her coloring book and crayons. When I couldn't take any more television, I picked up the coloring book.

This might sound strange, but I loved coloring the drawings of cats, and when I'd finished the book, I wished there were more.

Back to the television, I thought, but then one of my daughters dropped in. I showed her the book, said how much fun I'd had with it, and told her I was sorry to be finished with it.

"Well, Mom, maybe you're not quite finished with it." She pulled a pocket Bible from her purse. "Let's find an appropriate Scripture for each picture, a verse that expresses its feeling."

We started with a picture of two kittens lapping up milk and wrote, "God shall supply all your need..." We had a wonderful time, and afterward I wished I'd played this game with my children long before.

So, I'll have to play it with my grandchildren when they get a little older. Then they'll soon learn how to use the Bible, and they'll also learn how to look for the true feelings in life's little moments. And—so will I.

Father, please show me new ways to bring Your Word to light.
—MARION BOND WEST

*The priests made repairs [to the wall], each in
front of his own house.* —NEHEMIAH 3:28

*O*ne of Grandma's evening rituals was sweeping. She'd begin in the kitchen, careful to capture every crumb, and end on the front porch, sweeping our welcome mat with vigor. Once I asked her why she swept the porch every day, even when it didn't need it. She leaned on the handle of her broom and winked at me, as though she were sharing a secret. "If everyone would sweep in front of his own door, the whole world would be clean."

I was much older when I realized Grandma wasn't just talking about stray leaves and tracked-in sand. And now I remember her simple adage when I'm tempted to repeat what I heard about that single lady on the next block. Or when I complain about the neighbor's dandelions. I recall it when I begin a rampage on "other people's" kids. Or when I want to blame my mistakes on someone else. That's when I check for crumbs at my front door. And taking my broom, I get back to the full-time job of keeping my own porch clean.

*Forgive me, Father, for the times I've meddled in other
people's lives. With Your help, I'll tend to my own affairs.*
—MARY LOU CARNEY

January 4

*Always be prepared to give an answer to everyone
who asks you to give the reason for the hope that you have.*
—1 Peter 3:15

What matters most in a family these days?" a new mom asked our luncheon group, women of different ages and stages of life. Her question sort of hung there, suspended in silence over the table. It's the kind of question that doesn't have a quick answer because there are so many possibilities.

The momentary silence was soon filled by conversation that headed in a different direction, yet I continued to ponder her question. As a new mom, I used to wonder the same thing. But within five years, my husband Lynn and I had three children, and we hardly had time to pause and consider what mattered most. We simply did the best we could in the midst of our busy circumstances.

Now our children are grown, and we just celebrated the arrival of our first grandchild. I have more of life to look back on and a new reason to consider what matters most to our family and what I'd like to pass on to the next generation.

So as this new year begins, I'm carrying that question with me as I stir-fry some chicken for dinner, take a bunch of pictures off our refrigerator door and put them in our photo album, or stop everything I'm doing simply to sit and hold my new granddaughter. And I'm enjoying the process of thinking about all the possible answers.

*Lord, as I think about all the things that matter
most to our family, help me to remember what
matters most to You in the light of eternity.*
—Carol Kuykendall

JANUARY 5

*In the world ye shall have tribulation: but be of good
cheer; I have overcome the world.* —JOHN 16:33 (KJV)

*E*ach year in early January we invite all our godchildren and extended church family over for a potluck meal and one last singing of Christmas carols. Last year we included our ninety-four-year-old adopted grandma, whom we fondly call "Baba Draga." She bubbled with joy to "be with all you young people." (We middle-agers were pleased to be considered young.)

At one point my husband Alex was at the piano taking requests for everyone's favorite carols. Baba Draga astonished us all by requesting "Home on the Range." As we searched for the music, Draga explained it was her very favorite song because of the line, "Where seldom is heard a discouraging word, and the skies are not cloudy all day." She said, "I taught this to my boys, and when they would get into scraps or start complaining, we would sing this song." Chuckling, we sang "Home on the Range," while Baba Draga beamed and waved her arms conducting us.

A few months later, Baba Draga asked me to take her to the eye doctor. Her eyesight had been diminishing, and she was anxious to get some test results. To our disappointment, the doctor confirmed the diagnosis of macular degeneration. It was getting worse, and nothing could be done to stop her loss of vision.

Baba Draga insisted on taking me out to lunch afterward and surprised me by her good humor. When I commented on her happy mood despite the doctor's grim prognosis, she peered across the booth at me. "You know," she said, "everyone at my age has some loss or pain to bear. But I memorized something years ago that I tell myself every day: 'When cheerfulness is kept up against all odds, it is the finest form of courage.'"

*Dear God, thank You for Baba Draga and her example
of courage. Today, and all year long, please help me
refrain from discouraging words or thoughts.*
—MARY BROWN

JANUARY 6

For where your treasure is, there will your
heart be also. —MATTHEW 6:21 (KJV)

*C*hristmas thank-you notes are mailed, and the New Year's confetti swept out of the carpet. It's January, time to store the holiday finery and put out my regular decorations. To be honest, I've missed my accumulation of paintings, pottery, photos, and knick-knacks.

I set Great-grandmother's satin-lined spectacle box back on the rough-oak pie safe. My grandfather treasured this ivory box before it passed to me. I rehang *Little Arrow Maker* by Jerome Tiger, print number 656 of 1,500, bought by my husband Don at an auction. The red-black-yellow throw, a birthday gift from my friend Glenda, goes back over the edge of the divan. Since I welcome each piece like an old friend, the task takes half a day. When I place my mother's polished wooden fruit bowl on the dining room table, I have a sudden scary revelation: *I love my possessions. I love everything! My white wedding china, the Navajo pots, even the pillow that says* MY FAMILY TREE IS FULL OF NUTS. But hadn't Jesus clearly taught that all our treasures should be heavenly? I know people whose lives are centered on what they own—cars, clothes, houses. Was I becoming one of them?

I run my hand over the faded cover of Great-great-grandfather's Bible. As suddenly as the oppressive fear descended, it lifts. Yes, I love my possessions. But I love them because of the memories they bring to mind. Memories of dear people, some still living, others gone on to glory, who were loved and treasured parts of my life.

Lord, thank You for the precious memories
forever alive in my heart.
—PENNEY SCHWAB

*And the Lord, whom ye seek, shall suddenly
come to his temple.* —Malachi 3:1 (KJV)

As a child, I lived about twenty-five miles north of New York City. No trip to the city with my parents was complete without a visit to St. Patrick's Cathedral. We'd enter the darkened church, bathed in the flicker of candlelight. I felt so small beneath the towering archways and enormous stone columns that line the side aisles. Passing dozens of solid wooden pews, we'd pick a spot near the altar to pray. I'd say a simple prayer—"Help me to obey Mom and Dad"—then look up in awe at the tall stained-glass windows beneath a ceiling that seemed to reach to heaven.

I recollected all of this one January day when my family visited Flagstaff, Arizona, north of Phoenix. Driving outside town on the road to the Grand Canyon, we spotted a small wood-and-stone chapel, framed by snow and nestled among the pine trees. Walking through the unlocked front door, we breathed in the cold, fresh air and the scent of earth rising from the dirt floor. Bright sunlight streamed through the window behind the stone altar, and beyond, the snow-covered mountains stood as if reaching to heaven. We sat on an iron bench to pray.

My prayers are still simple—for health and a productive new year.

Yet in the rustic beauty, and in the notes and prayers visitors had tacked to the bare walls, I sensed God as near to me as in any of His grander houses. And He seemed to be telling me that the house itself is not important. What matters to Him is that I visit often.

*heavenly Father, be with me in Your house,
wherever that may be, for there I feel most at home.*

—Gina Bridgeman

January 8

For my mouth will speak truth. —Proverbs 8:7 (NKJV)

My grandson and I moved up to the airline ticket counter. His face shone with scrubbing. By some miracle both his shoelaces were firmly tied, and in one sturdy fist he clutched his small canvas suitcase. Jerry was about to embark on a big adventure, his first airplane ride to his home in an Eastern state from a visit to Grandma.

I inquired about the fare. *It will probably be a good round sum*, I thought, but this visit had been worth it. Nevertheless, I gasped when the clerk told me the latest boost in airfares. "That's for a child over twelve years of age," he added. "Half fare if the child is under twelve. How old is the boy?"

It was so tempting! How easy to shave off a few months! For a moment I hesitated. At that point Jerry spoke up: "I'm twelve-and-a-half," he told the ticket agent proudly.

That took care of that! A little later, waiting for Jerry's flight to be called, I opened the morning paper. On the first page were headlines about a prominent political figure indicted for lying and falsifying income-tax records. "Perhaps someone set a bad example when he was a little boy," I mused.

Jerry's clear-eyed, direct honesty had saved me from a shabby little lie. Silently, I thanked him with all my heart.

> *Dear Father, help us always to remember that children
> learn not by what we say, but by what we do.*
> —Frances Fowler Allen

JANUARY 9

Through love serve one another. —GALATIANS 5:13 (NASB)

My husband Leo answered the phone. "Hello? Oh yes, Frances, I'm feeling much better, thanks. My beauty queen took real good care of me!"

Beauty queen? Huh?

His words jolted me right out of the fever-induced stupor brought on by a bad case of the flu. The previous week, Leo had been the one burrowed under the covers, shivering and sweating from alternate bouts of chills and fever. The same vicious bug had then bitten me.

Blowing and coughing and wheezing, I had managed to crawl out of bed just long enough to shuffle back and forth to the bathroom. Even in my weakened condition, passing the mirror had been a shock to my system—red nose, sunken eyes, hollow cheeks, tattered sweater over baggy flannel pajamas, the bottoms tucked into big woolen socks. My hair was sticking out in all directions, and my whole being was enveloped in the strong fumes of a decongestant.

Some "beauty queen"!

As more of Leo's conversation with Frances filtered into my brain, it became clear that he wasn't referring to my physical appearance. (After fifty years of marriage, we both know I'm no beauty queen!) His perception of beauty was being conveyed in phrases like "hot soup ... tucking me in ... calling the doctor ... doling out pills ... stroking my brow," the many little things one does to nurse a loved one back to health—the many little things Leo was now doing for me.

Help me, Lord, to look beyond the physical and see
as You do the beauty that is soul-deep in others.

—ALMA BARKMAN

There is one body and one Spirit. —Ephesians 4:4 (nasb)

I t had been a challenging morning in my work as an infection control practitioner, and I'd never felt more alone. As I sat at my desk and tried to complete a report with accompanying charts, the required computer skills eluded me. Elsewhere in the medical center, two other members of a committee I chair were working on other parts of the report as a deadline loomed. There we were, three of us, all going it alone as we analyzed data on a new quality improvement initiative we'd implemented.

When I broke for lunch, Robin, the checkout clerk in the cafeteria, was furiously scribbling something on three-by-five cards in between ringing up customers. "We just got a new girl," she explained a little sheepishly, "and she's frantic about not knowing what to do. I'm making her cue cards." There on Robin's lap were cards showing how much to charge for a vegetable plate, a hot dessert, the caregiver's special.

Later, as I walked back to my office, I had my cue. The secret in getting the job done was in working together and helping one another, not going it alone. I telephoned my committee members right away to see if we could meet that afternoon. Thanks to Robin and some good old-fashioned teamwork, the three of us cranked out that report in no time.

Show me how to work with others to get the job done, Lord.
—Roberta Messner

January 11

Let me alone, that I may take comfort a little.
—Job 10:20 (KJV)

I have a new office. Well, it's really my son's old room, but now it's an office with a desk, a computer, and an old coffee mug filled with pens and pencils of all colors. I no longer spread papers all over the dining room table, drop scrambled eggs into my dictionary, or try to cook dinner and work at the same time. I have *a place of my own*.

Mothers rarely have this luxury, and I'm thankful I do. Everyone else in the family has always had a place of their own, but not me. For twenty-five years I've shared a bedroom, worked while children watched TV in front of me, taken business and personal messages, and tried to keep them all separate. Even while I worked, I was first and foremost "Mom."

Suddenly I'm getting some respect around here! People tiptoe into my office when they need me, instead of yelling, "Ma!" on their way to the refrigerator. The dog lies patiently at my feet until I get up from my desk before she bounds to the back door. I even know where my checkbook is now!

If you're a mother wondering what to do with an extra room, take my advice: Claim it for yourself. Let guests use it when they come, but the rest of the time make it a place of your own. You deserve it. You *need* it.

*Father, thank You for this spare room, and for giving
me the courage to claim it for myself. What I do in here
isn't earth-shaking, but the sense of personal identity
and worthiness this private place gives me is.*

—Toni Sortor

I call to remembrance my song in the night:
I commune with mine own heart. —PSALM 77:6 (KJV)

I was awake again at three o'clock in the morning. *Quick, Marion, before those troubling thoughts attack your mind. Sing!*

Singing the old hymns I learned as a child keeps away the "what-ifs" that like to attack in the middle of the night. I don't sing out loud, just silently in my spirit. After a while I can usually get back to sleep.

I sang my last song several times as I hovered on the brink of sleep:

Jesus is the sweetest name I know
And He's just the same as His lovely name.
That's the reason why I love Him so.
Oh, Jesus is the sweetest name I know.

Right then I was ambushed by an unexpected attack: *Jesus doesn't care about you or your stupid songs!*

Oh, Lord, don't let that thought stay with me and make me doubt.
Somehow, show me that You care.

"The piano tuner will be here by nine," my husband Gene reminded me the next morning. Neither Gene nor I play the piano, but he cherishes our baby grand. It's about ninety years old and has been in his family forever.

When Bobby Howington finished his work, he gave us our annual mini-concert. Gene and I sat side by side on the sofa listening intently as music from the perfectly tuned piano filled our living room and our souls. Bobby's skilled fingers lovingly played,

Jesus is the sweetest name I know
And He's just the same as His lovely name.
That's the reason why I love Him so.
Oh, Jesus is the sweetest name I know.

Your faithfulness amazes me, Father, time and time again.
—MARION BOND WEST

*I the Lord search the heart...even to give every man according
to his ways, and according to the fruit of his doings.*
—JEREMIAH 17:10 (KJV)

My son was driving me and two of my daughter Tamara's children to their home where I was going to spend "grandma time." Somewhere along the way I began handing out saltwater taffy to Caleb, five, and Ruby, four, in the backseat. The problem was I only passed them the flavors I didn't like. They got blueberry and licorice and raspberry; I got cinnamon and peppermint and chocolate. They didn't know the difference, but I did.

I began to wonder, *Is it really sharing if I'm giving something I don't want? Shouldn't I have a stake in it for it to be true sharing?*

We arrived at Tamara's, where every night Ruby and I read a book about what love is. One page said, "Love is sharing your umbrella in the rain."

There was no precipitation in Alaska's forecast the evening Tamara walked into Ruby's bedroom and rained M&Ms, my favorite candy, in my lap. Ruby was on red alert. Holding out her small hand, she announced, "Don't you know love is sharing?"

I parted with my M&Ms that night to a gleeful voice inside me that said, "Now this is sharing."

*God, Supreme Giver, prepare me for bountiful giving
by first keeping me generous in the small stuff.*
—CAROL KNAPP

JANUARY 14

He asked life of thee, and thou gavest it to him,
even length of days. —PSALM 21:4 (KJV)

The dinner party brought together various branches of the family. The seats of honor at the ends of the long table went to the two eldest, my grandfather Papa, then in his mideighties, and Grammy, my brother-in-law's grandmother, age ninety-four.

Isolated by deafness, Papa had become almost morbidly interested in the details of illness, both his own and other people's. The table was buzzing with lively conversations when he shouted to Grammy, above the chattering voices, "How's your heart?"

Grammy beamed down the long table at him, a beatific smile that encompassed the entire gathering and seemed to take in all of struggling humanity as well. She answered his question with a single word, "Enlarged."

Papa did not hear, and "enlarged" was relayed to him along the seats. Sitting beside him, I shrieked into his ear, "Her heart's enlarged."

Medically, of course, a serious condition. But as I said the words, I thought they also summed up God's will for all of us as our years increase. Grammy's answer has become for me a kind of shorthand prayer. Like Grammy, let me carry my aches and ailments lightly as I grow older! Each year let me care a little less about myself, a little more for others.

Father, enlarge my heart.
—ELIZABETH SHERRILL

Jesus Christ is the same yesterday and today and forever.
—HEBREWS 13:8 (RSV)

A few years ago, my sister's family underwent major changes when her little girls were three and five years old. One day the five-year-old was particularly cross. When she and her mother got into a rousing shouting match, my sister decided a time-out was necessary for both of them. A few minutes later little Erica came down the stairs. "Mother," she said matter-of-factly, "you must know that's not what I'm *really* mad about. I'm really mad about something else."

"Well then," said Tresa, smiling, "have you figured out what it is you're *really* mad about?"

"I'm mad," declared Erica, crossing her arms over her chest and emphatically stomping one foot, "because there's so much change around here! *And I don't like change!*"

Tresa thought for a moment. "Erica," she said, "let's think of things that *are* the same, while everything else changes. I'll start. We still sleep in the same house. Now your turn."

"It's still my birthday next week!"

"You still go to the same school."

"I still like gummy bears!"

Tresa's children have survived their family upheaval. And now, whenever the changes in my own life—children growing up and the years passing by—begin to upset me, I remember Tresa's wisdom and make my own list:

I still have two of my three children at home.

I still have my friends.

I still *don't* like gummy bears.

And I still have One who will never leave me.

In the midst of change, You, Lord, are my abiding constant.
—BRENDA WILBEE

JANUARY 16

Then did I beat them small as the dust before the wind.
—PSALM 18:42 (KJV)

My mother's coffee mug collection is reaching the two-hundred mark. Friends bring her decorated mugs from various vacation spots, and she herself brings them back from faraway and not-so-far places. She has one from my hometown of Walnut Creek and a delicate cup from a friend's trip to Belgium. Her collection lines the tops of her bookcases and cabinets, so I was not thrilled on arriving at Mom's house one day to have her hand me a rag and say, "I was just in the middle of housecleaning—would you like to help?"

I helped dust and polish, but I have to admit that all the while my eyes were on those mugs. I dreaded the moment I knew she would say, "Time to wash those two hundred mugs!" (Mom doesn't own a dishwasher, either.) But that time never came. Finally, I brought up the subject. Reluctantly, I asked, "Mom, didn't we forget something?" At her blank look, I said, "Your mugs."

She just laughed and said, "Oh, I have coffee from a different one each morning—that's how I wash them. One at a time! I could never face the thought of washing them all at once!"

Now *I* try that, too. Oh, not with mugs, but with cleaning my house, say. The whole thing seems overwhelming, but if I clean one room a day, it goes fast. Or my pile of mending—instead of letting it go, I do one small rip or tear every evening. Or in my Bible reading—I break down a book into verses or chapters and in a week or two (depending on the book), I've thoughtfully digested the whole book, day by day.

God, for today, let me do one piece
of one project—and be satisfied!
—LINDA NEUKRUG

"Your words have helped the tottering to stand, and you have strengthened feeble knees." —Job 4:4 (NASB)

I'm struck by how little I remember of what's been said to me in my lifetime. Childhood memories are now mostly impressions, and even last month's most profound conversations are filed away in loosely interpreted summaries, not in the actual words. But there are a few verbatim remarks, a few noteworthy word-for-word exchanges, that are indelibly imprinted in my memory. Sometimes, I admit, I wish they were not.

As I look over my childhood, for example, I can remember only fourteen words any teacher ever spoke to me. They were directed my way in the fourth grade: "*Any dummy can understand long division! What's the matter with you? Are you stupid?*" And I remember my father's antidote to those poisonous phrases: "*You can do it! You're the smartest girl I know!*"

And as recently as two months ago, preparing for major surgery, I couldn't seem to shake the memory of a well-meaning friend's ominous warning: "*Watch out for anesthesia. Your brain could turn to mush without enough oxygen!*" My husband, an encourager of the first order, provided the antitoxin: "*Who's in charge of your life? God or the doctors?*"

What amazing power in a few simple words! The old ballad sings the praises of a "home on the range...where seldom is heard a discouraging word." That's what I'm looking for. Aren't you? In a world full of wet blankets, I'm always hoping for a warming campfire. And that's what I'd like to be to the people who will remember my words one day.

Father, use me today to bring hope
and encouragement to everyone I meet.

—Susan Williams

JANUARY 18

*These things have I spoken unto you, that my joy might
remain in you, and that your joy might be full.*
—JOHN 15:11 (KJV)

"Bust the blahs out of your life by practicing more joyful facial expressions!" the professor encouraged the people attending his workshop on the importance of humor in our lives. "Our faces communicate more messages than our words, but starting about age five, we get self-conscious about using facial expressions, and our facial muscles start to atrophy. Loosen them up! Use them to express yourself. Open your eyes wider. Lift those eyebrows. Show some enthusiasm. Etch in a few laugh lines!" The man sounded a bit more like a barker at a carnival than a university professor, but he got me to thinking.

Driving home, I began to wonder what my face reflects and glanced up to catch a glimpse of myself in the rearview mirror. Looks kind of sullen and anxious, I decided as I pulled up to a red light. Is that what the person in the next car sees? How about the cashier in the checkout lane, or the gas station attendant? Do they know I have the Holy Spirit within me? Does my face reflect His joy? I couldn't shake the questions from my mind and I have to admit, since that day, I've been lots more conscious of my facial messages.

*Lord, I promise to smile more often today,
reflecting Your love. And who knows?
My facial messages might be contagious.*
—CAROL KUYKENDALL

JANUARY 19

No mere man has ever seen, heard or even imagined what
wonderful things God has ready for those who love the Lord.
—1 CORINTHIANS 2:9 (TLB)

He was only eight years old. For the past year he had been a cowboy and had slept every night with his stick horse Trigger. But now, after an August vacation with his parents in the Cayman Islands, he had a new ambition.

It was only the third day of school when he burst in the front door in tears. "Mama," Lowell wailed, "Carlos says he heard over the radio that we are all going to heaven on Friday! I don't want to go! I want to grow up and be a deep-sea diver." I sat in the wing chair in my daughter's den and wondered how she was going to handle this one.

She gathered her sobbing little boy in her arms and took him to the kitchen. I listened intently. She poured Lowell a glass of milk and gave him a gingersnap. "Lowell, honey," my daughter said softly, wiping away his tears, "I doubt that the man on the radio knows what he is talking about. But someday, Lowell, you are going to go to heaven, and if it should be Friday, you won't be the least bit sorry because the deep-sea diving in heaven is something beyond anything you have ever imagined. You won't have to wear a snorkel or an Aqua-Lung or even a wet suit." Sally snapped her fingers. "Besides, if you think the fish were colorful in the Cayman Islands, just wait till you see the fish in the oceans of heaven!"

When my daughter finally finished describing heaven, Lowell's tears had diminished to sniffles. "Well, all right, Mama," he wiped his sniffly nose. "I had better go call Carlos and tell him about heaven 'cause he doesn't want to go either."

How like Lowell and Carlos I am. Knowing what God has promised but still afraid of the unknown.

Dear Lord, I do not know what the future holds,
but I do know that heaven is eternity with You.
Thank You, Lord, for all the unimaginable,
wonderful things You hold for us on the other side.
—DOROTHY SHELLENBERGER

Weeping may endure for a night, but joy
cometh in the morning. —Psalm 30:5 (KJV)

*M*y grandmother died, unexpectedly and away from home. For me, there was a deep feeling of loss and a lack of closure. She had always been there when I needed her; now she was gone, and I hadn't been able to say good-bye.

A few days after the funeral, my sister Debbie came across a letter Grandmother had written to me. It was a single handwritten page with no indication of when it had been sent. But to me, the words seemed to have come from heaven.

> *Dear Libbie,*
>
> *I miss all of you down there. Not that I'm lonely or homesick; every day is a good one. Everyone is so helpful and kind.*
>
> *Just remember, when you are blue or lonely, you are not alone. Just stop for a moment and thank God for all things as they are, for they are working out something beautiful in your life. You may not see it today, but tomorrow is coming, and the sun will rise and shine down your path. Keep sweet. God loves you, and I love you.*
>
> *Your grandmother*

Neither Debbie nor I really knows when this letter was written. I think Grandmother sent it to me while my husband Larry was away for a year in Okinawa with the United States Navy. I have no memory of receiving it, and it doesn't matter now. What really matters is that God knew it would comfort me, and He saw that it was delivered right on time.

Father, You really do work in mysterious ways.
Thank You for the wonders You perform in my life.
—Libbie Adams

JANUARY 21

Don't you see how wonderfully kind, tolerant, and
patient God is with you? —ROMANS 2:4 (NLT)

Today I was with my twenty-two-month-old grandson Brock, feeding him his lunch. Between bites, he asked me the same questions over and over. Bite of cheese. "Nana, where Mama?" Bite of turkey. "Nana, where Papa?" Bite of bread and butter. "Elmo? Elmo?"

The first two I could answer: "At work," The Elmo one I winged: "Yes, Elmo." Brock took a drink of milk and the round began again.

"Nana, where Mama?" "Nana, where Papa?" "Elmo? Elmo?"

I gave the same answers over and over and over. Our conversation took on a predictable rhythm.

I thought about Brock's incessant questions as I drove home and was suddenly reminded of someone else who tends to ask the same questions over and over—me. And the recipient of this repetitive babble? God.

Year after year I keep imploring, "Why don't You answer my prayers?" "Where are You when I hurt?" "Why must my family face this trial?" "Would it spoil some divine plan if You made me tall and thin, or at least let me keep off those eight pounds I keep losing and gaining?"

And over and over the same answers come: *I hear you. Trust Me. I love you just the way you are.*

If God tires or grows weary of my endlessly repeated questions, He never shows it. I guess patience is something God—and nanas—have in common.

> *Open my ears and my heart, Lord, that I might hear and*
> *believe Your patient answers to my persistent pleas.*
>
> —MARY LOU CARNEY

*My mouth is filled with thy praise.... Do not cast me
off in the time of old age.* —Psalm 71:8-9 (rsv)

"Don't get old!"

That's advice I hear every Sunday from the ladies I pick up for
church as they struggle to get into the car. One turned ninety last year, and the
others are all in their eighties.

"Don't get old," they repeat, and we all laugh ruefully. Because we know
there's no help for it—we *are* getting old. And as I see them slowing down,
unable to do all the things they used to do, I know that eventually the same
thing will happen to me.

Yet in the things that count, my friends aren't getting old. They come to
church faithfully every Sunday. Several of them are faithful members of our
Thursday evening prayer meeting. Martha and Julia bake cakes and goodies for
our church coffee hours, and Vera always makes the coffee. Agnes crochets lap
robes to be given away. Viola makes hundreds of craft items for our semiannual
flea markets at which all of them help out. Their spirits have stayed young.

Then tonight I read Psalm 71. "An old man's prayer" is the title given to it in
The Jerusalem Bible. I was surprised to find that the Psalmist didn't protest his
getting old. He just asked for God's continued presence and blessing so he could
go on praising God for all His wonderful deeds, "even to old age and gray hairs"
(Psalm 71:18 rsv).

As I get older, I want to follow my friends' examples: to keep busy for the
Lord. But even more, I want to follow the Psalmist's example: "O God.... My
mouth will tell of thy righteous acts, of thy deeds of salvation all the day long"
(Psalm 71:12, 15 rsv).

Lord, keep me youthful in spirit, and always praising You.
—Mary Ruth Howes

January 23

Ye are the temple of God. —1 Corinthians 3:16

Anything over fifty years old is considered an antique, and the most valuable objects are those that are most rare," my mother once told me. I've never been an antiques collector, although I now have a couple of things from my grandmother's house that I treasure because they belonged to her.

I also have one very rare piece. In fact, it's a one-of-a-kind antique—me!

Anyone who has antiques knows the importance of taking care of them, so this fall I've started on a daily maintenance program for this single-issue, irreplaceable antique. I've made my three-part caretaking routine as simple and specific as possible, knowing I'm more likely to stick with it that way.

Body: Take a twenty-minute walk and eat two pieces of fruit every day.

Mind: Always read an informative book, even if it's only a few pages a day.

Spirit: Spend at least thirty minutes each day alone with God. No excuses.

That's it! I know it's minimal, but there's no rule that says I can't exceed these aims, and at least I'll do this much!

Whether your one-of-a-kind body is an antique or not, you may want to design your own three-part routine for preserving your priceless gift from the Creator. By taking good care of Grandmother's desk and rocking chair, I hope to preserve them for my children and grandchildren to enjoy for a long time. Maybe I can say the same about this one-of-a-kind antique called Marilyn.

Thank You for trusting me to be
caretaker of Your temple, Lord.

—Marilyn Morgan King

JANUARY 24

*G*randma Johnson was a tiny, energetic woman with a truckload of determination. Every member of the Johnson clan has stories to tell of her feistiness. My father talks about how his mother came to New York City alone in the early 1920s to earn a master of fine arts degree. My mother saw Grandma's single-minded drive when she came home one day to find Grandma intently painting the inside of some dresser drawers, oblivious to the three young children she was supposed to be looking after. My own memories of Grandma's visits include the time she took over my high school swim team's annual dinner, unperturbed by the fact that she was a complete stranger and that others had already planned the event. Strong-willed, determined, controlling—whatever you wanted to call her—Grandma Johnson was a force to be reckoned with.

Then while I was in college, Grandma became quite sick. She needed full-time care, so my parents moved her halfway across the country to live with them. She was in her eighties, and no one expected a full recovery. But her health slowly returned, and as it did, Grandma's arresting eyes mellowed into a softer, warmer blue. Her commanding arm now reached out primarily to clasp a hand softly in her own. She was gentler, sweeter, a pleasure to be with. It was as if her illness had released her from her need to be in charge, and the effect was transforming.

Surely there had been love there all along, yet something had obscured it. Perhaps our own prickly reactions to her had made us incapable of seeing it.

Dear Lord, thank You for grandparents, in all their
wonderful, human, and sometimes frustrating complexity.
—JULIA ATTAWAY

Beloved, it is a loyal thing you do when you render any service to the brethren. —3 JOHN 1:5 (RSV)

*W*hen Baltimore Orioles shortstop Cal Ripken Jr. broke Lou Gehrig's record for most consecutive games played (2,131), I read several articles about other great sports feats. But the one that stayed in my mind was about offbeat records, the ones that don't get worldwide publicity. Like the Englishman who ran nearly thirty miles in four hours and eighteen minutes—while balancing a fresh egg on a spoon. Or the man who holds the record for standing still, more than fifteen hours. How about 177,000 consecutive pogo-stick jumps? Or the woman who walked seventy miles balancing a milk bottle on her head?

It all makes me think about the "record holders" I know who also don't get the recognition they deserve. Like my friend Joann, who by calling and saying, "Can I have the kids this afternoon?" has come to my rescue more times than anyone. Or Grandma Hazel, who's cooked more meals and baked more cookies for lonely church newcomers than the record keepers could count. Or a man I know who surely caused a record number of smiles and giggles when he sent a box of toys and clothes to a family who had recently lost everything in a fire.

The feats of these people may not make any record books, but if statistics were kept for the works our Lord most values, like love, generosity, and compassion, they, and others like them—surely some you know—would go down in history.

Dear God, continue to bless and strengthen the record holders in our daily lives, and gently remind us to thank them for their selfless achievements.

—GINA BRIDGEMAN

January 26

Herein is love, not that we loved God, but that he loved us.
—1 John 4:10 (KJV)

*I*n a Western movie, my husband would be the heroic cowboy. You know the type: strong and silent, good looking, slow talking, quick drawing. I can picture the scene: dust swirling through an empty street, the sound of spurs jingling. In a flash, he would vanquish the bad guys, save the damsel, and ride off into the sunset.

Jacob is calm, stable, and thoughtful—qualities that most of the time I truly appreciate. But sometimes the fact that he doesn't tell me I look nice or say "I love you" leaves me feeling empty.

The other important man in my life, my grandfather, had been outgoing and affectionate. He always had a compliment, an "I love you," a hug, or a friendly joke.

One day I was feeling low, wondering why Jacob hadn't noticed my new haircut or said anything about the way I'd cleaned the kitchen. I decided to call my grandmother and ask her for some advice. After I told her how I was feeling, there was a long pause on the line. Then Grandma excused herself. Three minutes later she returned. "Honey, I should have read this to you a long time ago."

"What is it?"

"After your grandfather died, I was cleaning up his things and I found this note. Let me read you what it says: 'Dear Aliene, I never told you this often enough, you were the love of my life. I should have told you that more. Love forever, Gordon.'"

For a while we were both silent. "You see," she said, "your grandfather had a hard time saying he loved me too. But I always knew he did."

Lord, when my heart is heavy,
show me Your "I love you" in Your Word.
—Amanda Borozinski

January 27

"Let light shine out of darkness." —2 Corinthians 4:6

O ma, everybody will think we look so pretty!" my three-year-old granddaughter Gabi exclaims as we sit together on a bench in front of a big mirror in my bedroom, putting on our wigs—iridescent blue wigs.

Gabi doesn't know it, but our giggly little dress-up session is helping me through an extremely difficult life transition. I've lost most of my hair because of chemotherapy for my ovarian cancer, and I'm trying to get used to wearing a wig. Yet, even around my family, I feel terribly self-conscious.

I don't know why the hair loss was so hard. I suppose it's because my hair was one place where I had a sense of control. Cut it—or not. Wash it—or not. Color it—for sure! And when I lost control over what was going on inside my body, somehow this attack on the outside seemed especially harsh.

"My prayer is that you'll walk this journey in your own unique way," a friend told me. We both knew what she meant. "My way" meant finding something to smile about, some way to lighten up the dark, hard places.

So when I bought a couple of look-just-like-me wigs, I also purchased an outrageous blue one. Gabi's mother bought her one, too, knowing that this three-year-old might help me find something to smile about as I faced this transition.

Now here we are, sitting in front of the mirror, trying on our wigs and giggling as we imagine making a grand entrance into the kitchen where the rest of the family has gathered.

"Do you think we need some blue eye shadow?" I ask Gabi, who scrunches up her shoulders and nods. Finally, we're ready, and we parade down the hall and into the kitchen. "*Ta-da!*"

"*Ohhhhhh…* pretty!" everyone exclaims in unison.

Gabi doubles over, laughing so hard she can't walk. So I pick her up and together we twirl around the room, feeling very proud and pretty in our sassy blue wigs.

> *Lord, thank You that laughter helps lighten*
> *up the dark places on a difficult journey.*
> —Carol Kuykendall

January 28

Herein is love, not that we loved God, but that he loved us,
and sent his Son to be the propitiation for our sins.
—1 John 4:10 (kjv)

It's a boy!" our son Pat announced excitedly before I'd finished muttering a groggy "hello" into the telephone receiver. Ryan Patrick, our first grandchild, had entered the world at 3:45 a.m. A few hours later, I held him in my arms—surely the most beautiful baby in the world!

As I drove home from the hospital late that night, I replayed our first meeting in my mind, visualizing every detail of his tiny body, recalling every burp and yawn and cry, enjoying again the feel of him snuggled against my shoulder. We had been waiting for this child with a wonderful sense of anticipation. I thought I knew what it would be like when Ryan Patrick arrived, but I was not prepared for my strong feelings when I held him for the first time. God's love became more than an abstract concept, more than a promise from Scripture. With Ryan in my arms, God's love became a tangible, touchable presence. I knew with absolute certainty that God loved me!

"For God so loved the world, that he gave his only begotten Son, that whosoever believeth in him should not perish, but have everlasting life" (John 3:16 kjv). I praise and thank Him with my whole heart for using another baby, born on a cold January day, to reassure me of His love and make it real in my life.

heavenly Father, thank You for sending Your Son,
Jesus, as a baby so that we could better
understand Your great love for each of us.
—Penney Schwab

JANUARY 29

Oh that I were as in months past...
when my children were about me.
—JOB 29:2, 5 (KJV)

The people in my neighborhood are middle-aged. Where once we were all out walking babies, now we're out walking off the flab. Husbands who once climbed on roofs now search the Yellow Pages for younger men who will climb for them. The occasional roar of a teenager's car has replaced the everyday thunder of Big Wheels and tricycles.

It's quieter, that's for sure. When I look out my window, there's no knot of children rampaging around my front yard. The grass is healthy and untrampled. I haven't had to bandage a skinned knee in years.

When I was younger, I often daydreamed about the days when there would be peace and quiet in our neighborhood. Now that that day has arrived, I realize that I miss the sounds of children.

There are signs of hope, however. I heard a baby cry on the block behind us today. A young, childless couple recently moved onto our block, and they mentioned one room that they hoped would be "the nursery." And surely the house for sale next door is big enough for a large family.

My family is grown, but perhaps God will help me to reach out to that young family whose grandparents live far away. We can all benefit, and I'll bet I can walk off some of the flab as I'm taking a toddler for a ride in the stroller!

Father, I welcome the chance to make some new friends and
offer a helping, much-needed hand to a new acquaintance.

—TONI SORTOR

So let each one give as he purposes in his heart, not grudgingly or of necessity; for God loves a cheerful giver.
—2 CORINTHIANS 9:7 (NKJV)

Now that I'm in my sixties and working my way toward my nineties, when I hope I will finally be wise, I often ask myself, *Why am I here? Am I fulfilling God's purpose? Am I making a difference to the people who matter: my parents, children, grandchildren, friends, and neighbors?*

When I get introspective like this, I rev up my action plan. I may not be wise yet, but I do know this: in order to feel good about myself, I have to give more of myself.

So I make plans to fly home to Illinois to visit my dad and stepmom. I promise myself to phone them more often, at least once a week. I listen to Hannah and Zachary, the two of my eight grandchildren who take piano lessons, play their lesson pieces for me on the phone. I organize a nature event, picnic, lunch, or an arts-books-crafts fair for my neighborhood friends.

Am I making a difference? Yes, as long as I work at it every single day. You see, I've learned it takes work to make a difference.

Lord, You gave me gifts when I was born. Help me to use them every day to make a difference in this world.
—PATRICIA LORENZ

Those God foreknew he also predestined to be conformed to the likeness of his Son. —ROMANS 8:29

*M*y roommate Kathleen was in the car with her brother and his family, including her five-year-old niece Bright. They'd just come from church, where the minister had preached on imitating the qualities of Jesus.

The car radio played oldies music as the family cruised along on their way to lunch. When they stopped at a red light, Kathleen's sister-in-law caught sight of a woman in oversized curlers, bright red lipstick, and white-and-purple sunglasses in the car beside her. Unable to help herself, she burst out in giggles, then alerted the rest of the family to the spectacle next to them.

From the backseat a little voice piped up. "Mommy," scolded five-year-old Bright, "we are supposed to be Christlike. That is not very Christlike."

Bright's dad struggled to compose himself as he looked at his wife.

"Yeah, Mommy," he said, "Christlike."

A point had been made, by a preschooler, no less: The words we hear in church shouldn't be left behind the minute we step out of it. They're meant to follow us into our daily journeys—unto the ends of the earth or to the local Mexican restaurant.

Lord, thank You for the lessons
children remind us of each day.

—ASHLEY JOHNSON

February

February 1

But there was found in it a poor wise man,
and he by his wisdom delivered the city. Yet no one
remembered that poor man. —Ecclesiastes 9:15 (RSV)

There are about one hundred apartments in our building. Many of the residents are older and need help getting around, their mail brought to them, and little things around their apartments fixed. In addition, we have a large pool with a deck and seating area that requires maintenance, not to mention the rigorous opening and closing processes in May and October. Our plumbing and heating systems are always in need of some kind of care, and someone has to maintain the laundry machines and empty the coin changers regularly. The air-conditioning and ventilation systems are from the Stone Age and need constant watching. These are just a few of the tasks necessary to keep a big community like ours going.

You can't imagine what we pay our manager. Nothing.

Arnold is in his seventies, a former railroad man (as they say), and devoted to making everything run smoothly. From changing light fixtures in the lobby to pouring nasty stuff down the shower drains to keep them clear, he does all the grunt work. Heavy boxes addressed to us appear outside our door long before my husband has a chance to get home from work and fetch them from the mailroom. When Arnold isn't helping all of us, he's caring for an elderly friend who is bedridden.

Sometimes I think Arnold doesn't get nearly enough credit for all the things he does. But that doesn't seem to bother him. One afternoon this summer, I watched him replacing planks in the pool deck. He labored meticulously, contentedly in the sun, wearing pads to protect his bony knees. For Arnold, a job well done is reward enough.

Father, help me remember that good work,
well done, is Your work.
—Marci Alborghetti

*Come near to God and he will
come near to you.* —JAMES 4:8

I'd been out of town for several days, so it had been a while since I'd
seen my three-year-old grandson Drake. Now he and I were at my
kitchen table, late in the afternoon, eating apple slices. Since I only have two
chairs at my table, we were sitting across from each other.

Drake paused as he reached for an apple. "I want to sit there." He pointed
across the table to the place nearest me.

"Oh no, sweetie, you're fine where you are," I said. "Besides, there's no
chair there."

Without hesitation, Drake climbed down and with great care and effort
moved his heavy chair to my side of the table. Now our elbows were almost
touching. Drake didn't say a word. He just munched loudly on his apple slice
and smiled. Being near me—really near me—was important to Drake.

I thought about that when I read my Bible that night. *I want to be nearer to
God.* I closed my eyes and pictured myself climbing down out of my chair and
into the arms of my heavenly Father. *Let's talk about how to make this happen more
often,* He said. And I resolved to listen closely.

> *Draw me nearer, nearer, nearer, precious Lord!*
> —MARY LOU CARNEY

Holding faith, and a good conscience...
—1 TIMOTHY 1:19 (KJV)

I've just hung up the telephone, smiling from the latest story about my eight-year-old granddaughter Sherri. Apparently, she'd come in the door yesterday looking downcast, and her mother immediately knew something was wrong. "What's the matter, honey? Bad day at school?"

Sherri confessed to copying a word from another student's spelling test. "I wrote it down and it looked funny. Then I saw her answer and knew it was right, so I changed mine." A guilty conscience was bothering Sherri, and her mom's sympathizing words failed to console her.

Today brought a surprising turnaround. Sherri ran in the door after school. "You know what, Mother?" she said. "We didn't finish our spelling test yesterday and our teacher gave our papers back today." A smile spread across her face as she concluded, "I changed that word to the way I spelled it the first time!" The relief of a clear conscience outweighed a higher grade.

My granddaughter's example reminds me of things I sometimes overlook that can chip away at my spirit—the extra dollars the store clerk gave me in change the other day, or the unverified story about a friend that I passed on as gossip last week, or the critical comment I made to my husband this morning. Seemingly small and incidental things, but they can cause me to lose sight of important things—like trustworthiness, kindness, and love.

Thank goodness I can still rectify my behavior and make amends. I can pray for God's forgiveness and, with His blessing, start anew.

*Holy Spirit, keep sending me guidance
in the words of little children and always keep me
in good faith, in good conscience.*
—VIRGINIA POEHLEIN

FEBRUARY 4

The desire accomplished is
sweet to the soul. —PROVERBS 13:19 (KJV)

*W*henever I open what I laughingly call my "crafts box," an orange-colored cooler with wheels and a handle, I see unfinished projects. Here's two inches of ribbing that was supposed to be a sweater but never will be, since I don't remember how to do ribbing anymore. There's a pair of baby booties that have no openings where each foot should go. I was on a roll and forgot to stop knitting when I was supposed to.

"Just once I wish I could finish something," I told my friend Katy.

I held up a two-inch disk of red yarn that was supposed to be a hat—that was before I realized I never should have gotten involved with circular needles. "If I ever meet an elf," I joked, "this would be the perfect size."

Katy didn't laugh. "I think you have something here," she said.

"What? A clown nose?" I responded.

"No, seriously. My mother skis, and so many times I've heard her say that her nose feels colder than any other part of her body. Linda, can you knit two strings?"

"No, but I can crochet them."

"If you just attach one to each side of this disk…"

In less than five minutes, I had a disk with two strings that tied around a person's head.

"Linda, what you've got here is a nose warmer!" said Katy triumphantly.

Finally, a project that was just right—and finished! That winter, when Katy showed me a picture of her mom and two brothers wearing the nose warmers I had given them, I felt a warm glow of accomplishment.

Dear God, help me to see the possibilities
that are waiting in the most unlikely places.

—LINDA NEUKRUG

This is the confidence we have in approaching God:
that if we ask anything according to his will,
he hears us. —1 JOHN 5:14

How I love this computer/Internet/cell phone age! I know there are abuses, but most of the pluses outweigh them.

For example, here I am in Virginia furiously typing and through the speakers of this same computer I can hear our son Peter, live, directing air traffic from a control tower more than five hundred miles away. If I want, I can "Google Earth" the airport and zoom in until I can see a satellite shot of the control tower where he works. Or I can fly over the sky-lighted roof of our son Tom and his wife Susan's house in Georgia. Or follow, as I did, our son John on a week's trip in the mountains and by the sea in Croatia. I can find the grass landing strip in our son Dave and his wife Matti's backyard in Kentucky, and fly up Fort Valley inside our own Massanutten Mountain. What fun!

As the mother of four sons, I bless e-mail daily because I know from their college years that receiving "snail mail" letters from them is a pipe dream.

Then there's the Webcam. Bill and I bought two; one perches on a speaker by our computer and the other sits on a desk in Georgia. And our grandsons Jack and Luke look at the grainy square on their computer screen and see us, live, waving, laughing, playing peekaboo with them. And they respond, "Grandpa! Grandma!"

The cell phone—well, that goes without saying. How did I ever survive a trip to the grocery store without one?

All this communication and technology have enhanced my faith in how God can be close to and personal with me; He's had this expertise all along.

Lord, You know where I am. You listen and see and know
all about me, live. And You rejoice to hear from me as much
as I do when I hear from children and grandchildren.

—ROBERTA ROGERS

February 6

*It is a good thing to give thanks
unto the Lord.* —Psalm 92:1 (KJV)

I was a bit edgy grocery shopping with my two grandsons. It had been a long time since I'd pushed little ones along in a grocery cart. (How had I ever managed with four?) Alex, age four, was mostly quiet and helpful; Luke, nearly two, was excited, wide-eyed, jabbering constantly and determined to stand up in the cart. I tried to concentrate on my grocery list, but Luke seemed bound and determined to say something to me. I stopped and looked him right in the eyes. "What is it, Luke?" Delighted to have my full attention, he pointed happily over to the bakery section, which we were approaching.

"Thank you," he said to me in obvious anticipation and full trust. He pointed to the chocolate chip cookies.

"A dozen chocolate chip cookies," I said to the clerk. Each time the woman dropped a cookie into the white sack, Luke said loudly, "Thank you!"

There was something about Luke's thank-yous that took away my edginess, and a flush of gratitude swept over me. *Thank You, Father, for this little boy. And for Alex, too,* I prayed silently. *Thank You that I can take care of them today.*

That afternoon as I began the hour-plus drive home, more thank-yous popped into my mind. *Thank You, Lord, for this car that You helped me pick out when I was a widow. Thank You that it didn't rain today. Thank You that a husband who loves me is waiting at home.* What a wonderful feeling it was just to be grateful—and to know what I was grateful for! Why, it even felt good to say, "Thank You, Lord" for things I didn't particularly enjoy: a detour; having to stop and pump gas; red lights. I had forgotten what a remarkable feeling of joy giving thanks triggers somewhere inside us—that is, until two-year-old Luke taught his fifty-four-year-old grandmother a new thing or two.

*(A thank-you prayer I'd like to sing:) Thank You, Lord, for
saving my soul, thank You, Lord, for making me whole....*

—Marion Bond West

Go to the ant, thou sluggard; consider her ways, and be wise.
—PROVERBS 6:6 (KJV)

What a mess! We had had to move into our new home several weeks early, and extensive remodeling was still underway. Our walls looked like they had had major surgery, and plaster dust covered floors, furniture, and boxes.

"I can't take anymore," I wailed as I flopped into a chair. A small cloud of dust rose around me. "Lord, I just can't cope!"

As if to comfort me, Dusty, our new and obviously named kitten, reached out to pat me with one black paw. She left a white paw print on my jeans, climbed into my lap, and began to lick her paws clean. "You could sweep," her accusing eyes seemed to say.

"Sweep?" I asked her. "With all those rooms still left to sand, what good would that do?" Dusty merely went on licking. With a sigh, I admitted to myself that sweeping would at least stop the endless tracking from room to room. And it would give me *something* to do.

Seizing a broom I furiously swept not only dust but my own frustrations into a pile and dumped them into a bag. And as room after room emerged fresher and cleaner, I began to see other things I could do. I could wash slipcovers. I could move the furniture into rooms that were already sanded, and protect it behind closed doors. I could put down mats, and insist that people wipe their feet.

Gradually the house began to look more homey. I dug out candlesticks and candles, and found that candlelight dining not only lifted our spirits, but also hid the ugly walls.

Since that time, whenever a project seems overwhelming, I remind myself to find some tiny chore, some little thing I can grab hold of and do. And inevitably that one chore leads to others that finally lead to a solution to my immediate problem.

Dear Lord, save me from the inertia
that comes from self-pity.
—PATRICIA HOUCK SPRINKLE

FEBRUARY 8

*In you they trusted and were not
disappointed.* —PSALM 22:5

everal years ago, inspired by a book I'd read, I made a list of thirty
people I hoped to meet one day. The list was wide and varied,
including writers, motivational speakers, and celebrities. Amazingly, over the
past several years, I've met eighteen people on that list. Some of them were
everything I'd expected, and others were major disappointments.

Not long ago, after one such disappointment, I was complaining to God
about how disillusioned I'd been. Then God spoke to me in my heart: *Debbie,
you asked to meet these people, and I'm happy to send them into your life, but I want
you to make another list.*

"Another list?"

*This time leave the spaces blank. I'm going to send thirty people into your life
whom I want you to meet, and I promise you none of them will be a disappointment.*

This prayer-time conversation has had a curious effect on me. Now,
whenever I meet someone. I look at him or her with fresh eyes and wonder if
this is one of the people God is sending into my life. I find that I'm more open,
more receptive, waiting expectantly for those God wants me to meet. Since
then, I've been blessed in countless ways. I've still got my original list, but it's
not nearly as important to me as the one God asked me to keep.

*Father, thank You for the special people You have sent into
my life. Not a single one has ever disappointed me.*
—DEBBIE MACOMBER

February 9

*Add to your faith...patience; and to patience godliness; and
to godliness brotherly kindness.* —2 Peter 1:5–7 (KJV)

I had my hands in the meat loaf when the phone rang. Many cooks use spoons or forks to mix such ingredients, but my hands work better for me. That's why I had to snag a table knife then a couple of paper towels to scrape off the excess before grabbing the ringing receiver, which, by the way, still feels greasy.

"May I speak to Mrs. Wolseley, please?" the caller asked.

"This is she," I answered, trying to recognize the young woman's voice.

Five seconds later, I said, "Not interested!" and slammed down the phone.

Another telemarketer, this one pitching siding, for goodness' sake! I returned to the meat loaf mix, still grumbling in exasperation.

A few days later a letter arrived from my teenage granddaughter. "I finally found a temporary job. But it's a bad one," she wrote. Karen had spent weeks trying to find part-time work to help with her finances while carrying a full school load.

Well, you guessed it. She, too, had turned to selling by phone.

"Grandma," her letter continued, "people scream at me and call me names and slam down the phone. I don't want to bother them. I'm just trying to get through college."

Telemarketers have interrupted our dinner hour—yes, and meat loaf mixing, too—several times since Karen's letter arrived. But I no longer yell, "Not interested!" and bang down the receiver. You see, the voice on the other end of the line may belong to somebody's grandchild who's nearly as nice as mine.

*Lord, help me to be patient and to speak kindly
to everyone—even when I'm exasperated.*
—Isabel Wolseley

FEBRUARY 10

A merry heart doeth good like
a medicine. —PROVERBS 17:22 (KJV)

I tend to take myself far too seriously, overanalyzing, pushing myself too hard, feeling guilty if I'm not accomplishing something worthwhile all the time. So recently, my daughter Karen gave me a writing tablet with hilarious baby pictures on each page. Here were kids with expressions that looked like little old men or women, tough executives, primping prima donnas, pity-me Pattys, you name it. Each had a caption under it, spoken as though by an adult.

The one that really cracked me up was a kid with tight lips and intense, I'll-do-it-if-it-kills-me eyes. The caption: "Stress got me where I am today. WHERE AM I?" I laughed till my stomach hurt! Then I pinned the little guy on the corkboard over my desk. Whenever I find myself getting uptight, I just glance up at my little buddy and break into laughter.

Just in case you're one of those do-it-if-it-kills-me types, you might want to look for a cartoon that really cracks you up and pin it where you'll see it often. A merry heart might be just the medicine you need! Take it from one who knows, it'll do your heart good!

> *Lord Jesus, grant me the grace of a holy sense of*
> *humor. I'll begin by learning to laugh at myself.*
> —MARILYN MORGAN KING

Establish the work of our hands for us—yes, establish
the work of our hands. —Psalm 90:17

*E*very time I take out my mother's rings, I can see her hands. They were elegant hands, with long fingers, the nails perfectly shaped ovals. She painted them with brightly colored nail polish—usually red—that chipped and wore off so that the spots of color that remained were like ruby islands floating on her pale pink nails.

I look at my own hands and remember that I could only write a little after she was diagnosed with lung cancer late last fall, and that my pencil stopped when she died the following January.

Close to the end, I see my hands moving tentatively to lay a cool towel on her forehead. I see my hands lying on the arms of the recliner where I slept next to her bed.

Suddenly, I laugh when I remember my daughter Lanea's young hands fussing over her grandmother, moving with twentysomething rhythm to find music to comfort her or putting my mother's favorite movie into the video player.

Finally, I feel my son Chase's hand on my shoulder, keeping me steady and reassuring me while he and I sang "How Great Thou Art" at her funeral. His hands were no longer a little boy's hands; they were big and strong enough to keep me upright.

When I'm done reminiscing, I put away the rings. I grab my laptop and begin to work. The hands I see before me are my own. They are alive, and they are strong—just like my mother's hands.

Lord, thank You for generations who comfort,
teach, and strengthen one another.

—Sharon Foster

For we have great joy and consolation in thy love.
—PHILEMON 7 (KJV)

*M*y mother tells a story about her younger brother Bob, as a child in the late 1920s, running to lock the front door when it was time for his beloved grandmother to leave. A tiny Norwegian lady who wore her white hair swept up in a bun, my great-grandmother's arrivals were highly anticipated by her grandchildren, and her departures were deeply regretted.

No one has ever tried to lock me in to prevent me from leaving, but I also get chagrined end-of-visit reactions from my grandchildren. Sarah, three, disagreed when I announced I had to go. "No, Grandma, you do not have to go."

When my husband interrupted our play, three-year-old Clay, whose home is near ours, said, "No, Papa, Grandma can't go home yet. We're playing our game."

One time Caleb, five, rattled off his telephone number as I was leaving and said, "Maybe you can call my dad and he can give you a ride back here." A ride from Minnesota to Alaska is a long one!

Hannah, seven, reminded me as I was dropped off at the airport, "When you love someone, they're in your heart forever."

Yes, they are. The love between grandparents and grandchildren is like the Old Testament story of the oil in the widowed woman's lamp: no matter how much is poured out, it stays full.

God of the generations, whether it's 1929 or 2029,
a grandparent's love spreads joy and comfort.
—CAROL KNAPP

*"How can you say to your brother, 'Let me take
the speck out of your eye,' when all the time there
is a plank in your own eye?"* —MATTHEW 7:4

I picked up last night before going to bed. Honestly, I did. The children have only been up for an hour, so I've no idea how the file cabinet got covered in plastic animals or what the biology book is doing in the kitchen or when the fourteen-car pileup occurred on the living room carpet.

I am not a neatnik; my standards aren't stratospheric. I want things tidy enough that we can function and avoid major injury. I dole out chores, we vacuum daily, the kids pick up their rooms almost every night. But our apartment always looks as if it hasn't been cleaned in weeks.

Perhaps this is simply the fate of seven people living in five rooms. Perhaps it's because we race out the door—to ballet, to math group, to choir, to church, to something—every day of the week. I could put some of the blame on homeschooling: science experiments and pattern blocks and phonics workbooks do make a mess. Whatever the excuse, trust me: at the end of the day, it's clear this house is inhabited.

People tell me that there will be a time when I'll be wistful for the tiny blocks that now cripple me when I go into the boys' room at night. That's remotely possible. But one day there will be no one left to blame except my husband and me for the mess that's still here. Then I'll have to come clean and admit that my half-read book is among those on the sofa and my coffee cup is next to the computer. It might just be easier to pick up toys. Facing my own shortcomings is a lot harder than tackling someone else's.

*Is that a speck of dust, Lord, that keeps getting
in my eye? Or is it something bigger?*

—JULIA ATTAWAY

FEBRUARY 14

Be of good courage, and he shall strengthen your heart,
all ye that hope in the Lord. —PSALM 31:24 (KJV)

It was absurd that I had to wear a hat every time I went out my back door, down the pathway to the garage. A tiny hummingbird was dive-bombing me! The audacity of that little creature exhibited the courage of David to Goliath.

Her nest, the size of a walnut, was perched in a low-slung branch of the avocado tree outside my bedroom window. Her eggs had hatched, and two tiny beaks, like needles poking out of a minuscule pincushion, were barely visible. Within a few weeks the nest was empty.

Wrapped snug in a robe, sipping coffee in my favorite chair on the patio, I was treated to an aerial show like none other. The shimmering green and metallic red throats of a family of hummingbirds soared skyward, then dipped down to hover blossom-to-blossom through the clumps of bird of paradise and hibiscus. This four-inch bird cannot only soar, dip, and dive, but hover in place and fly backward at will!

I called upon that strength this morning. I'd found my energy diminishing. It seemed to take me twice as long to do half as much. Emotionally I was wobbly and apprehensive about fulfilling my commitments. I wondered where God was leading me and feared the future. A little hummingbird adjusted my perspective.

I will put my hope in the Lord and trust the One who has wondrously empowered small wings to strengthen my heart. I will soar in prayer to the highest heaven. I will hover in place as I wait for new direction. For affirming reassurance, I will fly backward and remember God's never-failing goodness and mercy.

Your perfect will for me...let it be, dear Lord, let it be.

—FAY ANGUS

"Before I formed you in the womb I knew you."
—JEREMIAH 1:5 (RSV)

When our granddaughter Kerlin phoned from Nashville, Tennessee, to say that she and her husband Jordan were expecting a baby, I was as excited as a great-grandmother-to-be should be.

"As soon as we learn the sex," Kerlin said, "we'll let you know."

This was a new dimension for me. When my children came along, you could only guess at an unborn baby's gender. They, in turn, expecting their own children, had opted not to know. Five months before the due date, Kerlin called with the news that she was carrying a boy. It was no longer "when it's born," but "when he's born."

Soon Kerlin and Jordan chose a name. Somehow, awaiting Adin Marshall Richter was different again from waiting for "the baby" or even for "him" to come. He had an identity, a name to sew on a blue blanket. I even wrote him a letter: "Dear Adin..."

The birth was still four months away when they set the date for his baptism. "We thought you'd like to make plane reservations ahead," Kerlin explained.

So much planning, so many details already decided—how strange it all seemed to me! Strange...and troubling. "Is it right, Father," I prayed, "to know so much so far ahead?"

I knew you, the answer came at once, *before you were born. Before you were conceived. Before the mountains and the seas were in place.*

Is five months too early to plan ahead? For an awestruck moment I had a sense of the unimaginable vistas of time as matter was flung into space, and galaxies formed, and the components of the Earth were forged in exploding stars. How far ahead did God plan for the creation of life...of humankind...of you and me?

Take away my fears for the future, Father.
It is already in Your care.
—ELIZABETH SHERRILL

Freely you have received; freely give. —MATTHEW 10:8

I'd been in a quandary for days. I was scheduled to be lay leader in our worship service on Sunday—a time to ask for and bless the offering—and I couldn't come up with an idea about what to say. Other lay leaders usually used personal stories or examples of stewardship.

I was still stewing over this challenge when my daughter-in-law and two granddaughters stopped by our house on Thursday.

"Oma, can I please have a cookie?" three-year-old Gabriella asked me. The question is a predictable part of our first few moments together.

As I handed her a chocolate chip cookie, her mom asked, "What do you say, Gabriella?"

"Thank you." She grinned, twirling around with her treat in hand. This exchange was so automatic that I hardly noticed; a parent teaching a child to say *thank you*. I did the same with my children, just as my own mother did with me, hoping not only to teach good manners and gratitude, but also to teach our children to become generous givers because they have been receivers.

The "thank-you habit": a good idea that is also God's idea. So as Gabriella twirled around the kitchen, I knew I had my Sunday stewardship story.

Lord, You are the "Giver of all good things," and we say
thank You by giving back out of what we've received.
—CAROL KUYKENDALL

*"Out of all the gifts to you, you shall present every
offering due to the Lord, from all the best of them."*
—NUMBERS 18:29 (RSV)

*O*n our twentieth wedding anniversary, my husband walked in the door
with a dozen red roses. I went to the living room cabinet for a vase and
saw several of our wedding gifts sitting on the shelf—china, crystal, silver—as
though they were museum pieces. "We'll save them for a special occasion," I'd
told Paul. But in twenty years we'd hardly used them. Most of the time they sat
waiting on that shelf. *Well, if this isn't a special occasion*, I thought, *I don't know
what is*.

Reaching for a vase, I thought of other gifts I might have stored away,
waiting for just the right moment. Like my gift for music. I hadn't sung in the
church choir for years; I always said I was too busy. But just like those wedding
gifts, weren't God's gifts meant to be used and enjoyed?

That night we set the table with our best tablecloth, our silver flatware, and
a cut-crystal vase filled with red roses. The kids especially enjoyed drinking
sparkling juice from etched crystal goblets that they'd never seen on our dinner
table. We laughed as the four of us clinked our glasses together. "Let's do this
more often," my daughter said.

"We will," I replied, as I made a mental note to go to choir practice that week.
After all, if every day is a gift from God, then all of life is a special occasion.

*Give me one more gift, Lord: the courage to
use all You've given me for Your glory.*

—GINA BRIDGEMAN

"Then listen to me; be silent, and I will teach you wisdom."
—JOB 33:33

Grandma lived with us all of my growing-up years. No one ever said it was easy for three generations to share one roof. We had our ups and downs; we kids found her old-fashioned notions ridiculous, and she considered our newfangled ideas equally absurd.

But it was not the generation gap between us that I remember most about Grandma. It was her total, unshakable faith and confidence in us. I can still picture her, tilted back a bit to see better through her glasses, shaking her head with its small knot of white hair as she read the daily newspaper.

"Tch! Tch! Tch!" was the sound her tongue made against her teeth any time she read of juveniles in trouble. "I am so glad this is not your name here." And then those blue eyes would pierce straight into me. "Oh, but of course it couldn't be. You would never do anything so bad like that."

And you know, she was right. I had my share of temptations, of course, but any time I felt my resistance weakening where something really *bad* was concerned, Grandma's words would stop me. Somehow, there was no way I could bear to break her trust in me.

Today, I proudly bear the name of "Grandma," and I feel that same confidence in my two grandchildren. I keep reminding myself that I must make them aware of my trust in them. I must give it to them as a buoy to cling to when the going gets rough.

I think this might even be the biggest job God has for us grandparents to do.

Lord, no joy, such as being a grandparent,
comes without responsibility. Help me to
fulfill mine in a way pleasing to You.
—DRUE DUKE

FEBRUARY 19

Now is the day of salvation. —2 CORINTHIANS 6:2

*M*y friend Helen works in a retirement home. One day she was telling me how most of the folks she works with tend to be good-natured and pleasant, praising the workers and enjoying the meals. The others tend to be unhappy and negative in their outlooks, railing at God and complaining about the surroundings.

"What do you think makes one person cheerful and upbeat, while another's outlook is doleful and sour?" I asked her one day.

"I wondered about that for a long time," she confessed. "So I started asking their relatives and friends. The one thing I'd consistently hear was, 'Oh, Mom has always been cheerful!' Or, 'He's the same old Dad I remember from when I was little.'" She laughed. "That's when I came up with my very own unscientific theory: *The way to be a happy* old *person is to be a happy* young *person*."

Her words really hit me. By the time I am eighty, I'll have lived 29,200 days! That's plenty of time to practice being cheerful about my lot in life!

Dear God, whatever my age, I want to be someone people enjoy having around. So let me start practicing today!

—LINDA NEUKRUG

"I have given you an example to follow." —JOHN 13:15 (TLB)

The game was on the line when my grandson David, eleven, came to bat in the top of the ninth inning. There were two outs and a runner on second base, and his team was behind by one run. I held my breath as David fouled off the first pitch, swung at and missed the second, took a ball low, and fouled off the third ball. Then he drilled a high fastball past the diving first baseman, batting in the tying run. He stole second and ended up scoring to give his team a 13-12 victory. I don't know who was more excited, David or his cheering grandma!

But the next game was different. David batted 0 for 2, and had trouble getting the ball over the plate when he pitched. He was pulled from the game in the fifth inning, and his team was knocked out of the tournament.

Still, my young grandson is able to keep baseball in perspective: The main thing for him is doing his best and having fun. He accepts his successes and failures, his wins and losses, for what they are—an inevitable part of the game. He did the same thing after the loss as after the win: he practiced batting to improve his skills. That's a pretty good example for living life, wouldn't you say?

> *Lord Jesus, thank You for loving me just as much*
> *when I strike out as when I hit a home run.*
> —PENNEY SCHWAB

For ye shall go out with joy, and be led forth with peace.
—ISAIAH 55:12 (KJV)

I put baby Henry into his stroller and bundled up four-year-old Solomon for our walk. Solomon donned the bright orange furry top hat he'd found in a secondhand store. Together, we walked down our country road to the town road that has a sidewalk and traffic.

Solomon helped push the stroller, and I kept my hand on his just to make sure he was safe. As a car approached, Solomon tugged his hand away and waved. The driver seemed a little surprised and waved. His wave was all the encouragement Solomon needed.

When the next car came, Solomon giggled. As it got closer, he jumped up and thrust his arms high and wide as if he were shipwrecked on a desert island, hailing a passing ship. The driver, passenger, and some children in the backseat waved back. Another car came. This time Solomon waved before they were close enough to see. The car approached: a tiny tap on the horn made Solomon double over in giggles.

In town, we bought the newspaper and some drinks. The man behind me at the register tapped Solomon's orange hat. "You're quite an ambassador, young man," he said. "I see you waving at all the cars, making people's day."

"What's an ambassador?" Solomon asked. "Someone who makes people happy?"

On the way back home, Solomon started to wave and I joined him.

It felt silly at first, but it was fun watching the faces perk up. I looked down at Henry in his stroller, wondering when he'd learn to join us in wishing the world a good day.

Lord, help me to be an ambassador
of Your joy to all I meet today.
—SABRA CIANCANELLI

FEBRUARY 22

*"I [wisdom] was his constant delight, laughing and
playing in his presence."* —PROVERBS 8:30 (TLB)

Rusty is a purebred papillon, with large ears and long fur at his jowls
that gives his face the look of a brown-and-white butterfly. He's the
neighbors' dog, and they're away at work most of the time. Rather than whine
and whimper at being left alone, Rusty has found someone to visit—us. Each
time he crawls through the hole he dug under our fence, he brings fun and frolic
into our lives. And that is often.

So much so that we're all agreed he's a time-share dog. If our neighbors aren't
home when darkness falls, Rusty "sleeps over" with us. Whether he's running to
catch a toy we've tossed or flirting with his own reflection in the swimming pool,
he's our much-looked-forward-to entertainment. If I'm stressed or just plain
down in the dumps, I follow Rusty's lead and take time to play, or I grab the
leash and we go for a walk—tonics that lighten me up. And when I'm feeling
lonely, like him, I visit a friend.

> *How lovely it is when unexpected blessings come into*
> *my life to cheer me up and put a smile into my heart.*
> *Help me to pass them on, dear Lord.*

—FAY ANGUS

But lay up for yourselves treasures in heaven,
where neither moth no rust doth corrupt, and where thieves
do not break through nor steal. —MATTHEW 6:20 (KJV)

A beloved grandmother who became ill was taken into the home of her daughter and family and tenderly cared for. She enjoyed the bedside visits with loved ones, especially her four-year-old great-granddaughter, Jill. Jill smoothed the covers, discussed the things she and her doll Moppet had been doing, and often brought Moppet with her to visit, too.

One day, the door to the bedroom was softly closed and Jill's mother told her gently, "Grandmother just went to heaven."

"In her nightgown?" Jill exclaimed, "She should have got ready!"

What Jill didn't understand was that grandmother had gotten ready a long time before. For this great and final journey, Grandma had packed days with prayers for family and friends; she had gathered up knowledge of God's greatness and shared it with many; she had given her love, her testimony, her time, and her tithes, witnessing to Sunday school classes, to strangers, and to any seeking the way. She had mended hearts, had lifted her voice in songs of praise in the choir and in her kitchen.

For this journey she had joyfully "got ready"—and had left behind a clearly marked road map as to where she'd be.

May we heed Your admonitions, Lord,
and lay up for ourselves treasures in heaven.
—ZONA B. DAVIS

White hair is a crown of glory and is seen most
among the godly. —PROVERBS 16:31 (TLB)

In my family it happens at age forty-two. Reading glasses. When my dad turned forty-two, he got them. Two years later, at age forty-two, my mom got them. And a couple years ago, when I turned forty-two, I was no different.

Before I turned forty-three, I noticed my knees started cracking every time I walked upstairs. Then my left shoulder ached whenever the humidity rose. Not long after that, my son Andrew announced, "You sure do have a lot of gray hairs on top, Mom."

My mother said it best when she recited her favorite poem shortly after she got her first pair of reading glasses:

I can see through my bifocals,
My dentures fit me fine.
My hearing aid does wonders,
But Lord, I miss my mind!

I laughed with her when she recited it years ago, and now that I'm reaching middle age myself, I've decided to keep my mother's sense of humor about it. I've also added this to my favorite quotes about aging:

"Age is a matter of mind. If you don't mind, it doesn't matter."

Lord, whether I'm thirty-two, forty-two, or
ninety-two, remind me to look for the positives
and not dwell on the "reading glasses" of life!
—PATRICIA LORENZ

*He wakens me morning by morning, wakens my
ear to listen like one being taught.* —ISAIAH 50:4

A few years ago, I took a long-awaited trip to Italy, spending a week in the Tuscany area. As we neared the end of our time there, our tour guide arranged for a "Meet the Locals" night. Five people from the town of Cortona came to give us a slice of what their lives were really like.

We met an artisan who worked in gold and his new wife, who had given up country life to live in town. There was an aged pastry maker. And a batik artist and her daughter, who sold handmade sweaters. We asked them questions about their genealogy, education, real estate prices, and opportunities for young people there. Then someone asked, "What do you think of tourists like us?"

The batik artist shook her head as soon as the question was translated. "Not the word! Not the word for you. A *tourist* is someone who comes to eat lunch. A *traveler* is someone who comes to make a discovery." Her gesture took in our entire group. "Ah, travelers!"

Today I am far from the quaint streets of Cortona, with its ancient doors and geranium-filled windows. But while I cannot choose to stroll in the plaza or visit the Etruscan museum, I can choose how I will spend this day—as a *tourist* who goes routinely from activity to activity or as a *traveler*, intent on discovery. And that decision, rightly made, can transform every day into a vacation from the ordinary!

*Thank You, Father, that You have given each of us a sense
of wonder and curiosity. Help me to exercise mine today.*

—MARY LOU CARNEY

FEBRUARY 26

But be ye doers of the word, and not hearers only.
—JAMES 1:22 (KJV)

*M*y friend Sharon was struggling in her new business. With the bills piling up, she was considering closing the doors and filing for bankruptcy. She was tired and fearful from the constant stress. I prayed for her every day, but her problems only worsened. So one day I just "laid it on the line" with God.

"What are You going to do about this, Lord?" I asked, angry that Sharon was still suffering.

Just that quickly, I heard my question come back. "What are *you* going to do about it?" God asked me.

Then I remembered something I'd read about three levels of prayer.

The first level is *Give me*. The second level is *Help me*. And the third and highest level is *Use me*. I was stuck at the first level.

How could God use me to help Sharon? I couldn't solve her business problems, but I could take on some of her daily tasks, giving her more time to devote to the business. I wrote checks and balanced her checkbook, even shopped and cooked dinner so she could relax at the end of a particularly trying day. It doesn't sound like much, but it meant fewer worries for her and a good feeling for me to know that I was really helping.

Now I strive always to pray, "Use me." It's hard, but I find that if I let God use me, the answers to "help me" and "give me" just follow naturally.

*Dear Father, use me today to help make my
world and someone else's a little better.*
—GINA BRIDGEMAN

February 27

And Moses was an hundred and twenty years old when he died; his eye was not dim, nor his natural force abated.
—Deuteronomy 34:7 (KJV)

Her old, elegant hands reach for the grand piano's polished keys. Fingers find familiar patterns. Love songs to God, love notes for her husband—gone these fifteen years—ripple and eddy around her petite body. Lustrous white hair forms a feathery halo in the lamplight.

Deep-set eyes—blue behind closed lids—are submerged in reverie. She is in conversation with her music, communing with her past. There is her "precious Bill," the handsome tennis player she still can't believe fell in love with her; her mother Nanny, who saved her minister-husband's meager wedding and funeral earnings to give her oldest daughter a start at college; her friends in China, with whom she weathered perilous World War II years on the mission field; her three accomplished children—and maybe, too, the infant daughter she buried on foreign soil.

"I don't feel old when I play my piano," she tells me. "It's like I have a friend who talks to me and I talk back." She needs this friend who won't leave her, who keeps her secrets, harbors her sorrows, and releases her joys.

She is my aunt, Elizabeth Blackstone. And she is one hundred years and two months old. As I watch her fingers swirl across the piano keys, I know why I traveled 2,500 miles to Monte Vista Grove in Pasadena, California, to be her caregiver.

Her hands grow tired and the music slows. Her eyes open. "The Lord's been good to me," she says, rising gracefully from the piano seat.

Silently, I thank her real Caregiver for inviting me to join Him.

As I grow older, Lord, may I continue to pound life's keys with passion.
—Carol Knapp

February 28

Then shall I know even as also I am known.
—1 Corinthians 13:12 (KJV)

*P*atsy's house is always immaculate," my sister-in-law said. "Patsy's dinner parties are divine!" another friend raved. So when Patsy stopped me after church and invited me for coffee the next day, I hesitated. If I accepted, I'd have to reciprocate. And there was no way I could be the perfect homemaker she was.

But I was new in town, so on Monday, after lecturing my children about not touching, running, shouting or *breathing* in Patsy's house, I rang the doorbell. She greeted me with her sunny smile, sent my children off to play with hers, and led me into the kitchen. There, spread all over the counter, were breakfast dishes, toast crumbs, open cereal boxes, juice spills, and a trail of toys. *Just like my house*!

I stared. Patsy laughed. "Because I used to be a home economics teacher, everyone thinks my house is always in apple-pie order," she said. "Well, some mornings it looks like this." She poured coffee and led the way to the living room. "I'll clean up later. Right now let's have a nice visit."

And we did. And I learned just how "perfect" Patsy really was—perfect in that she allowed herself to be open and vulnerable with me. There's a risk in letting others know what you are really like. Patsy made the first move, and the rest is history. It's been twenty years of friendship, and although we now live hundreds of miles apart, we still feel like next-door neighbors.

Lord Jesus, You revealed Yourself by becoming one of us.
Today, let me show my true self to a potential friend.
—Penney Schwab

February 29

Certainly this is the day that we looked for;
we have found, we have seen it.
—Lamentations 2:16

oo often, when my "to do" pile threatens to topple, I excuse my inefficiency
with "I could get caught up on all these tasks if I just had an extra day!"

Well, today is that day—a whole extra twenty-four hours to spend as I please!
It's one of those every-four-year days inserted in our calendar to compensate for
the quarter-day difference between man-made years and astronomical ones.

I must confess that as a senior citizen, I've had more complementary extra
days than those who haven't reached my age. In fact, I've even had a few freebies
that can't be attributed to leap year but instead to crossing the international
dateline. On one of those trips, I even had two birthdays when one February 17
came back-to-back with another. But that gained day was "lost" on the return a
week later when February 23 jumped to 27, so I can't really count that as an extra.

So what will I do with today's gift of twenty-four hours? I wonder if, by
midnight tonight, I'll tell myself, *I got my "to do" list done*! Or will it be, *I can't
believe I wasted all that time*!

Thank goodness, Lord, for the time
You give me that I can spend just with You.
—Isabel Wolseley

March

MARCH 1

"Return to Me with all your heart." —JOEL 2:12 (NASB)

*S*pring didn't hold much promise for me. It seemed that one of my sons had turned his back on God and was headed full steam in the wrong direction. I'd tried praying, Bible reading, counseling with friends, and talking to him. Nothing seemed to be helping him turn around. Everything looked dismal.

My husband Gene, picking up on my mood, said, "Let's walk down to the lake. Some Canada geese have been visiting. I've been feeding them every other day for more than two weeks." Silently we walked hand-in-hand to the lake. Gene had grabbed a sack of cracked corn in case the geese happened to be there. Just before we reached the water, we saw and heard the geese soaring overhead—in the wrong direction.

"Hey, guys!" Gene called loudly, cupping his hands to his mouth. "You're missing dinner. Come on back. Turn around."

I couldn't help but smile at the way Gene pretends the geese, ducks, and an occasional heron understand him. We stood still, watching their perfect V-formation sailing almost out of sight.

At first I thought it was my imagination. But, no, the lead goose turned and the others followed. They did a perfect U-turn high above and returned to Gene's call. They all touched down in the water and hurried toward the bank where their trusted friend waited.

> *Lord Jesus, if wild geese can return when called*
> *surely sons can, too. Please call his name.*
> —MARION BOND WEST

MARCH 2

Fear thou not; for I am with thee: be not dismayed;
for I am thy God. —ISAIAH 41:10 (KJV)

*S*oon after my husband Keith and I moved into our new house, our gray and white cat Pi got out through a badly fastened screen and vanished. Naturally, I panicked. For hours I went around the neighborhood calling her name, looking under cars and under bushes with equal scrutiny. When it got dark, Keith made me come home, but I was in tears that something terrible had happened to her.

The next day we made up flyers describing Pi and offering a hundred-dollar reward for her safe return. We went from door to door in our cul-de-sac and several of the streets nearby, passing out the flyers and telling our neighbors how much we really wanted our cat back. No one had seen her.

Two days later, Mary, who lived three houses down from us on the same side of the street, showed up at the door with Pi in her arms. "She was hiding in my backyard, and I found her when I was pruning my bushes," she said.

I snatched up Pi and ran for my checkbook.

"No, no," Mary said. "I'm happy I could return her to you."

I insisted that I wanted to give her something.

"Just be my friend," she said. "That'll be more than enough."

I hugged her and thanked her for bringing back Pi. And then I hugged Pi and thanked her for my new friend.

Lord, thank You for bringing good out of the things I fear.
—RHODA BLECKER

MARCH 3

Unto him that loved us, and washed us from our sins.
—REVELATION 1:5 (KJV)

I'll probably never meet Kara, now four years old. But one day she made a beautiful observation that has helped me:

"We had been standing on the hillside watching the airplane's skywriting," her grandmother wrote me one day. "When the words began to disappear, she asked, 'Why, Grandma? Where do they go?' Then, as I groped for an answer, her little face brightened, and she suddenly exclaimed, 'Maybe Jesus has an eraser!'"

I smiled as I read, but my eyes filled and suddenly I wanted to hug that little girl. For that morning I had been grieving over past mistakes. A cruel thing I had said to my mother the day I left for college. And Dad...if only I'd invited him to that luncheon where I was to speak—he'd have been so proud. One tender but painful memory releases others: the time I'd punished a child unfairly, humiliated my husband, let a friend down....

No matter how much we mature as people, grow as Christians, try desperately to compensate, memories of our own failures rise up to haunt us, and sting—how they sting. For me, it's not the unkindness of others that hurts so much or lasts so long, it's the burden of my own. Yes, I ask God to forgive me, and try to believe that I am forgiven. But the memory won't go away. And if I can't forgive myself, how can God?

Then a little girl, in her innocence and wisdom, makes me realize: like that writing on the sky that simply disappears, Jesus has wiped away all the things I so bitterly regret. Jesus does have an eraser.

Dear Lord, thank You for that child. Now I can forget,
because I am forgiven. I too have an eraser.

—MARJORIE HOLMES

MARCH 4

Lord...you have made my lot secure. The boundary lines have
fallen for me in pleasant places. —PSALM 16:5–6

Three-year-old Kyle, my nephew's son, lives on seventy acres covered with woods and pasture. Within view of his front door there's a farm pond with quiet fish and noisy bullfrogs. Kyle has never seen my city apartment, shaded by a few maple trees sheltering noisy mockingbirds.

I visited my sister, Kyle's grandma, last month, and Kyle was there.

He wanted to play a pencil-and-paper letter game with me. He doesn't know how to write letters, but he's obviously grasping the concept.

"What's the first letter of your name?" he asked me.

"E," I said. He wrote down some indistinguishable squiggles. "What's the first letter of your father's name?"

"J."

"What's the first letter of your mother's name?"

"F."

"What's the first letter of your frog's name?"

"My what?" I thought I'd misheard.

"You know, your frog—in your pond."

It took me a second to figure it out. "Babe, I don't *have* a pond." Or a frog. "I'm not as blessed as you."

Since then, when I've needed a smile, I've thought of Kyle's blind assumption that everyone has a personal pond. That everyone has the same good fortune as he.

But as I walk my small yard and hear the mockingbird's songfest, I also know I was too quick in my comeback that Kyle is more blessed than I. I have my own good fortunes. Some are in my natural environment: my maples and songbirds. Some are in my family: my siblings who eagerly share joys and sorrows. Another is three years old with a pond of his very own. The first letter of his name is *K*.

Lord, my good fortune may not seem to be as
expansive as someone else's. But in Your good grace,
help me to see how very blessed I am.

—EVELYN BENCE

MARCH 5

Encourage one another. —1 THESSALONIANS 4:18 (NKJV)

I dried my hands and answered the soft knock on the door. There stood Richard, the handsome ten-year-old from next door. In his arms he lovingly held a kitten of the ordinary alley cat variety.

Richard beamed as he said, "Mrs. Duncan, isn't he beautiful? I named him Tiger because he has stripes."

Sure enough, the kitten was striped in tiger fashion, but as I looked down at him I thought he had a long way to go to be worthy of that name.

Then Richard held him higher so I could see him better and said, "Look at his eyes. I love his eyes! They are just the kind I hoped he would have!"

Instantly I saw Tiger in a different light. With all that love to surround him, I knew he would be a wonderful pet. Richard hurried away to show Tiger to the next neighbor. I stood in the open door a few moments, looking out into the dusk and wondering how many people I knew who—with love and the proper encouragement—could step up from their "alley cat" roles to be "tigers."

Lord, help us recognize the power of love to
liberate the potential in those around us.
—MILDRED BROWN DUNCAN

March 6

*For therein is the righteousness of God
revealed from faith to faith.* —Romans 1:17 (KJV)

Recently I heard a story about William Randolph Hearst, the famous newspaperman and collector who filled his mansion with art masterpieces. One day he learned of a painting that was supposed to be especially valuable and commanded his scouts to search for it. At last, one of them came back and reported that he had located the painting.

"Buy it!" commanded Mr. Hearst.

"You already own it," replied the scout. "It's in a crate in one of your warehouses."

My initial reaction to the story was amazement. How could Mr. Hearst lose track of such a treasure and not put it to use? Then I remembered the restless night I'd spent in a hotel the week before, worrying about the keynote speech I was to make the next morning at a conference. *Have I prayed about the speech?* No. *Have I asked for God's support and placed my faith in Him, so I can relax and get a much-needed good night's sleep?* No. *So where is my faith, my greatest treasure of all?* Locked up, I decided, in some dusty warehouse.

I resolved right then to get my faith out of storage, polish it up, and put it to use.

heavenly Father, today and every day I put my faith in You.
—Madge Harrah

"You are to judge your neighbor fairly."
—LEVITICUS 19:15 (NASB)

There's an old joke that says, "If the doctor tells you that you only have six months to live, join your homeowners' association. It will be the longest six months of your life."

I only wish that I had heard that joke before I joined the board where I lived. I faced the first meeting with eager anticipation and the following meetings with dread. By the end of the third meeting—to decide if potted plants on the balconies had to be in pots under twenty-four inches or thirty-six inches—I was ready to jump off a balcony. Instead, I silently invented nicknames for the other participants.

There was Dina, the "Detail Woman," who would wave a copy of the rules and regulations as she let us know about every tiny loophole in whatever we were discussing; "Lucy Late," who dashed in halfway through and insisted on a recap of every topic; and Bruce, the "Big-Picture Guy," who kept saying, "We're not seeing the big picture here!"

After the meeting droned to a close, Julie, a longtime neighbor, walked alongside me as we left the meeting room. "That was dull as a butter knife," I commented.

"You made your feelings pretty obvious," she told me.

Stung, I stopped in my tracks. "But I didn't say a word!" I protested. "No," she agreed. "You just rolled your eyes, sighed a lot, and drummed your fingers on the table." More kindly, Julie continued, "Long ago I realized that these meetings would never be entertaining. But they *are* necessary. So if I'm going to participate, I need to be there, body and soul."

I had to admit that Julie had a point. And while the meetings never became interesting, I did learn that I could respectfully listen as we took care of the necessary business of living in a neighborly way.

God, sometimes my silence can speak more sharply than my words. Help me listen to everyone respectfully.

—LINDA NEUKRUG

MARCH 8

My soul thirsts for You.... When I remember You on my bed,
I meditate on You. —PSALM 63:1, 6 (NKJV)

I keep a glass of water by my bed to sip during the night and first thing in the morning when I wake up. By doing this faithfully and by drinking more water during the day, I think I stay healthier and succumb to fewer viruses.

How I long for water in the morning! After gulping down the glass by my bed, I head to the shower. The forceful spray rids me of my sluggishness. My stiffness fades, my lethargic mind awakens and begins to burst with ideas and enthusiasm for the day ahead.

Morning prayer has the same effect on my soul's thirst. Recently I told my pastor that I yearned for more time to pray in the morning and regretted how long I snuggle under the warm comforter before I get out of bed.

"Use that time when you're still in bed," he advised. "When you first awaken, begin praying. Turn your thoughts to God right then and there. Offer Him your day and talk to Him about any anxieties you may have. Whatever thoughts come, turn them to God."

I've been following his suggestion, and what a difference it's made in my "soul health"! Like my first sips of water, that initial groggy turning to God often quickens my sense of thirst for His presence. And when I get up early enough to have a longer time of prayer before the day's work begins, that morning prayer is like a long shower—cleansing, refreshing, and invigorating to my soul.

Dear Lord, help me be more faithful to prayer
each day. Thank You for quenching my thirst
and washing me with Your living water.

—MARY BROWN

MARCH 9

"I tell you the truth, unless you change and become like little children, you will never enter the kingdom of heaven."
—MATTHEW 18:3

Last Sunday I attended church with my friend Lurlene. By the time we arrived, the sanctuary was almost full. "We like to leave the back pews for the families with little children," Lurlene said as she steered me toward the front of the church.

I glanced into the rows as we passed. Young mothers and khaki-clad fathers sat with children between them. Small quiet toys were on the floor, and little hands were already busy scribbling on scraps of paper.

After the opening Scripture and hymns, the pastor moved on to the prayer. It was a long and sincere prayer, starting with the missionaries and moving on to the concerns of the church, including supplications for the well-being of several local women who were expecting.

At the end of his prayer, the pastor invited the congregation to join in the prayer that unites all Christians: "Our Father, who art in heaven..."

The mature voices droned out a subdued recitation of the familiar prayer. But coming from the back rows were smaller and brighter voices. "Our Father, who art in 'eaven, hawoed be thy name." Word for word, the children offered the Lord's Prayer, a bright descant to our more plodding, predictable rendition.

I listened to the children and thought about what they were saying.

Our Father. Already they were learning that they had not only an earthly father but also a heavenly One.

My mother used to say that "God has no grandchildren, only children." I thought about that as I listened to the final strains of those little voices. And I was pretty sure that the tiniest seekers in the building were also those closest to their Father.

Thank You, God, for children. Even as we teach them,
may we be open to the things they can teach us:
innocence, simplicity, and absolute trust.
—MARY LOU CARNEY

March 10

*You are a letter from Christ delivered by us, written not with
ink but with the Spirit of the living God.*
—2 Corinthians 3:3 (rsv)

*I*t was nearly midnight when I climbed into bed, exhausted. As my
eyelids closed in preparation for blissful oblivion, my hand touched
something hidden under my pillow. A piece of paper, folded up. I pried my eyes
open and turned on the light. It was a letter—typed—from Mary, age five.

"I HOP WE KAN GIT TOO GETR AGIN SUNE. MARY JULIA"

I smiled. Mrs. Julia is Mary's persona when we have tea parties.

From time to time I buy a box of fresh cookies at the bakery around the
corner, get out the good china, and invite my kids to tea. They pretend to be
adults, and we sit and chitchat about their children and the challenges of
parenting. The kids love it. I do, too, especially when they share their insights on
what causes children to misbehave or feel loved.

It was kind of silly how loved I felt at that moment, sitting in bed in the
middle of the night. We'd had a tea party that afternoon. It was fun, but almost
lost to memory after bulldozing the kids through evening chores, keeping
night prayers on track, and making sure teeth were brushed, stories told, and
monsters banished.

It was awfully nice to have a love note. I'd like to have more of them. For that
matter, I ought to write a few myself.

Jesus, let's get together again soon. I love You.
—Julia Attaway

MARCH 11

Trust in Him at all times, O people;
*pour out your hearts to him. —*Psalm 62:8

I saw a robin!" My mother's voice on the phone had the singsong quality of smug victory. She might as well have added, "*Na-na-na-na-na!*" She likes to win this game.

Mom and I have an annual competition to see who can spot the year's first robin. It started the year I left home, and it's been going on for more than two decades. Here in Connecticut, the first robin is a big deal. It means that the winter will, indeed, end, even when we're convinced it's going to go on forever. Mom and I are not winter lovers by any stretch of the imagination. For both of us, it's always been a long, gray crawl from Christmas to Easter. So the first robin is an important signpost, and even more so this year.

My grandmother has been ill for months, and my mother's older sister died shortly after Christmas. Our lives have been touched by melancholy, and the road ahead looks bumpy and gray as mortality looms large in our lives. To make matters worse, it's also been the coldest winter in a decade. It's hard even to imagine Easter. Then Mom's call came. I couldn't remember the last time she sounded so excited.

This year's sighting was the earliest yet. Three days later, I saw a dozen robins gathered together in some undergrowth by the road. A dozen! It was nine degrees out. Mom may have had the victory, but we both won this year.

God's lesser creatures know what we advanced folk sometimes forget: Easter and spring always come. Sometimes, we just have to wait awhile.

Lord Jesus, let me never forget that You are risen
and present in all circumstances and in all seasons.
—Marci Alborghetti

MARCH 12

The Lord receives my prayer. —PSALM 6:9 (NASB)

*E*very morning I sat down in front of my computer with eager anticipation and pressed the "send and receive" button for my e-mail, waiting to hear from our youngest son Glen and his family, who live way out West on Vancouver Island. Had they tried the recipe I'd sent them for old-fashioned cookies? Had they chuckled at the joke I'd forwarded? Did the children explore the website I thought would be of interest to them?

No response.

Oh, they're probably just so busy they haven't got around to answering yet, I tried to console myself.

Several days passed. I sent them a few more e-mails. Still no response.

I began to worry. Maybe they were all sick in bed. Worse yet, maybe there'd been an accident. Maybe...well, you know how mothers are.

I picked up the phone. "Hello, Glen?"

"Oh, it's you, Mom. Say, what's happened to the e-mails? We haven't heard from you in a dog's age!"

"You haven't? But I've sent all kinds of messages. I was wondering why you weren't answering."

That was the day I learned that just because I send an e-mail message doesn't mean that it arrives. After several phone calls, our Internet service provider discovered a glitch in the system. My messages were being intercepted and scrapped as junk mail ("spam" in computer jargon). The very idea!

Once the problem was cleared up, it didn't take long before Glen was responding.

"Yum...the cookies turned out great."

"Check out this website."

"Here's a funny for you."

How grateful I am that there are no glitches in God's system. When I send Him a prayer, He not only receives it, He responds. He always gets the message.

Thank You, God, that none of my concerns are "junk mail" to You.

—ALMA BARKMAN

MARCH 13

And now these three remain: faith, hope and love. But the greatest of these is love. —1 CORINTHIANS 13:13

I was visiting my daughter Laura on Whidbey Island in Washington, where she was a part of the AmeriCorps community service program. I wanted to feel close to her, and yet not be too much of a mother—1 didn't want to be a walking suggestion box. More than that, I wanted to be able to put aside the differences we have in our outlooks on life.

Laura met me at the ferry, her long dark hair and sparkling blue eyes standing out in the crowd. We hugged and laughed, then roared away in her noisy pickup. As we talked, I swallowed hard at some of her free-spirited opinions.

We stopped to walk a trail she'd helped build. At the entrance was a kiosk she'd built and painted. "I hurried to get it finished before you came," she said. On it she'd painted a colorful outdoorsy scene with an enormous sun pouring down over all.

"It's beautiful, Laura," I said.

She always did favor the sun, even as a small child. As we walked the trail, I told her a story about her childhood. *Does she even want to hear this*? I wondered. But when I finished, she said, "Mom, thank you. I like it when you tell me things from back then. No one else can give those things to me but you."

The whole week was like that, a twining of old and new. At week's end, when we parted at the ferry, she said, "I love you, Mom. You'll always be my mother."

We laughed and hugged tight. "I love you too, honey," I said. "I'll be praying for you."

"I'm glad," she said. I could tell she meant it.

As the boat pulled away from its moorings, I waved at Laura, feeling the strong sunshine of her grown-up love—and the grace that allowed me to get out of the way to receive it.

> *Lord, help me to keep letting go of my daughter,*
> *while holding her in prayer.*
> —SHARI SMYTH

*And this is his command: to believe in the name of his Son,
Jesus Christ, and to love one another as he commanded us.*
—1 JOHN 3:23

*W*hen our dog Cookie was about eleven years old, we got a puppy,
another white puffball named Dolly. I was used to my comfy
old dog and had forgotten how mischievous an energetic puppy is. Every day
I chased after Dolly with my shoe in her mouth, or yelled at her to not pull
Cookie's tail, or picked up the tissue snowstorm after Dolly had emptied and
shredded an entire box.

One rainy day after Dolly had burst through the doggy-door with mud-
covered feet, I yelled to our daughter Maria to catch her before she painted half
the house with mud. Maria grabbed her as I reached for a towel. "What am I
going to do with this dog?" I asked in frustration.

"Love her, of course," Maria answered, hugging Dolly tightly as she carried
her to the kitchen sink. Her simple admonition was absolutely right. No matter
how I may feel about what Dolly has done, I need to love her. Discipline and
train her, yes, but at all times, love her.

Even with her adorable puppy face, that's easier said than done, because she
simply isn't lovable all the time. Who is? Yet I know God loves me always, not
just when I please Him. Jesus' command is to "love each other, as I have loved
you" (John 15:12 NIV). I need to remember that when I get annoyed with my
husband or frustrated with my children.

God's love for me never changes. How comforting to know He simply loves
me, no matter what.

*Gracious God, amid life's messes and irritations,
help me to love as You have loved.*
—GINA BRIDGEMAN

Even when I am old and gray, do not forsake me, O God.
—PSALM 71:18

We were moving my mother from her Connecticut house of forty years into a retirement community nearby. She hadn't balked at selling and giving away and cleaning out. In fact, she seemed fairly cheerful in accepting that in her eighties she couldn't keep up the house and yard anymore.

"I don't mind this move," she told me. "It's the next one I dread. That will be the one to the nursing home, I'm afraid."

Mom was wrong. Her next move, after recuperation from colon cancer at ninety-one, was to private care in Virginia a few miles north of me. Then she moved, at ninety-two, to a fine assisted-care facility in Pennsylvania. But that was too far away, so at age ninety-three, we moved her to another assisted-care place near us. She had now had three "next" moves, none of them to a nursing home.

In the meantime, however, Mom took out her dusty faith and began to reassess it. She decided really to believe that God loved her, personally; that the Bible's teachings on eternal life were accurate and that Jesus really was the Savior; that in trusting Him she would find the ultimate confidence for her "next" move. With joy, I watched my mother come to a peace about death and dying—the peace that passes understanding, the peace Jesus alone gives.

Lord of all life, thank You that no one is ever too old to come to You in new or increasing faith.
—ROBERTA ROGERS

MARCH 16

*D*on't throw anything out!" the voice on the phone instructed. I was in the melancholy last phase of clearing out my mother's home in Miami Beach. Everything she could use in the nursing home—clothing, furniture, photographs—had already been shipped, other things labeled for sending to various family members. Now only odds and ends remained.

"Nothing of value," I apologized to the lady who'd answered the phone at the thrift shop.

An hour later she pulled into the driveway, followed by two men in a truck. "We'll take everything!" she told me. End tables, dishes, a lamp, old magazines, even a worn bathroom rug went out to the truck. But...a handle-less cup? A chess set with missing pieces? In growing amazement, I watched the three of them carry away broken clothes hangers, a card table with only three legs.

"You have no idea," the woman told me, "what treasures these will be for someone." They served elderly people living alone in single rooms, poverty invisible on Miami Beach's sunny surface. "With a few repairs and some ingenuity on their part, anything you give us will be used."

Anything? Surely there was *something*, somewhere in the house they wouldn't accept! I found it under the kitchen sink, a dishrag so full of holes we'd been using it to wipe the floor. Even this was carried triumphantly to the truck.

"How—who—" I began.

"We'll wash it," she said, "put a one-cent sticker on it, and someone cooking on a single hot plate will have a way to clean it."

Nothing of value? From that day on I have not called "worthless" anything that need and imagination can turn into treasure.

*Bestower of blessing, let me learn from the needy
of the world to value each and every provision.*
—ELIZABETH SHERRILL

March 17

The priests who carried the ark of the covenant of the Lord
stood firm on dry ground in the middle of the Jordan.
—Joshua 3:17 (NASB)

After my father died, his parents chose me to handle their personal affairs when the time came. For years, I'd dreaded the responsibility. Then, years later, my ninety-one- and ninety-two-year-old grandparents were admitted to the hospital.

My hands trembled as I drove to my mom's holding a vase of flowers for my grandmother. Stacks of terrifying documents sat on the floor of my Jeep—power of attorney papers, bank statements, Social Security information, brochures from assisted-living facilities. Each time I glanced over at the piles, my heart skipped a beat. *How am I ever going to handle all of this?*

Just as I turned into my mother's driveway, I tipped over the vase, spilling flowers and water all over the papers on the floor. *Don't You see, God?* I cried. *I can't do this!*

I carried the sopping wet mess into the house. "I've only just gotten started," I told my mom, "and I've already ruined everything!"

"I know just what you need," Mom said. "You'll see." She ran back with a beige briefcase with a long strap. "When I began working years ago, your sister gave this to me. I want you to have it." She handed me the briefcase, took the wet papers, and spread them out to dry.

The instant I slipped the strap of Mother's briefcase over my shoulder, I stood taller and my breathing slowed down. "Now you look like you can handle anything," Mom said.

I asked Mom for some file folders and started sorting the papers. Later that day when we went to the hospital, my confidence in my ability to care for my grandparents seemed as real and close as the briefcase on my shoulder.

Thank You, Father, for the tangible signs of
Your presence—and of my mother's love.
—Julie Garmon

March 18

And I John saw the holy city, new Jerusalem,
coming down from God out of heaven, prepared as a bride
adorned for her husband. —REVELATION 21:2 (KJV)

On my drive to work I have to pass through an area of the highway called T-REX, which stands for Transportation Expansion Project.

We're two years into the five years it's supposed to take the city to build a mass transit system right through the heart of Denver. To city officials, it's an exciting answer to our congested highways. To me, it's a nuisance.

I see it for what it is today; they see it for what it will be tomorrow.

They have vision. And over and over, on television and in the newspapers and with signs along the highways, they try to communicate that vision to people like me. As I sit in bumper-to-bumper traffic, I need to know that the suffering is temporary and the best is yet to come.

God is the creator of vision. He who knows the end from the beginning promises us over and over again that what's in store for us is to be in heaven with Him.

He keeps telling us the best is yet to come. So we should be encouraged while we endure disappointment or pain—or traffic snarls. God gives us His vision of heaven to hold in our hearts.

Father, help me to see Your vision,
so I can look forward to what will be.

—CAROL KUYKENDALL

MARCH 19

And looking upon Jesus as he walked, he saith,
Behold the Lamb of God! —JOHN 1:36 (KJV)

*W*e had taken our young grandson to the zoo and had watched with delight his excitement and awe as he had viewed tigers, lions, elephants, kangaroos. On our way home, we stopped to visit young friends who had a little boy just Robbie's age.

"I went to the zoo," Rob announced proudly.

His little friend looked envious. "What did you see?"

I wondered which animal would be named first—the ferocious lion that had roared so obligingly or the huge elephant that had delicately lifted a peanut out of Robbie's fingers.

"A chipmunk," Robbie answered, affection and pleasure warming his voice. "When we were having our picnic, a chipmunk ran right across the grass."

For a second I felt astonishment and a touch of disappointment.

With all the great exotic animals to choose from, why had he chosen a tiny creature he had seen every summer of his life?

But Robbie's friend saw nothing unusual about the choice. "A chipmunk," he echoed, his face glowing. "I wish I had been there."

It was because the chipmunk was small and familiar, I decided.

The lions and elephants were really too large and exotic to really be believable.

Isn't it that way with God? I thought. The idea of a God so vast He can create a universe is sometimes almost beyond the mind's grasp. But Jesus was man as well as God—familiar and real and within the scope of our understanding.

Father God, thank You for sending Your Son in a
form I can recognize, identify with, and understand.

—LOIS T. HENDERSON

And encouraged them with these words.
—2 CHRONICLES 32:6

I've never thought of myself as a funny person ever since I tried to tell a joke at a party years ago and a strange man told me I'd gotten the punch line wrong.

But for one week last year I had the experience of feeling I was a good storyteller. It happened like this: When shopping in an antiques store with my mother-in-law, she picked up an old plate with an exorbitant price tag and whispered to me, "The cost is ridiculous! Why, my grandmother had the same thing."

I said, "*Shh*! I once saw a sign in an antique store that said: 'We Charge Fifty Percent Extra If We Have to Listen to What Your Grandmother Had.'"

My mother-in-law thought that was so funny that during my entire visit with her she told practically everyone "the funny sign Linda told me about." Every single time we were in a group, she'd say, "Linda told me the funniest thing today." Then she'd nudge me, "Tell them." I basked in her encouragement, and by the end of the week I felt like a budding Bob Hope. I even got up the courage to tell a small joke back at work.

Since then, I've applied that kind of encouragement to others. When I said to a student, "You used such a vivid example in your writing," I began to see more vivid paragraphs in that young man's work. When I told a sometimes gruff employee, "You have such a pleasant manner on the phone," in just a week I wondered why I had ever considered him to be gruff.

Just as I'd lived up to my mother-in-law's praise so, too, did everyone else around me live up to mine.

Let me congratulate, not correct, someone today,
God—a coworker, a spouse, a child.
—LINDA NEUKRUG

Will you be my prayer partners? —ROMANS 15:30 (TLB)

I simply can't work with that woman another day!" I wailed to a friend. "She's always right, has a sharp tongue, and is incredibly stubborn."

"You could fire her," my friend said when I paused for breath. "But is that the best solution? Have you done everything you can to help her do her job?"

"Of course!" I replied indignantly. "I've coached, I've sent her to seminars, I've provided written instructions, I've—"

"Have you prayed for her?" he asked.

I hadn't, I confessed, because I didn't think God would change her. But as I set myself to pray for her anyway—diligently and daily—something else happened. I began to change, to view her behavior in a different light. Yes, she had a sharp tongue—but she spoke from frustration, not anger. She was stubborn—but a more fragile person would have broken under the workload she carried. And she *was* right—most of the time!

As I gained understanding, I was able to appreciate her dedication, talents, and significant contributions. When I concentrated on the good points, I was able to deal more effectively with her shortcomings. In time, we were able to work together harmoniously and productively.

"Prayer changes things" reads a plaque on my office wall. When I go to God in prayer, He sometimes changes situations, and even other people. Most often, however, He changes me.

Lord Jesus, thank You for the privilege of
praying for others, and for the refreshment and
renewal that comes through prayer.
—PENNEY SCHWAB

MARCH 22

We are the children of God. —ROMANS 8:16 (KJV)

I was a happy child, but I longed for one thing that I never had—my own bedroom. When my husband Gene and I bought a new home, my granddaughter Jamie, nine, helped me select wallpaper for one of our guest rooms. Excitedly, she picked out a pattern with a bouquet of blue and pink flowers held by a blue ribbon.

"This is what I'd want for my bedroom," she said.

"Me, too," I joyfully told Jamie.

Now there's a bedroom in our home that suggests a little girl lives with us. A quilt nearly matches the paper and covers an old, painted iron bed. Dolls, pillows, and handmade stuffed kittens are piled on the bed. Old-fashioned storybooks are spread out on it, and an old trunk holds some ancient paper dolls, waiting to be dressed. There's even a deck of well-worn "Old Maid" cards. In a corner, small animals and dolls enjoy a tea party set up on miniature wicker furniture. The white wicker baby scales that I was weighed on as an infant hold some of my children's first shoes. Little girl clothing hangs about the room. There's a child's straw hat for dress-up occasions. A pair of china dolls sits primly, waiting to be picked up and loved. This, at last, is the room I wanted as a child.

But it's more than that. It's a room where I can go and feel the freshness of youth again. It's a special place for talking to God about our children and our ten grandchildren. In my little girl room, I pray them into His care.

Thank You, Father, for loving all the little children
of the world no matter how old we are.

—MARION BOND WEST

MARCH 23

Like arrows in the hand of a warrior are sons born in one's youth. Blessed is the man whose quiver is full of them.
—PSALM 127:4–5

My husband Wayne and I were blessed with four children in a five-year span. By the time Dale, our youngest, was born, I hadn't slept through the night in three long years. The house was in constant chaos, and in those pre-disposable-diaper days, the washing machine was going day and night. My hands were more than full with the demands of our growing family. Thankfully, I was blessed with wonderful parents who visited us often. Soon after Dale's arrival, my mother came to help.

Early one morning, when our newborn woke for his feeding, his older sisters and brother came looking for attention. Jody sat on one knee and Jenny on the other, and Ted shared space with his infant brother on my lap. All too soon, the older three started squabbling and whining.

My mother woke up and joined us in the living room. "Oh, Debbie," she said with a smile, "these are the happiest days of your life."

Aghast, I looked at her and said, "Mom, you mean it gets worse?" Now, in retrospect, I can see how very blessed I was. Mom had the perspective to see it then; thank God, I can see it now.

Lord, give all parents the patience, the prayer, and the sense of humor they need to raise their children in Your grace.

—DEBBIE MACOMBER

*If our earthly house of this tabernacle were dissolved, we
have a building of God, an house not made with hands.*
—2 CORINTHIANS 5:1 (KJV)

I was born and raised in Ireland, and for the first ten years of my life I lived in my grandmother's farmhouse. How I loved that house! Every inch of it reflected my beloved grandmother's taste and talents, from the delicate lace curtains she wove to the splendid patchwork quilts she made from scraps of cotton. I always thought of the farmhouse as home, and after I moved to America, vacations to Ireland included long visits with Grandma.

When Grandma died at the age of eighty-six, her house and its contents were sold. I wanted to buy the home but couldn't. For many years afterward I harbored a longing for it and was saddened to think of it occupied by strangers.

Then, one year, I returned to Ireland with my young son. I wanted him to see where I was born, so we drove to the farmhouse. As I parked the car near the front gate, the new owner came out and when I introduced myself, he very kindly invited us in for tea.

But once inside, I felt strange. The house that had been a cocoon of happiness to me now seemed different. It was as if I had never played, laughed, and loved there.

As we were leaving, my host said, "Come back any time." I smiled at him and realized that without Grandma living there it wasn't the same house any longer. It was *people*, I now saw, that brought the love and warmth to make a house a home. And the memories of "home" was something I always would carry *within* me. As we drove away, I hoped the new owners would be happy making this house their home.

*Lord, help me to accept change and move with the seasons of
life, holding in my heart the joys and warmth of things past.*
—STEPHANIE ODA

MARCH 25

Behold, children are a heritage from the Lord, the fruit of the womb is a reward. —PSALM 127:3 (NKJV)

Mama! You say the weirdest things!" my daughter protests, and I laugh while she groans.

"What did I say so wrong?" I feign innocence, pouring it like syrup on pancakes. Lanea is now twenty-seven and I'm forty-six, but we giggle long distance on the phone like schoolgirls—schoolgirls talking way past their bedtimes. We gab each night, mostly about nothing, but each word says we love each other. Each conversation is a choice to be friends.

It was so difficult to leave her when I moved to Chicago. I packed way too quickly, laughed too loudly, and left too many things behind. We drove to the airport pretending that my excitement over my move was also hers and that neither of us was fearful in any way.

We hugged good-bye at the curbside check-in, and I saw the same look on her face she's probably seen a thousand times on mine. Looking down at me from her six-foot height, her expression said, *Are you sure you know what you're doing?* When the woman checking me in told me that my flight was delayed because of snowstorms in Chicago, Lanea's doubtful expression became more pronounced. Her eyes widened and one of her eyebrows lifted higher. "I'll be okay, baby," I reassured her.

She hugged and kissed me again, waved, and then drove away, looking like a mother dropping off her child at school for the first time.

My oldest baby is grown up, and I am far away. To my mind, our separation was as much about giving her a chance at independence as any adventure I might be having in the big city. I can laugh with her now and not worry how each sentence, each word, will affect her future. Now each time I call and we laugh and giggle, she knows that while I'll always be her mother, I'm also her friend.

Lord, thank You for giving us the courage to be friends.
—SHARON FOSTER

Mine eyes are ever toward the Lord. —Psalm 25:15

My granddaughter Tirza recently turned one. During my daughter Kelly's pregnancy, I'd hoped for a brown-eyed girl. In my father's family the boys had brown eyes and the girls their mother's blue. I'd inherited my dad's darker eyes and passed them on to my daughter. I even purchased an elegant brown-eyed doll for Tirza before she was born and shared with the doll's designer my dream for a third-generation girl with chocolate eyes.

In the weeks after Tirza was born, I studied her eyes whenever I held her. They were a tantalizing mystery. While flirting with earth tones, that pesky blue wasn't giving in either. Finally Tirza's eyes cast their vote. Did brown win? Not exactly. But they sure weren't blue. They ended up slate gray with brown flecks. My wish hadn't been completely ignored!

Someday I'll tell Tirza the story of her grandma's thwarted dream. And I won't leave out the most important part: brown, blue, green, or gray, as long as they look to Jesus, the Lord of life, her eyes are the right color.

> *Jesus, Son of God, the eyes that see and*
> *love You are beautiful beyond telling.*
>
> —Carol Knapp

MARCH 27

"And if you greet only your brothers, what are you doing more than others?" —MATTHEW 5:47

While visiting the library the other day, I picked up a book on the architecture of houses in America. One of the earliest design elements, I learned, was the porch, connecting the house to nature and the world outside. While the tall stone structure of a castle is designed to keep the world out, the porch welcomes the world to the front door. The porches pictured were wide and inviting, reminding me of the "front-porch people" I've met, whose open arms and inviting smiles seem to say, "Come and sit for a while, and we'll get to know each other."

So I ask myself, *Am I a front-porch person*? I think of the time in our Sunday-morning service when the pastor asks us to greet people around us. It's too easy to smile and say "Good morning" without much thought behind it. Do I ever introduce myself or ask their name? Do I greet them as I would a visitor to my own front porch? Or do I smile and shake hands automatically, creating an impenetrable castle wall that sends the clear message, *Don't get any closer*?

Jesus seemed to encourage the front-porch attitude as part of what it meant to follow Him.

Welcome to my home, Lord. Welcome to my heart.
—GINA BRIDGEMAN

Be strong and of good courage; do not be afraid,
nor be dismayed, for the Lord your God is with
you wherever you go. —JOSHUA 1:9 (NKJV)

*E*very summer when I was a child, Grandma Kobbeman presided over our annual family reunion at Sinissippi Park in northern Illinois surrounded by her five children, their spouses, and her twenty-four grandchildren.

One year, when Grandma was well into her seventies, she decided to ride her grandson's motorized go-cart. We held our breath when she squeezed into the seat, pressed the accelerator to the floor with her heavy brown oxfords, and threw the little engine into World Cup competition. She flew across the track and down into the baseball field, barely missing the popcorn stand. As she headed for a row of poplars at the edge of Rock River, she released her foot from the accelerator and came to an abrupt halt at the edge of the water.

For a woman who had watched our country change from horse-and-buggy to men-on-the-moon, Grandma had adapted with a remarkable sense of adventure.

I later asked her, "Why aren't you afraid to try new things?" She just smiled and said, "Faith in the Lord is all you need, honey."

I'll always be grateful for Grandma's example—and the faith that never fails to inspire me when I feel afraid or am filled with doubt. Last year I soared down a steep waterslide with my children, rode on top of an elephant, and took my first helicopter ride.

Isn't there something you've always wanted to try but were afraid? Do what Grandma did. Depend on your faith in the Lord and plop down on that go-cart!

Lord, with Your help I'll keep a spirit of
adventure alongside my "go-cart of faith."
—PATRICIA LORENZ

MARCH 29

*For whom the Lord loves He corrects, just as a father
the son in whom he delights.* —PROVERBS 3:12 (NKJV)

*S*ome years ago my daughter surprised her artist great-grandmother
with a fistful of hastily colored pictures. Grandma looked them over
carefully, then remarked gently, "You know, these aren't really pictures. They're
more like scribbles!"

I had always greeted Rebecca's efforts with a casual, "How pretty, dear," and
was afraid her feelings would be hurt by Grandma's bluntness. But Rebecca took
the criticism evenly. "I'm not too good at coloring," she admitted.

"You could be," Grandma told her. "Bring me your crayons and lots
of paper."

The two, separated by more than eighty years, spent a happy hour exploring
the world of color and design. Rebecca learned to color, and I learned a lesson,
too: criticism, offered in love and followed by constructive action, is far more
valuable than empty praise.

*Dear Lord, may I learn to give and
receive criticism in Your spirit of love.*

—PENNEY SCHWAB

MARCH 30

Jesus answered, "I am the way and the truth and the life."
—JOHN 14:6

*M*y grandson Drake and I were standing outside church one Sunday morning, waiting for the rest of the family to join us. I was, as is my custom, dressed up—a lacey top, a gauze broom stick skirt, and a great straw hat with a band of tulle and a cluster of silk hydrangeas. Suddenly, the sun disappeared and it started to sprinkle. "Oh no," I wailed, "my beautiful hat will get wet!"

Drake looked at me, considering this for a moment. Then, with perfect three-year-old logic, he said, "Nana, your flowers will like it. They need rain!"

I laughed, even as the drops became thicker. All Drake knew about flowers was that they needed water. And in this summer of drought, he had watched his mother and me water, water, water. He wasn't aware that silk blossoms this perpetually full could be had for $3.99 at craft stores.

Knowing what's real and what's not is pretty much a lifelong quest, whether you're seeking true love, testing the waters of a new friendship, or choosing which tub of butterlike substance to buy for your morning muffin. I'd like to say that age has rendered me an expert at sniffing out the fakes in life—the friend who will desert you just after you tell her your dearest secret, the designer blouse that will fray the third time you wear it, the "special offer" that isn't quite as special as it claims—but I still make mistakes in judgment.

I have learned, though, to cling tightly to those things that have proven themselves good and true and real: my husband Gary, my family, my closest friends, and, most of all, my faith. There's nothing fake or fleeting about the way God has seen me through the traumas and temptations of my life.

In this world of confusing decisions and
clamoring options, You, Lord, are the one true thing.
—MARY LOU CARNEY

MARCH 31

In the world ye shall have tribulation:
but be of good cheer; I have overcome the world.
—JOHN 16:33 (KJV)

I've been getting more forgetful lately. For instance, between dialing a telephone number and waiting for someone to answer, I can totally forget whom I'm calling. When someone asks if I'm free at 3:00 p.m. on Wednesday, I sometimes can't remember without checking my calendar. And when my daughter impatiently tells me her math teacher's name *again*, it doesn't even sound familiar. Most people joke that forgetfulness is merely a common sign of aging. "At our age you start wondering more about the *hereafter*," a friend jested. "You walk into a room and wonder...now what am I *here-after*?" I laughed, but part of me didn't think the joke was funny. At forty-five, I don't like the idea of aging.

Last week, something happened that changed my perspective. Our dear minister Dr. Bob died of a rare lung disease at the age of seventy. At his memorial service, a family member passed on his final message to us, the flock he shepherded for twenty-five years. "Tell them," he whispered near death with a faint smile, "*the best is yet to come!*"

I now repeat that hopeful promise to myself whenever I start worrying about aging—or any other problems, for that matter. And even when I'm forgetful, I vow not to forget those comforting words.

Father, with the promise of heaven in my future,
the problems of the present seem more tolerable.
—CAROL KUYKENDALL

April

APRIL 1

God has surely listened and heard my voice in prayer.
—PSALM 66:19

I've been noticing young mothers with their children lately. Maybe it's because my own children are now in their thirties and forties, and I like to remember what they were like when they were little.

On Easter morning I enjoyed seeing all the children dressed up for church in new pastel colors. The little girls wore hats, and the small boys sported new suits. The young fellow who sat in front of us each Sunday wore a solid white suit with short pants. His hair was combed perfectly, and I couldn't help but steal glances at him sitting attentively next to his mother. When we stood to sing, he climbed up on the seat so he could see better. That's when I saw he was wearing very old but obviously beloved cowboy boots with his new white suit. Had his mother forgotten to have him change shoes? He sang loudly and clapped along with the lively music about a risen Savior. He and his mother exchanged looks of pure love.

Sadly, I knew I would never have allowed one of my sons to wear those boots with a brand-new suit on such a special Sunday. We would have fought all morning, but I would never have relented. My unhappy child would have worn matching shoes to church, probably asking himself what a loving God had against cowboy boots.

As the pastor prayed, I peeked at the little boy. His head was bowed and his hands folded underneath his chin. He didn't move an inch. He may have been only four, but he had obviously come to worship with a happy heart.

Dear Lord, help my inside and outside
to match when I come to worship You.
—MARION BOND WEST

APRIL 2

Behold, I make all things new. —REVELATION 21:5 (KJV)

*M*y family's Easter message that year came unexpectedly. Tindy, our gray-and-white Persian cat, leaped nimbly to the kitchen stool and from there to the refrigerator top. She sniffed at the hard-boiled colored eggs that had been left in a rack to dry. *Crash!* The eggs, intended for the children's Easter baskets, rolled on the floor. I gathered them up, but cracks and lines now spoiled the colorful surfaces.

"They're ruined!" cried Jenny.

Granny thoughtfully studied the situation. Then she sat down, picked up an egg and a wax crayon, and began following the crack with a line of green. Soon a vine circled the egg. Then she added tiny green leaves and red and yellow flowers. Like magic, the cracks were transformed. She then went to work on the others and soon all were bright with colorful designs.

"Why, they're prettier than before," Jenny cried.

And they were.

The Easter message? Broken eggs, like broken people, can become more beautiful than ever. The eggs needed Granny. Broken people need Jesus Christ.

Because I love You, Jesus, and because You have died for me,
I am made whole and beautiful once again.

—DORIS HAASE

Now they were on the road, going up to Jerusalem, and Jesus was going before them; and they were amazed. And as they followed they were afraid. —MARK 10:32 (NKJV)

They had reason to be afraid, these disciples following their stubborn leader into the stronghold of His enemies. To me this reluctant trip represents the journeys in my own life that I don't want to take.

One of them was to the nursing home in Sudbury, Massachusetts, where my elderly mother was dying. I'd made the five-hour drive from New York many times, but this one, I knew, would be the last. Our son had brought two-year-old Lindsay up from Florida, so I could show Mother her great-granddaughter. "Before she dies" were words we didn't say.

In Mother's room, Lindsay sat very quietly on my lap. I'd worried that the sights and smells of a nursing home might be frightening for her or that Mother's beautifully wrinkled face might seem forbidding.

After perhaps half an hour, Lindsay began to squirm. "She's sat about as long as a two-year-old can," I apologized to Mother.

I set Lindsay down and took her hand to lead her to the door. She pulled free and ran straight to where her great-grandmother sat bent in her wheelchair. Reaching up a tiny hand, she stroked Mother's cheek. Again and again, that gentle stroking. Mother's eyes opened, blue as the little girl's, and the two smiled at each other.

Watching, it seemed to me that Jesus was showing me Mother as He saw her—not an old and ailing woman, but a wide-eyed young girl at the beginning of life.

This vision of Mother has stayed with me through all the years since: Jesus' gift delivered by a child on the journey I didn't want to take.

"Jesus went before them." As He goes before each of us down every fearsome road.

Help me follow Your steps, Lord Jesus.
—ELIZABETH SHERRILL

APRIL 4

I am listening carefully to all the Lord is saying.
—PSALM 85:8 (TLB)

I love a good movie. I've lost count of the many times I've seen television reruns of *The Sound of Music, My Fair Lady, Chariots of Fire,* and Sir Anthony Hopkins playing C. S. Lewis in *Shadowlands,* to name a few. Currently, I've taken to watching a TV program that features actors, actresses, and directors in hour-long interviews that give inspirational insights into their childhoods and their struggles to get to where they are.

The high point of the program comes toward the end, when as part of the regular format, the featured personality is asked, "When you get to heaven, what do you want God to say to you?"

The answers vary from, "Whew, I'm glad you made it!" to "Welcome, come on in" or, as in one original response, "We're not ready for you yet. Go back down to earth!"

The answer that left the greatest impression on me came from the director who said that throughout his childhood, in his home, the Scriptures were read aloud every day. He wasn't given a choice. Day in and day out, he had to sit and respectfully listen to the Word of God, so much so that when he gets to heaven he would like God to say to him, "Thanks for listening!"

I've thought a lot about that director's answer. Because the Word of God is the voice of God to me, I've now taken to reading my daily devotional passages of Scripture aloud so that I might better listen, not only with my inward ear, but also with my outer ear. When I get to heaven, I hope God also says to me, "Thanks for listening!"

> *What an awesome and magnificent voice You have,*
> *O Lord! Help me listen daily to the beauty of the Psalms,*
> *the wisdom of Proverbs, the promises spoken through the*
> *prophets, and, most of all, the voice of Christ.*
> —FAY ANGUS

APRIL 5

*"My God, in whom I trust!" For it is He who delivers you
from the snare.* —PSALM 91:2–3 (NASB)

I'd had it with Willie, our fat gray-and-white tomcat. If we let him sleep inside during the night, he'd wake me up around one o'clock with a constant *meeeeeoow* until I let him out. Then, promptly at four o'clock, he'd stand at the front door and demand to come back inside. When I let him in, he'd meow relentlessly at the side of our bed until I stomped upstairs and topped off his bowl with a few more pieces of dry food. During the day, Willie paced in my kitchen window boxes, trampling through my flowers, his wide eyes seeming to say, "Meet my needs. Meet my needs."

I complained to Jamie, our twenty-year-old daughter, who had just finished house-sitting for us for a weekend. "I don't know what you're talking about, Mom. While I was in charge, Willie behaved like a perfectly normal cat. He slept at the foot of my bed all night. I fed him once each morning. He purred a lot, but I don't think he meowed much at all."

Is it just me, God? I prayed. *What am I doing wrong with Willie? Even our cat has begun to control me!* God's gentle spirit seemed to impress an unwelcome truth on me: Too often, I handled friends and family just the way I handled Willie. I'd zoom in to fix people's problems, until my constant "helping" made them think I was at their beck and call and left me feeling exhausted and irritable.

Then I came up with a simple plan: From now on, I'd shut our bedroom door at night and turn on the humidifier so I couldn't hear Willie. He could meow as much as he wanted; I wasn't going to jump up to get him more food. In a few days, Willie learned the new rules. So did I.

*Lord, before I start trying to fix everything and everyone,
remind me to pray and share my problem with You.*

—JULIE GARMON

APRIL 6

Let them do good, that they be rich in good works, ready to give, willing to share. —1 TIMOTHY 6:18 (NKJV)

*W*hen we moved into our new home, the first thing on our agenda was to redo the garden in the front yard. We dug up overgrown boxwoods and ligustrum, and replaced them with colorful camellias and lantana. We even planted a holly tree. Our hard work paid off—our garden was beautiful—but we had exceeded our budget by hundreds of dollars.

The next summer, wiser about our needs and committed to staying within our budget, we mapped out a more realistic garden in the backyard. I had my doubts that it could match the fabulous garden we had created in the front yard.

"We're calling it 'gardening on a budget,'" I explained to my friend Lee.

"What a great idea!" she exclaimed. "I've got some agapanthus I've been wanting to separate. You can have as many as you can pull apart! And call my daughter Cindy. She's ready to thin her daylilies."

Jeannie and Hilly gave us Louisiana irises from their front yard, and Steve and Kathleen brought over pots of hostas and begonias. Another friend alerted us to a plant sale at a local university where the agriculture students offered great deals.

"Not only did we stay within our budget, but we now have flowers with a history," I explained to my daughter, a new homeowner. "When the time comes, I'll divide up my flowers for you, and then you can do the same one day."

Now when I look at my bucket daisies, sweet Williams, and the rest of my flowers, not only do I see a beautiful garden but also the generosity of my friends who made my gardening on a budget more meaningful than I ever imagined.

Lord, what can I share with others today?
—MELODY BONNETTE

The eternal God is your refuge, and underneath are the
everlasting arms. —DEUTERONOMY 33:27 (NKJV)

*M*y daughter's call from the hospital emergency room reached me at the convalescent home where I was visiting my ninety-three-year-old mother. My granddaughter Robin, just turned six, had fallen from the high bar at school, injuring her mouth severely. I picked up her sisters, aged two and four, and spent a hectic, tense afternoon supervising the little ones while awaiting Kris's return with Robin.

The doctor had put eight stitches inside Robin's mouth, six on the outside. As the littler ones swarmed over their mother, Robin sat squarely in the biggest chair in the living room. Her face puffed almost beyond recognition, her long hair still ropey with dried blood, she looked tiny and forlorn. Still, I approached her cautiously, for Robin is the least demonstrative, the most private of children.

"Is there anything you want, darling?" I asked.

She looked me firmly in the eye and said, "I want a hug."

Me, too! I thought, as I cuddled her on my lap. *But how and whom does an exhausted grandmother ask?* As we rocked gently the words came: "I will pray the Father, and He shall give you another Comforter, that He may abide with you forever" (John 14:16 NKJV).

So I asked, just as simply as Robin had done—and just as simply felt the everlasting arms enfold us.

Holy Spirit, thank You for Your role as Advocate,
as Intercessor, as Counselor; but thank You most especially
for Your tender warmth as Comforter when I need a hug.
—ELAINE ST. JOHNS

APRIL 8

Choose the good. —ISAIAH 7:15 (NKJV)

I wish I had beautiful fingernails like you," I remember saying to Irene Solomon as I snuggled near her on the living room couch. Mrs. Solomon was a family friend who had come to stay with my brother Davey and me, so that my mother could go on a trip with my father. As far as I was concerned, everything about Mrs. Solomon, from her lovely red nails on, was perfectly wonderful.

Holding my seven-year-old hand in hers, she said, "Well, we can do something about that."

Soon Mrs. Solomon was patiently painting my scraggly fingernails that same bright red. "You know, Pamela," she said, "your fingernails are either being bitten off or they are growing long like mine. You can choose which way you want them to be."

I don't think I ever bit my fingernails again. And that's not all I learned from Mrs. Solomon. In the mornings, she put bright red cherries in the middle of our grapefruit; she let me wear my Sunday shoes to school; and at night she made us cola floats in my mother's crystal goblets. Later, on my eighth birthday, when everyone else was giving me useful things, she gave me an evening bag made of woven silver.

Though Mrs. Solomon worked well past retirement age in downtown Chattanooga, Tennessee, rode back and forth to work on a city bus, and lived in a tiny house in a modest neighborhood, she never stopped eating her cereal out of china bowls, painting her fingernails red, or (even in her late nineties) giving outlandish birthday presents to her friends.

The truth is, a cherry makes a grapefruit sweeter, china and crystal are made to be used, presents don't need to be practical, and you and I are either making life nicer or we're not. The choice is ours. Mrs. Solomon taught me that.

Father, in every moment of every day,
a choice waits. Help us to choose the good.
—PAM KIDD

APRIL 9

You will surely forget your trouble. —JOB 11:16

Although my Grandma Rae was housebound because of severe arthritis, she never let it get her down. She was well-read, informed on news events, and through TV was up on all the latest trends. Visitors dropped by daily, myself included. One time a friend came to spend an hour cheering up Grandma. But it seemed that all she wanted to do was complain—about the weather, about a lazy husband, about a son who didn't visit often, about....

Grandma listened patiently, but when the woman began listing *Grandma's* troubles ("Oh, you poor dear, you can't walk"), Grandma put a stop to that right away. "I make it a point," she said firmly, "to forget my troubles as easily as most folks forget their blessings."

I remember being shocked at Grandma's blunt words and wondering how her friend would take them. But after a short pause, the woman laughed and began talking about the pleasure she got from her gardening and other hobbies!

I've always remembered these words. They come to me whenever I'm tempted to let my troubles cloud out a clear and sunny day. And so I pray:

> *Dear God, let me be as quick to forget my*
> *troubles as I tend to be at forgetting my blessings.*
> *And help me to remember Your goodness always.*
> —LINDA NEUKRUG

APRIL 10

The earth is the Lord's, and everything in it,
the world, and all who live in it. —PSALM 24:1

As I sit on my porch, the world according to the morning paper lying heavy on my lap, grim news fills me with a sense of doom. The world, I think, is spinning out of control. *Lord, where is the hope?*

Across my long porch, a male finch perches on the edge of a hanging fern, warbling his heart out. His tune, I think, also carries news. Grabbing my binoculars, I look inside the fern at the tiny nest cradling three pale blue eggs. The eggs have somehow survived cat-stalking, storms, and at least one bird of prey. My newspaper slips to the floor. Through my lenses, I watch the plain, brown female pecking at the eggs. *They're hatching!*

I wait awhile, then I creep closer, climb on a railing, and angle the binoculars to peek inside. The hatchlings are twined together, the size of a nickel, naked, helpless, and mud brown. They cannot feed themselves and, left alone, their shallow, exuberant breathing will soon cease. But their parents are hovering nearby to nurture their brood, so they can grow up and fly and sing their song and propagate their species all over again.

Here, in this little backyard miracle, I see the hand that holds the world. An event too small, too ordinary to make the morning paper. But, light as a feather, soft as a whisper, its good news lands in my soul. God is in control.

Creator God, thank You for the works of Your hand
that cry out the awesome truth of Your care for me.
—SHARI SMYTH

APRIL 11

Jesus...said..."I have come as light into the world."
—JOHN 12:44, 46 (NKJV)

One evening, while I was taking care of my little granddaughter, Saralisa discovered a most spectacular toy: Grandma's flashlight! She found out that just by pushing a lever she could cause *light* to shine! Of course, we turned off all the lights and played with our new toy, flashing it all over the room, across the ceiling, into Grandma's mouth, into her own eyes, shining it through our fingers to turn them red, giggling and squealing with delight through it all. Next she shined it on my old dog Oscar, and then, one by one, on the photographs of family members that hang in my family room, naming each one.

Later, after my little one was asleep, I sat there quietly thanking God for the shining wonder I'd seen in Saralisa's eyes and for the joy it gave me to be "in on" her marvelous discovery. Then it occurred to me that prayer is like that light beam. Even in the darkest passages of life, we can shine the light of Christ on those we love, and upon ourselves as well.

I'm going to make this a part of my evening prayer time, and it will be a good way to teach Saralisa how to pray for others, too.

Loving Christ, Light of the world, may my
prayers tonight beam Your love into the lives of

_____.

—MARILYN MORGAN KING

*I am reminded of your sincere faith, a faith that dwelt first
in your grandmother.* —2 TIMOTHY 1:5 (RSV)

O utside my grandparents' home one day, a neighbor's child suddenly
announced, "I don't like you."

Well, I ran crying to Grandma, who wrapped her arms around me and kissed
me. "Let's see if a cookie will help," she said. Grandma was right. A cookie, plus
a glass of cold milk, did help. But soon anger replaced the tears.

"I'm going back out there and telling that Emily I don't like her either!"
I announced.

"Tell you what," Grandma answered. "Why don't you ask her to come inside
and have some cookies, too. Remember, the Bible says we should return good
for evil." I glowered in skepticism but finally gave in.

Grandma was right again. The promise of another cookie did it.

Soon Emily and I were cutting out paper dolls in the front room, then playing
jacks on the sidewalk. That was the beginning of our being "best friends."

Now here I am a grandmother, nearly seventy years later, and not much has
changed. I still believe that returning good for evil is the best way to treat others.
I'm thankful that I learned that early in life from my dear grandmother. It is the
seed I want to plant in the tender hearts of my growing grandchildren.

*Father, thank You for the lesson my grandmother taught
me—and for her faith. Help me to pass my faith on to my
grandchildren today and every day.*

—ISABEL WOLSELEY

April 13

For it is written, "As I live, saith the Lord,
every knee shall bow to me." —Romans 14:11 (KJV)

One of my most vivid teenage memories is of my father, a pastor, kneeling to pray beside our living room sofa. For him, respect for the majesty and authority of God meant kneeling when he came into God's presence through prayer.

I, on the other hand, have taken a more informal approach to prayer.

I encouraged my own four children to pray openly and spontaneously as they were growing up, but we never knelt to pray. Our son Philip developed an especially deep and meaningful prayer life, along with a hunger to study the Bible. I often thought how that would have pleased my father, who died when Phil was just two and a half years old.

After we moved from Alaska to Minnesota, Phil, then twenty-four, came to live with us for a few months. Every day he would shut himself away for a time of prayer in our upstairs guest bedroom. One morning, after he had left the room, I noticed that the bedspread was rumpled at the foot of the bed. I walked in, and as I bent to smooth it, I saw two distinct indentations in the soft rose carpet—the impressions of my son's knees.

Almost shyly, I knelt down on the same spot and settled my own knees into the carpet. With tears of joy and gratitude, I thanked the Lord for His generosity in giving me a father and a son who loved Him in the same way—on their knees.

Lord God, help me carry the blessings
of prayer into my family's future.
—Carol Knapp

April 14

God revealed these things by his Spirit.
—1 Corinthians 2:10

*P*arakeets were never at the top of my favorite pet list. But when someone I know needed a new home for her two birds, Hercule Poirot and Miss Jane Marple, I took them, wire cage and all. The birds nuzzled and chirped all day long—until the time I left the cage open and Hercule and Miss Marple made a run (or should I say, fly?) for it.

I tried catching them with my hands; they flew across the room. I tried throwing a light cloth over them; they seemed to be laughing as they flew by it. I put cups of birdseed on the curtain rods. Then I got a broom, taped it to a blue plastic laundry basket, covered the basket with some pink netting torn from a dress I hadn't worn in a decade, and thought, *They'll never get away from this*! Well, they did.

My neighbor, to whom I'd never said much more than "hello," knocked at my door. "I heard such a racket through the wall," she said, "that I wondered if everything was all right."

It's hard to say "everything's fine" when you're answering the door, holding a blue laundry basket festooned with pink tulle and fastened with duct tape to a broom handle, two parakeets flying feverishly around your head, and cups of birdseed falling to the floor. But with my neighbor's help—she somehow got Hercule to land on her finger, and Jane followed shortly after—I got the birds back safely to their cages.

What did I learn from my adventure? Well, I don't know very much about parakeets. And never say no to a helping hand—or finger—no matter the embarrassment.

God, thank You for birds that fly as they were
meant to and for good-hearted neighbors.
—Linda Neukrug

April 15

If you are wise, your wisdom will reward you.
—Proverbs 9:12

Before my daughter Lindsay and her new baby were discharged from the hospital, her doctor came to check her out. Her husband was taking a load of flowers down to the car, so she and I listened together as he reviewed some precautions for Lindsay's first week at home. Then he sat on the edge of her bed and gave her one last piece of advice.

"Let your husband take care of the baby—and let him do it his way," he said. "If you always tell him how to change her or dress her or burp her, he'll simply stop helping. Babies adjust. And in most cases, the difference doesn't really matter."

Lindsay nodded, probably not yet understanding the wisdom of his words. I nodded knowingly. After all, my husband Lynn and I have been married for thirty-seven years.

A few days later I was back home, watching Lynn cut a cantaloupe in half—the wrong way. Everyone knows you cut a cantaloupe the short way, through the fat middle, like a lemon; not the long way, end to end, like a watermelon. I told him so.

He paused, looking at the cantaloupe. "Why does it matter?" That's when I remembered the doctor's advice. The circumstances change, but the challenge to accept each other's differences remains the same through all the seasons of marriage.

Lord, help me to see what doesn't matter,
which will help me know what matters most.
—Carol Kuykendall

*"I will send down showers in season; there will be
showers of blessing." —*Ezekiel 34:26

Bless you!" a stranger said to me as I sneezed loudly in the supermarket once again. It must have been the tenth time I'd heard it that day as I suffered with yet another winter cold. *I don't feel all that blessed,* I thought, sniffling and reaching for another tissue. I appreciated her kindness, but suddenly the phrase seemed silly. Who's really thinking about God's blessings when somebody sneezes? I've read that the origins of this tradition go far back in history, to a superstitious belief that an evil spirit could enter the body to steal the soul or to the fear that a sneeze signaled oncoming illness, requiring God's protection for the sneezer. Whatever its origin, the average "Bless you" is little more than a courtesy today.

Still, all those "bless yous" made me think about the many times each day when I do feel blessed in small ways. I was blessed when a truck driver let me in ahead of him to make my left turn, instead of speeding up to beat me to the intersection. And I was blessed when a woman held the door open and waited for me as I struggled with my arms full of boxes for a school project. These weren't big events, but little kindnesses that eased my way and brought much-needed help.

Yet I've discovered something about these small, everyday blessings. They seem to mean the most to me when I'm on the giving end. The other day I was waiting in the checkout line with my full cart, and I let a man with a huge box of diapers go ahead of me. "Thank you. You're a blessing to me today," he said. But instead I felt blessed, privileged to be able to pass on even the tiniest bit of God's love that might make someone's day go a little smoother. It's one of God's wonderful ironies:

The more blessings I give others, the more blessed I am myself.

*heavenly Father, show me the ways I might shower
others with blessings as You have showered me.*
—Gina Bridgeman

Be honest in your evaluation of yourselves,
measuring yourselves by the faith God has given us.
—ROMANS 12:3 (NLT)

I want that," declared Sophia, my two-year-old granddaughter. She had chosen a pluot, a reddish-colored sweet fruit that is a cross between a plum and an apricot.

We were at French Market Produce, a wonderful open-air seafood and produce market in Mandeville, Louisiana. Tables were piled high with dark green seedless watermelons, pink-skinned nectarines, oversized, sweet Vidalia onions, and jars of local honey. Large green ferns hung from the rafters. And wafting throughout the market was the pungent aroma of boiled seafood.

We bought our pluot and walked over to a bench next to the snowball stand. Sophia took a bite, the sweet juice running down her chin. Minutes later an elderly gentleman sipping a spearmint snowball sat down beside us.

"Whew," he said. "Shopping with my daughter and her boys gets a bit hectic. Those boys go a mile a minute."

"I know what you mean."

"I was going to buy them snowballs." He shook his head. "But those boys have better things to do."

"Don't sell yourself short," I said. "We're important to our grandchildren, even if they're too young or too busy to know it. Some of my fondest memories are of my grandmother. I remember her helping me get dressed on chilly winter mornings in front of our fireplace. One Christmas she ate all my homemade cookies that my brother and sisters wouldn't eat."

The gentleman stood up to leave. "Time to go?" I asked.

He winked at us. "I'll be right back. I know a couple of boys who might just love a snowball."

Lord of the young and old, help me to see the value in my
relationships with others, especially my grandchildren.
—MELODY BONNETTE

APRIL 18

Consider the lilies how they grow. —Luke 12:27 (KJV)

I often see birdwatchers in my neighborhood because I live next to a bird sanctuary where there are miles of fields surrounding a big reservoir. But the woman I began to see almost every morning wasn't your typical birdwatcher. Most of them stand still, peering through binoculars. This woman had binoculars hanging by a cord around her neck, but she didn't always use them. What made her different was that she would stop and peer intently at the ground, or up at the trees on the ridge. Sometimes she just stared at the sky. She must have liked what she saw, because she was always smiling.

Since we passed each other so often, we nodded. Then we said "Hi," and finally she asked if she could say hello to my dog. My curiosity got the better of me, and I asked her what she was looking for.

"I'm interested in everything," she said. "The different grasses, the birds, the deer peeking out from the bushes." I felt a little embarrassed because I've lived here fourteen years and I've seen the same things, but they didn't stop me in my tracks. I think the woman must have read my expression because she told me she had recently moved from the city to live with her son and his wife. "It's so beautiful here!" she said, looking around.

"Didn't you like the city?" I asked.

"I loved it!" she said. "I used to walk around, just as I do here, looking in store windows and at the fronts of houses, even little alleyways, marveling at it all." She stopped to look at some geese flying toward the reservoir. Then she smiled and said, "I feel as if each day is a gift, and I get to open it."

Dear Lord Jesus, thank You for the gift of this day.
—Phyllis Hobe

The Lord is good to those who wait for Him.
—LAMENTATIONS 3:25 (NASB)

I don't like waiting for anything. I abhor waiting rooms or recipes that say, "Wait about two hours and...." I pace the floor waiting for phone calls to be returned, or even for our daily mail delivery.

My husband Gene moves at a different pace. He's methodical, sure, careful... and *slow*. Everywhere we go, no matter how hard I try to slow down, I end up sitting in the car and waiting for him. We start out the door together, and then he disappears and I sit in the car and fume, and even if I don't complain, my grim face gives me away when he finally arrives. It makes us both miserable.

One of my friends has a photograph of a magnificent rose hanging in her home. It was taken by Everett Saggus, a widely acclaimed photographer who lived in Elberton, Georgia, where I grew up. He had wanted to take a picture of a rose just as it opened in the very early morning. Getting to the garden before sunrise hadn't been good enough for Sag. He spent the whole night by the rosebush, waiting and watching. His amazing patience paid off: he not only captured the pale yellow rose as it opened, he actually caught the dew as it fell onto the thirsty flower. I visualized him crouched there in the dark, chilly hours waiting quietly, doing nothing—absolutely nothing—except waiting.

A few days after I heard the story of the rose, Gene and I were leaving on a short trip. As usual, I found myself in the car nearly ten minutes before Gene arrived. This time, though, I began to fill my waiting time with prayer. *Father, thank You for my husband. Thank You that I have someone to wait for....* I wasn't finished thanking God when Gene opened the car door and sat down, smiling. I smiled back. Maybe it's never too late to learn to wait.

Teach me more about the quiet power in waiting, Father.
—MARION BOND WEST

APRIL 20

Noah walked with God. —GENESIS 6:9 (NASB)

I got a laugh today while waiting with my aunt in a restaurant. A tall, athletic man who'd learned Aunt Betty was one hundred years old wanted to know her secret for long life. Ninety-two pounds of spunk looked up at him and said, "Well, I guess I just kept on breathing!"

There's a little more to it than that. My aunt's quick wit is hard to beat, and she's also independent and adventurous. She drove her mother and five siblings cross-country in a seven-passenger car when she was barely sixteen! And she worked her way through college in the 1920s peeling potatoes at 4:00 a.m.

She's a lively student and teacher. The other night she sat leaning forward, arms wrapped around her legs like a teenager, listening intently to her daughter Jeanne read aloud from her doctoral dissertation. If she caught a grammatical error, she said so.

The most inspiring thing I've seen Aunt Betty do happened in a medical lab: She helped hold open a heavy door for a woman pushing a patient in a wheelchair. Wobbly herself, steadying her steps with a cane, yet trying to ease the passage for someone else—this is her way.

It's a combination of things that gets a person to the century mark.

Fundamental for my aunt is prayer. She's a great believer in "going to my knees." Maybe that's how she's stayed so limber in body and spirit. Her knees don't meet the floor these days, but her heart bows to the Lord she loves.

I wish I could find that man from the restaurant. I'd like to tell him the whole story of how my aunt made it to one hundred.

> *The roads we travel are different distances, Lord. Please*
> *walk mine with me, whatever its length or terrain.*
>
> —CAROL KNAPP

There is precious treasure and oil in the dwelling
of the wise. —PROVERBS 21:20 (NASB)

I arrived at my friend Scarlett's house with a heavy heart. Life seemed off track, out of control. I'd allowed my worry to overshadow my prayer time for weeks.

I let myself in her front door. "Be right down! Grab some coffee! I put out a mug for you!" she hollered from upstairs.

Scarlett and I meet for simple things—coffee, long walks, and to get acquainted with each other's children. The thing I love most about Scarlett is her daily passion for God, even though her life is far from carefree. Scarlett often grabs my hand and prays out loud no matter where we are or what we're doing. Once she began praying as we ran laps around the mall parking lot. It didn't matter that we were covered in sweat and wearing tennis shoes. We didn't even close our eyes.

Sitting down with my cup at her kitchen table, I noticed Scarlett's brown leather Bible lying open to Proverbs 21. Scarlett reads the matching chapter of Proverbs for each day of the month, and today was April 21. Quickly, I flipped through the worn Bible. Smiley faces, exclamation marks, colored markings, and notes crammed the margins. I ran my hand over the pages, soft from hundreds of touches.

"Hey, girl. You ready to walk?" Scarlett pulled her long hair into a quick ponytail.

I slid the red ribbon marker back to Proverbs 21. "Always ready to walk with you, girlfriend."

Father, thank You for the people who
draw me back to the richness in You.

—JULIE GARMON

April 22

*Since we are surrounded by such a great
cloud of witnesses...let us run with perseverance
the race marked out for us.* —Hebrews 12:1

I do not sew. Not even a little bit. But I lost buttons this week—from my coat, my jeans, and my favorite sweater—and I have to try.

I stand on a stool and stretch to reach Grandmother's sewing basket on the top shelf of the guest closet. I pull back the lid and see bright spools of thread lining the bottom in colorful disarray. "*Always keep a good supply of thread laid by, so you can match your cloth.*" Grandmother's voice is so clear I want to turn to see if she is peeking over my shoulder.

I settle into my reading chair and begin to thread my needle. I can almost feel Mother's hand on mine, guiding it toward that silver sliver's eye—the way she did the summer I was eight and tried to make clothes for my doll. After a few initial fumbles, my needle slips in and out of the buttons, attaching them securely. Suddenly, my hand becomes my sister's as she sews rows of buttons on the sleeve of my wedding gown—a gown she made for me by cutting up her own wedding dress.

Later, as I tuck the sewing basket back on that remote shelf, I feel connected to the women in my family in a way I haven't in a long time; connected to their resourcefulness, patience, generosity. And if my clumsy attempts with a needle and thread are what prompts this closeness, I'm almost eager for my next loose button!

*Thank You, Lord, for the threads that bind me to my past
and to those I love. May I learn from them even now.*

—Mary Lou Carney

APRIL 23

The flowers appear on the earth; the time of the singing
of birds is come. —SONG OF SOLOMON 2:12 (KJV)

*M*y computer sits on a desk in my home office, its back to the windows that show me the view of my front lawn and the street on which we live. Below the windows are beds with green plants in them: calla lilies; a broad-leafed plant whose name I don't know; some cacti in terra-cotta bowls; and a large bird-of-paradise plant, which every spring produces exotic orange and purple blossoms.

This past spring, Perky, the little Australian shepherd mix who lives in my office because she can't get along with the other dogs, took to standing on her hind legs and looking out the window at the street. I thought she probably did it because she was lonely when I wasn't in the office with her. Then I discovered she had a friend.

I was sitting at the keyboard, typing one morning, when I saw an iridescent green hummingbird at the bird-of-paradise blossoms, wings moving impossibly fast, long beak probing for nectar in the vivid blooms. I stopped working to watch; there is something about a hummingbird that makes me marvel at creation. Perky came over to the window and stood to put her paws on the sill. I thought she would bark at the hummingbird, but she didn't, and I didn't want to shoo her away because I thought it would startle the little bird.

The hummingbird left its flower and came over to the window, hovering on the other side of the glass just beyond Perky's nose. They looked at each other for almost thirty seconds, and it was possible to imagine that they were communicating, asking how things were going, wishing each other well. The meeting done, Perky dropped back down to the rug, the hummingbird went back to breakfast, and I returned to my work, feeling privileged to have been eavesdropping on a natural scene I could never have imagined.

Thank You, God, for the glimpses
You give me of the glory of Your creation.
—RHODA BLECKER

APRIL 24

"Pour out your hearts to him, for God is our refuge."
—PSALM 62:8

've always admired people who are disciplined in prayer. But despite my best intentions to set aside a time for earnest prayer each day, it doesn't always happen.

One day as I was driving home from town I thought, *perfect time for praying.* I began to formulate a prayer, but it sounded wooden and phony. I made a few more attempts, but the words just wouldn't come.

Finally, in desperation, I gave up. "Lord Jesus, I just can't pray today," I said. "Is it okay if I just look out the window for a while and say nothing?"

As I climbed Marshall Road, I drove past a pink splash of Japanese cherries in bloom. "I like that," I said out loud. "Thanks, Lord." At one house, a neatly landscaped yard was ablaze with red azalea bushes. My heart leaped with joy. "That's neat, Lord," I exclaimed. At a roadside garden, clumps of bright yellow and red tulips swayed gently in the wind. "You did a great job when You made tulips," I said. Almost home, I crested a hill and spread out before me lay Mount Baker, its rugged snowcapped peaks mellowed by a late afternoon sun. "Wow, God!" I whispered. "You must be incredibly great to create a scene like that."

And so it went all the way home. I wasn't praying, mind you, I was merely expressing my delight in the pristine beauty I saw and telling the Person I felt was responsible for it.

When the words won't come, Lord, open my eyes
to the prayer-starters You've put all around me.
—HELEN GRACE LESCHEID

Better is an handful with quietness, than both the
hands full with travail and vexation of spirit.
—ECCLESIASTES 4:6 (KJV)

*I*t's getting harder for me to read. I may soon have to go to large print. My hearing is slowly fading, too. My body seems to be gradually closing some of its windows to the outside world as I grow older.

But there's another side to that page of life. As my sensory input diminishes, I'm less easily distracted by external things and more inclined to turn to God's presence within me for nourishment and spiritual companionship. I now have more time to savor silence, to spend an hour sitting on the mountain or by the stream, soaking up God's presence in nature, and to open myself to the life of the spirit in prayer and meditation.

Could it be that the dimming of our senses in age is made for this quiet turning inward? I have to admit that it's not an easy time in life. Body parts are wearing out, endurance is diminishing, short-term memory has started to fail. Yet in their place has come the priceless gift of contemplation.

My husband Robert and I have decided that now is the best time of our lives!

God of grace and mercy, may I stop dreading the
losses of age, and accept with thanksgiving the special
gifts You have provided for this time in life.
—MARILYN MORGAN KING

APRIL 26

*In the day of prosperity be joyful, but in the day of adversity
consider: God has made the one as well as the other.*
—ECCLESIASTES 7:14 (RSV)

When our son lost his job, he and his family moved in with us. Our daughter, also jobless, joined us, too. Then my parents and my husband Larry's mother became ill, so Larry and I took turns traveling to Missouri to help them. When our parents' illnesses were pronounced terminal, our children moved out of our home, and Larry and I brought in our parents, whom we cared for over the next ten months as they died, one by one. Sometimes I felt besieged, like Job, and questioned God's purpose.

Then I heard a motivational speaker talk about attitude. She said, "When you face adversity, do you wallow in misery and whine, 'Why me?' Or do you examine the problem while asking, 'What good can come from this?'" She added that it's possible to grow and change for the better because of the pain we experience, but we have to choose to do so.

"All right, God, help me see the good in this," I prayed.

So He showed me. During the months that our children and grandchildren lived with us, we developed a closeness that will stay with us the rest of our lives. When our parents lay dying, our children came often to visit them, creating new bonds of love.

Time of adversity? No, a time of togetherness, with one another and with God.

*Thank You, Lord, for the troubled times
that strengthen our souls and help us grow.*
—MADGE HARRAH

April 27

Is it a small matter? —Genesis 30:15 (KJV)

I once had no trouble believing that God cared about little things—parking places, a lost recipe, a sick pet. But lately that seemed foolish. That's what I was thinking about when Jan ran up to me at church.

Tears filled her large blue eyes. "Oh, Marion, pray! I have to take the last two puppies to the dog pound. We can't find homes for them. The children don't know yet."

When I'd rescued a puppy from underneath the church nearly a year before, Jan had taken it home, despite already having a dog and several cats and chickens and two horses. Now it had puppies of its own. Jan's five children loved the new dog, especially the puppies.

"They'll kill them, Jan! Puppies never really find good homes there."

She sobbed, "But I prayed, and God promised they'd be adopted."

I felt horrible, apologized profusely, and prayed that week that Jan's family would adjust to their loss.

At church the next Sunday, Jan exclaimed, "Oh, Marion, I took the puppies to the pound. I was crying, and so were the children. When we arrived, I ran to the head of the line and begged the lady to let me just put the puppies inside and leave. She said no.

"When I got back to the car, a man came over from his truck and asked me what the problem was. I showed him the puppies. The children were wailing now, and he said, 'I only came to adopt one puppy, but I'll take them both. I live on a farm, and they can run. I'll take them to the vet regularly, and we'll love them. I promise!'

"He took them. We never even went inside the pound! Can you believe how much God cares about the little things?"

Father, forgive my unbelief. I believe!
—Marion Bond West

APRIL 28

Serving the Lord with all humility.... —ACTS 20:19 (KJV)

*G*randma Hazel is an "adopted" grandma to dozens of us in our church and community. At eighty-eight years old, she's an untiring worker for the Lord. She's either dishing out meals at the Salvation Army dining room, driving a friend to a doctor's appointment, knitting blankets for babies with AIDS, or making meat loaf for church suppers. When she has health setbacks or family problems, she keeps moving forward with faith, saying, "To worry is to insult the Lord."

Once I worked hard on presenting a dramatic program for Holy Week at church. I thought I could make a difference for the Lord with that program, but only a handful of people attended. I was discouraged. *Why did I even bother? I asked myself.* When I shared my disappointment with Grandma Hazel, she listened thoughtfully, then told me, "I guess I never think about making a difference. I just try to serve the Lord and let *Him* make the difference."

She was right, of course. When I looked back at my church production, I saw that the people who were there had really enjoyed it. Several even told me how much it had blessed them. And I certainly grew from the prayer and planning I put into it.

So now when I'm inclined to give in to disappointment, I remember the strong working faith of Grandma Hazel and others like her who know how to trust the Lord. I take my eyes off of myself and how I'm doing, and try to please God instead. No project is ever a failure, no opportunity is ever wasted, I'm learning, when we let the Lord make the difference.

> *Lord, help me serve You joyfully and*
> *faithfully, leaving the results to You.*
> —GINA BRIDGEMAN

The Lord recompense you for what you have done, and a full reward be given you by the Lord. —RUTH 2:12 (RSV)

*M*om, can you help me find a snack?" sixteen-year-old Derek called from the kitchen about ten last night as he opened and closed the refrigerator door. I had about twelve reasons why I couldn't. I was reading a book. I was tired. I'd already finished my kitchen duty for the day. Besides, a familiar parenting rule echoed in my head: "Don't do for them what they are capable of doing for themselves." Yet a maternal instinct flickered within me. My boy needed me. And he didn't need me for much these days. No rides home from school. No hugs and tucks into bed. No advice at the shoe store. We hardly had opportunities to talk. I hesitated only a fraction of a second and then put down my book.

"How about a flour tortilla with melted cheese?" I suggested, coming into the kitchen.

"Great," he grinned, settling down on a stool, happily letting me take over for him. "Mom, Homecoming's coming up. I was thinking of going...but if I ask a girl out and she says 'no,' what do I say next?" The question was a tough one, but what followed was a preciously important conversation that I would have missed if I had refused to help with his snack. Some may call that coincidental timing, but I call it God's way of tucking His blessings into our acts of kindness, especially when those acts are chosen over the rules.

Lord, help me choose Your rules all through this day.
—CAROL KUYKENDALL

APRIL 30

Because you are precious in my eyes, and honored,
and I love you. —ISAIAH 43:4 (RSV)

*I*t was time to say good-bye to my little granddaughter Hannah. Our far-flung family had gathered for a rare reunion. Now Hannah was continuing on to visit her other set of grandparents. As she waited in her car seat in the rented van, I leaned in and said, "You have lots of fun with Grandma Patti."

Hannah was quiet for a moment. I could tell she was thinking hard about something: perhaps she was visualizing the special things she and her other grandmother would do. Then she looked at me intently, and in her no-frills four-year-old style she said, "But I will still love you." Hannah's heart held a space for me no matter who else was there.

I've thought about Hannah's words a lot since then. They remind me of the way God loves me. He has billions of people to attend to, but He still loves me. He sees all my failures and mistakes, but He still loves me. He knows my every thought and doubt, but He still loves me. And I have the sure sign of His love for me in the shape of the Cross on which His Son died.

Lord, in all the times and places of
my life, Your love never leaves me.
—CAROL KNAPP

May

May 1

O Lord, you are my God; I will exalt you, I will praise
your name; for you have done wonderful things.
—Isaiah 25:1 (NRSV)

I walk every day. When I have a lot on my mind, these walks can become intense. I've been told that friends regularly pass me in their cars, waving like NASCAR signalers, and I don't even notice.

Lately, I've been battling my self-absorption by mixing a little conversation with God into my daily exercise. Since my purpose is to be less focused on myself, I pray for others.

If I see a gorgeous, well-tended garden, I thank God for the people in that house and pray for their continued success.

When someone in a car passes too close to me or speeds by, instead of getting furious, I ask God to keep the driver and everyone he or she encounters safe.

If I see a Coast Guard ship or one of the submarines from the base downriver traveling out to sea, I pray for the safety of the cadets or the submariners.

When I pass the houses of those I know who oppose me on issues like school spending or the homeless shelter in our city, I ask God to keep them well.

If I see a work crew painting a house or mowing a lawn, I pray that their work will go well and that their skin will be safe from the sun.

As I pass the local college, I ask God to help the young people and their professors lead us to a better tomorrow.

When I see some nurses from our city's hospital power walking along on their break, I pray for their continued strength, health, and gentleness.

And suddenly my walk is over!

It's amazing how many people I can put in my prayers...especially when I'm not thinking about myself.

Lord, help me to be selfless in my prayers.
—Marci Alborghetti

MAY 2

Consider it pure joy, my brothers, whenever you face trials
of many kinds, because you know that the testing of your
faith develops perseverance. —JAMES 1:2–3

*Y*esterday, my four-year-old granddaughter Cassie came to spend the
day with me. In true grandma fashion, I planned all her favorite treats,
the highlight being to rent her favorite video *Cinderella*. But when we were settled
in front of the TV, Cassie confessed that the mean stepmother always frightened
her. Concerned, I said, "Maybe we should have rented something else."

"Oh, no, Grandma," she said, patting my hand reassuringly. "I just fast
forward past the scary parts." And so she did, zipping past each scary part and
looking up at me with a serene smile.

I couldn't help speculating on how blissful it would have been to fast forward
past certain parts of my life until I got to the good parts. Things like my brain
surgery for an aneurysm when I was thirty-two. But no, not that part. That's
when I learned that instead of praying frantically when I'm afraid, sometimes
I need to be still so I can hear His reassurance. Then how about that endless
year I struggled to overcome my addiction to cigarettes? No, because that battle
taught me the importance of being in daily contact with God.

I shook my head. No fast forward for me. It seems I need the scary parts if
I'm to continue growing spiritually. And the next time you run into a scary part,
remember it's just a rough spot that eventually leads you to the good part: a
clearer perspective and a wiser point of view.

Dear Lord, help me face life's problems as they come,
with the sure knowledge that You'll always be there,
even and especially in the scary parts.
—BONNIE LUKES

MAY 3

I came that they might have life and have it abundantly.
—JOHN 10:10 (NASB)

Our dog Sterling loved nothing more than to go for a ride in the car. But one afternoon when we stopped to run a quick errand in a neighboring town, she got loose, hightailed it down a busy street on the trail of another barking dog, and didn't find her way back.

We were heartsick, but despite days of searching for her and the ads we placed in local newspapers, she was never found. Then one day we got a telephone call. "I think I may have your dog. Terrier-poodle mix? Gray? Bark bigger than her bite?"

"Yes. Yes. Yes."

"When I found her, she must have been in the wild for a while," the lady said, "all tangled up with a mess of briers. But she's sitting pretty here on the sofa with the rest of my brood now. You can come and take a look."

It was indeed Sterling. But not the Sterling that had flown out of our car that afternoon and in a mad dash for freedom lost her way. This Sterling had little pink bows in her hair, and her nails were painted a matching pink. She sat poised like a queen on the lady's best furniture, an esteemed member of the family.

Days before, Sterling had been a common stray. But her kind benefactor had treated her to an appointment with the groomer and lavished her with love—the abundant life. Just as Jesus offers us when we lose our way.

> *Some folks are so generous, Lord, that they point*
> *me back to You. Help me to bask in Your abundant*
> *life and freely share it with others.*
> —ROBERTA MESSNER

MAY 4

And he showed me a pure river of water of life.
—REVELATION 22:1 (NKJV)

*W*hen I walked into the break room at 8:00 a.m. and saw that the coffee machine was broken, I gasped. "What am I going to do without my coffee?" My coworkers laughed, pointing to the huge, hand-printed sign tacked to our barren coffeepot:

Yes, the coffeemaker is broken. No, we don't know what's wrong with it.
Yes, we've ordered another one. No, we don't know when it will arrive.
And, no, we don't know what you are going to do without your coffee!

I laughed too. Obviously, I wasn't the first to utter those remarks.

My coworkers and I were still huddled in the break room when the next caffeine-deprived soul entered. And when Anna wailed, "What will I do without my coffee? I *need* coffee in the morning!" a coworker began singing "*Ohhh*, I *neeeed* coffee in the morning" to the tune of "I Love Paris in the Springtime." The rest of us joined in enthusiastically, if not melodiously.

When our manager walked in and said, "Oh no, the coffee machine's broken!" the whole room roared. And then almost as one, we stood up, ready to begin our workday fueled by laughter...almost as good an energy-giver as caffeine!

God, I'm thirsty for laughter. Please show me
how to pour some refreshing humor on the minor
irritations life may bring my way today.

—LINDA NEUKRUG

MAY 5

The spirit of a man is the lamp of the Lord.
—PROVERBS 20:27 (NKJV)

*E*llie, dear!" Gramma exclaimed happily as she threw open the door to her new apartment. "What perfect timing! The coffee just finished perking, and I'm all set to whip up some blueberry pancakes!"

I stepped into the tiny foyer, into a Gramma-size hug. Peeking over her shoulder, I looked into the living room/dining room/bedroom/den—four rooms in one, with large, north windows.

Gram and I both loved the sun. She used to say that we were like cats—always looking for a sunny corner where we could curl up and read. But not a sliver of delicious sunlight was ever going to make it through those north windows. *This place is really going to depress her*, I thought.

But I was so wrong.

While I was there the phone rang; the doorbell buzzed. Friends came by for lunch, and Gram made plans to go on a daylong river trip with her church group. All around us were pictures of family and friends. A stack of letters and postcards covered her desktop. And the afghan she was crocheting tumbled out of a basket next to her recliner.

I didn't have to worry about that apartment. Friendship and sharing chased away the shadows. Laughter and joy lit up all the corners. Love and warmth radiated throughout those tiny rooms. Gram didn't waste one minute brooding about the lack of sunlight; she simply went ahead and made her own!

> *Dear Lord, when darkness comes into my life,*
> *help me to see the sun in Your loving presence*
> *and radiate it out to those around me.*

—ELLEN SECREST

My times are in thy hand. —PSALM 31:15 (KJV)

I stopped at the foot of the stairs and set down the vacuum. I'd been running up and down, getting a bedroom ready for guests. The phone had rung nonstop, the breakfast dishes were still on the table, and none of this was getting that writing assignment done.

It was time for a minute vacation. I stuck a CD into the player, dropped into a chair, put my head back, and for a moment let Gregorian chant transport me to an unhurried world.

I discovered the wisdom of these brief getaways when my husband and I were on an actual vacation. In the Florida panhandle, we had stopped for the night at a motel set in a grove of ancient live oaks. Printed on the breakfast menu of the adjoining restaurant we noticed "The Oaks Prayer for Today":

"Slow me down, Lord. Ease the pounding of my heart by the quieting of my mind.... Teach me the art of taking minute vacations: of slowing down to look at seashells, to chat with a friend, to pet a dog.... Let me look up into the towering oaks and know they grew great and strong because they grew slowly and well."

Minute vacations—could I really recapture, in the workaday world, the release of pressure we felt on that rambling, no-special-destination car trip? For a few days we really were stopping to look at seashells and make friends with playful dogs. I copied down the prayer and, back home, set out to experiment. A two-minute stretching exercise turned out to be a quick way to relax. So did a stroll around the yard. Or a few minutes with a crossword puzzle. I developed a score of instant escapes, like preparing a cup of Lapsang Souchong tea with my best china, or opening a photo album and spending a moment in another time and place.

It isn't only the minute vacation, I'm finding, that's different. To stop, to step aside, to lay down—even for a moment—the pressures to achieve is to see all the other minutes in a new way, to receive time itself as a daily blessing.

Lord, teach me to walk today in Your unhurried steps.
—ELIZABETH SHERRILL

New wine must be put into new bottles. —MARK 2:22

My friend Cheri and I had been walking at the mall three mornings a week for a couple of years, when she suggested trying something new. "How about swimming at the Y?"

Immediately, a whole list of excuses came sputtering out of me. "Oh, I haven't been swimming in years. Besides, I don't look good in a swimsuit anymore! And I'd get chlorine in my hair." And the final insurmountable obstacle: "It's *winter*, for goodness' sake!"

"Well, never mind then. I just thought I'd ask." I think my answer was what Cheri had expected from me, someone who is eighteen years older than she. But as I was driving home, some words I'd heard from an energetic church friend in his eighties floated across my mind: "We grow old by consent." *Why should I consent?* I thought. *I used to love to swim. Why not enjoy it now? Indeed, why not? Every day I am a new person in Christ!*

Cheri and I have been swimming regularly for months now, and though I may *look* like an old wineskin, when I'm splashing around in the water I feel like a kid again. Besides firming my upper arms and tummy a bit, the swimming experience has taught me to question my "can't dos." No matter what your age, before turning down the opportunity for a new adventure, ask yourself, *Why not?* If there's no good answer, at least try it once. It may keep you young!

*When I hesitate to try something new, Lord, remind me
I'm a new creature in You. Then I'll ask, Why not?*
—MARILYN MORGAN KING

MAY 8

Be content with such things as ye have.
—HEBREWS 13:5 (KJV)

One of my favorite pastimes on a Saturday morning is reading the garage sale ads in the newspaper. If one is close by, I will often include it in my round of errands.

One weekend an ad jumped up at me:

Nine-ft, curved-front, buttoned-back leather sofa. Mellow, forest green, glowing and unspotted. Rich in emotional history. Negotiations, whisperings, rumors, raconteurs. Understandings, misunderstandings, tears, and treaties. Tinkerings, tidying-ups, pleadings, and fiascoes, all tucked into its cushions. Moving. Must sell.

What come-hither and buy-me appeal! I could just feel myself sinking into the sofa, listening to the tales it could so obviously tell. Desperately, I wanted that sofa!

"*Harumph!*" said my husband John. "The last thing we need is another sofa." With a chuckle, he reached for a pen and started marking up the ad. "Here, now read it," he said.

Six-foot, wood trim, wing-back sofa. Mellow, golden-brown, glowing, and slightly spotted. Velour crushed here and there from much family sitting and cuddling. Rich in emotional history. [*Here the wording was the same, with one important addition:*] *MANY PRAYERS tucked into its cushions. Not moving. Cherished. Should never sell.*

Sheepishly I looked at him. Of course! The sofa I so desperately wanted I already had! It had been part of our family for years. As we sank into the warm comfort of its cushions, John put his arm around me. "Listen to the tales it will tell!" Fun and frolic. Fellowship of friends. Come-and-sit-awhile-and-talk tales. Bible studies. Prayer....

The rewritten ad was right. "Cherished. Should never sell."

Thank You, Lord, for the comfort of our dear,
familiar things and our cozy corners—
to share with others, and to share with You.
—FAY ANGUS

*"Then I will purify the lips of the peoples,
that all of them may call on the name of the Lord
and serve him shoulder to shoulder."* —ZEPHANIAH 3:9

I had just finished speaking to a Christian Women's Club in Williams Lake, Canada, and was saying good-bye to the women at the door, when my host came into the room clearly agitated.

"Your son was on the phone. He and his wife are passing through town, and he wants to know if you'll meet them for lunch at the White Spot."

I was stunned. My son, who hadn't wanted to talk to me in three years, who would visit in our hometown and not let me know that he was there, now wanted to see me. "Where did he call from?" I asked. "When am I to meet them?"

"I don't know." I left the meeting room in a hurry and waited by the telephone hoping my son would call again to give me the particulars. He did, and we had a wonderful reunion. Not much was said, but both of us sensed that we had begun the healing of a strained relationship.

In my talks with women, I find that many a mother's heart has been broken because a son or a daughter is avoiding her. I pass on to them what has helped me during this difficult time.

Often an estrangement develops during a traumatic time such as a death or a divorce. Raw emotions take time to process. We need to give our children time and space to sort them out. No amount of talking will help the situation. In fact, too much talking makes it worse. It's like egg whites: the more you beat them, the bigger they get. We can't hurry up the healing process in ourselves or in others.

In the meantime, though, we can be grace-givers. Grace lets another person be, gives him or her the freedom to grow, to make decisions, to fail, and to mature at his or her own rate. We can pray for our children and wait expectantly for Jesus, the great Reconciler, to bring us together again. And when He does, we can be there with a warm embrace.

*Jesus, my children and I are Your people, the sheep of Your
pasture. Help me to trust You with them.*

—HELEN GRACE LESCHEID

May 10

*Lead a life worthy of God, who calls you into His own
kingdom and glory.* —1 Thessalonians 2:12 (RSV)

When I volunteered to work several hours a week as a caregiver for an elderly woman in our community, I felt quite smug about my decision. I envisioned the loving friendship that would develop between the woman and me. She would be gentle, she would be kind. And grateful, of course.

Instead, she proved to be an angry, bitter person who did nothing but complain about everyone she'd ever known. Soon she included me in those complaints. All my attempts to make her comfortable and content met with verbal abuse.

One day as I was standing in my kitchen, putting together a box of food and supplies to take to the woman, I exploded in rebellion. "God, I don't like being around this woman. I don't think I'm worthy to serve You in this area with an attitude this bad. Maybe I shouldn't try to help her. Maybe I should just quit."

God's answer sounded as clearly inside my head as if I'd heard the words spoken out loud: *Don't worry about your attitude. She needs you, and that's all that matters. Get to work.*

A weight lifted from my shoulders. God already knew my limitations, of course, but He could use me anyway, worthy or not. Eventually my attitude toward the woman changed, and I was able to view her with a little of the love and forbearance I'm sure God had felt for her—and for me—all along.

*Father, help me reach out today to someone who is difficult to
be with, even as You reach out to me when I'm not at my best.*

—Madge Harrah

May 11

Beloved, let us love one another: for love is of God.
—1 John 4:7

Conversations with my six-year-old granddaughter Olivia resemble the old game of Twenty Questions. This one took place while we waited for my hamburger and her chicken strips at a local cafe.

Olivia: "Who are your children?"

Me: "Your mom Rebecca and your uncles Patrick and Michael. You know that."

Olivia: "Are Emilee and Aaron your children?"

Me: "No."

Olivia: "Is Katie your child?"

Me: "No. Katie is your mom's birth mother, and Emilee and Aaron are her children. You know that too."

Olivia: "Well, my mom is adopted, you know!"

Me: "Yes, I know."

Olivia: "How did you decide who got her?"

Me (thinking quickly): "I got her because I was older."

Olivia: "Who loved my mom more, you or Katie?"

Me: "We both loved her the same."

Our food arrived. Olivia stopped talking to dip her fries in ketchup. I spent the momentary silence thinking about love. Despite what I'd told Olivia, surely I loved Rebecca more than Katie did! After all, Katie wasn't part of her life for twenty-three years.

But love is a two-way street. In order for Rebecca to be a beloved part of our family, Katie had made the heart-wrenching decision to place her for adoption. I'd told Olivia the truth after all: Katie and I loved Rebecca the same, and that love had given us the added joy of knowing and loving each other. Love multiplied, because none of us can ever out-love our generous, giving, amazing God.

Loving Lord, thank You that we're all
beloved parts of Your precious family!
—Penney Schwab

May 12

Mortify therefore your members which are upon the earth.
—Colossians 3:5 (KJV)

John, don't pick at that!" Foam rubber poked out of the arm of the sofa, and my son was plucking off small pieces. It was driving me crazy.

Our flowered sofa was already a major eyesore: nine years of use, one cat, and four kids had worn it to shreds. One day about a year ago a frayed spot appeared on one arm. That small spot quickly became a rip, the perfect hiding place for little toys. The rip grew, exposing foam rubber that begged to be pulled and poked and torn. Beneath that was fluff, ideal for a snowball fight when Mom wasn't looking.

At the time, we didn't have money to replace the sofa, so I bought a bedspread to cover its wounds. The spread tended to slip whenever my husband Andrew sat down quickly, and it fell off completely when the kids bounced around on it. I ended up rearranging it a dozen times a day, snapping at whoever messed it up. *This is more than embarrassing,* I thought one day as a neighbor graciously pretended not to notice. *It's mortifying.*

The word *mortifying* set off a little alarm bell in my head. Didn't Paul say we should mortify our earthly desires? My desire for nice-looking furniture was definitely not spiritual. It was so earthly that it had me growling at the people I love.

I pulled off the bedspread and faced the not-so-ugly truth: Our sofa had been worn out by years of rich family life. From cowboy forts to sickbeds, from pillow fights to snuggly read-alouds, this sofa had done it all. Smiling ruefully at my vanity, I turned to my son.

"John," I said, "when we get a new sofa, I'm going to let you completely destroy this one!" His eyes grew wide with anticipation. Now *that* would make this sofa memorable!

Jesus, appearances aren't everything.
No sofa's going to get me to heaven; only You are.
—Julia Attaway

MAY 13

After years of dreaming about remodeling our house, we finally knocked down the walls between our kitchen, family room, and dining room. But I still have one item on my wish list: a new family table.

I want a user-friendly, sturdy table that people are drawn to, not only to eat, but to read the newspaper or have a cup of coffee or play games. I call it a family table because it's the kind of place where family "happens."

The family table of my childhood was an oblong glass table that my mother inherited from an aunt. My mother insisted it set a proper tone for our family with four rambunctious children. It was the only place where we came together regularly.

Then there was the family table we had when our children were growing up—a heavy wooden trestle table with a bench along one side so we could add people without scouring the house for chairs. Our photo albums show what happened around that table: birthday parties, pumpkin carvings, Valentine's Day dinners, science projects, love.

Now I want a family table with comfortable chairs that beckon both adults and children. I may not get my dream table for a while, so in the meantime I'm taking note of what else beckons and connects people, like our big comfy couch in front of the fireplace, a bunch of stools pulled up to the kitchen counter and, most of all, the presence of God in the words and attitudes of the people who live in our home.

Father, may Your presence bless
our newly remodeled home each day.
—CAROL KUYKENDALL

Into thine hand I commit my spirit. —PSALM 31:5 (KJV)

Are you ever frazzled? Webster's dictionary says it means "worn, weak, and frayed." The word suited me perfectly when our sons were young. My husband Jim worked long hours, and I sometimes felt very lonely. I'd fret and "fray" when I had a quick decision to make and I saw myself as a "weak" parent. There was neither time nor energy left for activities I'd always enjoyed, like the piano.

One day my husband suggested I enroll in a neighborhood quilting class. He offered to babysit on those evenings and I agreed to try it.

As I discovered the beauty of the old patchwork patterns, I thought of hands busier than mine, long ago, sewing late into the dusky evening—perhaps in our own little eighteenth-century house. Those amazing women, in their hardship and poverty, created intricate masterpieces with a needle, some recycled thread, and hundreds of little scraps of cloth.

As I learned quilting, I realized something else: I am not unique; everyone's life is a segmented experience. The secret of becoming *un*frazzled is not a change of circumstances, but a change of attitude. Our little patches of time can either be tossed on the scrap heap, or be used to form a lovely, colorful masterpiece of memories, bringing warmth and happiness to those we love.

Help me, Lord, to choose to be contented
with my now, knowing it's from You.
Pattern my whole life into a work of beauty.

—VICKI SCHAD

MAY 15

Behold, thy mother. —MARK 3:32 (KJV)

*W*hen I was a little girl, the Saturday before Mother's Day always included a trip to the florist. There we would pick up white cardboard boxes. Inside were carnations—a white one for Grandma and red ones for my mother, my sister, and me. "This is to honor your mother," Grandma would say as she pinned the bright flower to my dress before we left for church on Sunday. "Red says that your mama is alive. White means she's already gone on to heaven." She touched her own pale flower tenderly.

It was Anna M. Jarvis of Philadelphia who—almost a hundred years ago—began a letter-writing campaign to a variety of influential people, which eventually resulted in establishing Mother's Day as a national holiday. It was Anna, too, who championed the wearing of carnations. Her own dear mother had loved white carnations, and Anna thought that the flower represented the purity of motherly love. Later, red carnations were added for those whose mothers were living.

I don't see red and white corsages on Mother's Day anymore. But this year I think I'll go back to that tradition—with a bit of a change. I'll wear a white *and* red carnation. White to show that my mother "has gone on to heaven," but red to show that she's very much alive there!

> *Unlike even the fairest flower, Lord, a mother's love never dies. Thank You, thank You, thank You!*

—MARY LOU CARNEY

MAY 16

In hope of eternal life which God, who never lies,
promised ages ago.... —Titus 1:2 (RSV)

My daughter Maria and I were watching the dogs play at the park. We used to bring our bichon frise Cookie here to watch her play with all the other dogs, but that seemed long ago. At twelve, Cookie is long past rambling in the park. Her sight almost gone, she can barely amble from her bed to our backyard, her legs stiff and tired. Watching the dogs scamper around, I wondered how the time had gone so fast since Cookie's playful puppy days. I wasn't as quick and limber as I had been twelve years ago, either, nor was I so carefree. Age seemed to bring with it more worries, more concerns.

Just then a little white puppy ran past, snapping me out of my reverie. She dashed right up to a small brown dog, then took off at full speed, pink tongue flapping, little legs running all-out with the joy of being a puppy at the park on a warm, sunny spring day. Suddenly I saw a flash of Cookie's sweet old face. Tears sprang to my eyes, but then another thought came just as quickly. *That's what Cookie will be like in dog heaven*. Her old legs fast and young, she'll be able to see and run after a ball as in the old days.

In that moment I understood God's great promise. One day—a never-ending sunny spring day—we'll all be young pups again, pain gone, fear forgotten. The infirmities burdening this life will disappear. We'll be perfect, yet best of all we'll spend eternity with the Perfect One.

Lord Jesus, spending the day with You is the very definition
of heaven. Thank You for Your promise of eternity.
—Gina Bridgeman

May 17

Let each of you look out not only for his own interests, but also for the interests of others. —Philippians 2:4 (NKJV)

To me, my grandparents had always been models of marital devotion. When I was a child that love warmed me, and the sparkle in Grandpa's eyes when he looked at his wife prompted me to search for his brand of tenderness in the young man I chose to marry. But when my wedding day came, Gramps was desperately ill and Granny was constantly at his side. "I can't go through with the ceremony without them here," I mourned.

I was apprehensive and ill at ease as I slipped into my wedding gown. "I'll go by the hospital and show Gramps how I look," I said to Mother. But Gramps's eyes were closed, so I kissed his cheek softly.

"I'll be there," Granny promised, seeing the mournful look on my face.

She arrived at the church just as the wedding party was starting down the aisle and slipped into the small room where I was waiting for my cue. "Here's a kiss from Grampa, too," she said, kissing me twice and smiling. But there were tears in her eyes, and mine were misty also.

When Tim and I returned from our wedding trip we hurried to Gran's house. "How is Gramps?" I asked.

"Oh, my dear," Gran said, "he died shortly before your wedding."

"But you came!" I cried. And then the enormity of her gift to me overwhelmed me.

"Yes," she said in her gentlest voice. "Grandpa sent you his last kiss."

*Lord, somehow You taught Gran how to put aside
her own feelings and help others. Show me, too.*
—Maxine Montgomery

A word of encouragement does wonders.
—PROVERBS 12:25 (TLB)

*M*y friend Jewel has two dogs, Me-First and Me-Too. Me-First is a fluffy white miniature poodle, a bouncing bundle of energy. At the ring of the doorbell, he's the first there, yipping, yapping, skidding on the doormat, and jumping up and down, clamoring for attention as the door is opened.

"All right, Me-First," I say as I hunch over to pet him. "Good dog, nice dog… now settle down." In the background, Me-Too, part collie and part who-knows-what, sits quivering with excitement as he waits his turn to be noticed. If I don't take time to notice the dogs, the rambunctious interruptions continue until Jewel puts both dogs out in the yard.

The fact of the matter is that we all like to be noticed. When our son Ian was seven years old, he was at his Me-First worst! He would butt his way into a conversation—especially when company came to visit—sit and fidget or rampage around the house. He needed to be noticed.

I know how he felt. There were times when I felt that the family was taking me for granted. I didn't rampage around the house, but I did turn quiet and brood.

I decided we needed "look at me" time. If any of us were feeling unappreciated and wanted a pat on the back, during dinner they could put up their hands. This was the signal for the rest of us to give them a few moments of glowing tribute and encouragement.

The good news is that in the heart of God there are no me-toos. Each one of us is a me-first, reassured and loved beyond measure.

In the hustle and bustle of daily living, it's so easy,
Lord, to take one another for granted. Help me to remember
that appreciation and words of encouragement do indeed
work wonders, especially with my children.
—FAY ANGUS

May 19

A merry heart has a continual feast.
—Proverbs 15:15 (NKJV)

"What if no one sits by me on the bus?" Karla asked as we walked to the bus stop on her first day of first grade. *Good question*, I thought. I was worried, too. It was my first day of seminary. I'd changed outfits three times that morning, not sure exactly what seminary students were supposed to look like. Karla interrupted my thoughts, "What if nobody likes me, Tammy?"

As we waited for the bus, I told her a story I'd heard about two travelers who passed through a small community. The first, stopping by a farmer at the edge of his field, inquired as to the character of the town, as he was looking for a place to settle down. "What were the people like in the town you left?" the farmer asked.

"Oh, bitter, jealous, and nosy," the traveler replied.

"Same kind of folks here," the farmer said. Disappointed, the traveler journeyed on.

A few days later, a second traveler approached the farmer, asking the same question. Of the town he'd left, the traveler reported, "Oh, they were lovely people, kind and warm!"

The farmer replied, "Same kind of folks here." The traveler found a home.

The school bus drove up, and Karla squealed with delight as she spotted her kindergarten friend Precious waving enthusiastically from a window. As I drove to school, I thought of the many transitions I'd already made—first grade, college, parenting, and now seminary. Driving into the school's parking lot, I spotted a pickup basketball game going on among my new classmates. *These are my kind of people*, I thought, as someone passed me the ball. Just the kind of people I expect to find anywhere I go today. What sort do you think you'll find?

Lord, as I venture out into the world today, help me to expect
beauty, wonder, and holiness in everyone I meet.
—Tammy Rider

MAY 20

The name of the Lord is a strong tower;
the righteous run to it and are safe. —PROVERBS 18:10

I often find myself awake at 3:00 a.m. Although I usually pray for a while, sometimes worries sneak up on me and before I know it, my mind is wide awake and whirling with problems. My husband Bill not only finds it easy to sleep but is able to put his concerns off until morning. I envy him this gift.

Knowing how I dislike my sleepless hours alone, he came up with a gentle illustration for me. One morning, as our son John's calico Manx picked deliberately at the back screen, Bill let her in and set her breakfast bowl on the floor. As she somehow managed to both gobble and purr in each mouthful, he said, "You know, honey, I watch Caddy do this almost every day of the year. She's out all night, on duty so to speak, alert every minute in the dark and dangerous world. Then she asks to come in, is served a good meal, chooses a warm, soft place, washes herself all over, and curls up for a long, deep nap. She can go off-duty.

"It can be like that for us with the Lord—we come in from a world of problems and fears to where it's safe and we are cared for, and we can curl up in His love and let go. We are utterly safe, just like Caddy."

Lesson learned.

Father God, how quickly I forget how safe I am in Your love.
Help me come in from the dark and my fears, and simply
curl up and rest in the safety You provide.

—ROBERTA ROGERS

MAY 21

I have fought the good fight, I have finished the race,
I have kept the faith. —2 TIMOTHY 4:7 (RSV)

One spring morning in May, my daughter Brenda and I set off down the meandering country roads of Willow, Alaska, in the annual Walk for Hope. We hoped we could last for all twenty-two miles! It was a "rejoice-and-be-glad" kind of day...in the beginning. Brenda and I bounced along, chuckling over the cartoon blow-ups of Garfield the cat, which measured each mile of our progress.

About the ninth mile, our feet began to protest, but lunch up ahead at mile eleven lured us on. At mile fourteen, Brenda was ready to quit. I agreed to climb in the rescue car with her if she felt she couldn't continue, but she switched to autopilot and we plodded on. The last miles were excruciating. I could barely lift my feet. And every time I passed a grinning Garfield, I wanted to rearrange his teeth! We limped proudly to the finish line nine hours after we had begun.

That night I overheard Brenda confide to her dad, "Mom said she'd get in the rescue car with me, but I wanted her to make it so I kept on going." Now, months later, her words still echo in my heart. Sometimes the path before me seems long and tortuous. I am tired and hurting and I want to give up. Jesus, in His earthly life, grew weary, too. There must have been days when He longed to quit and return to heaven, but He didn't, so that you and I could make it to the finish line.

Do you feel like giving up? Whatever your circumstances, Jesus Christ walks with you. And maybe—just maybe—someone else will reach that finish line because you kept going.

Walk with me, Lord.
—CAROL KNAPP

MAY 22

A man's own folly ruins his life. —PROVERBS 19:3

I have a large cardboard carton of recipes that I've clipped from newspapers and magazines over the years, but I'm ashamed to say I've tried only five or six of them. I guess habit causes me to keep making the same meals even though I have the directions for hundreds of new dishes.

One day, a friend of mine phoned just after I finished reading a book about an exciting woman who traveled to England by ship and hitchhiked once she was there. "My life is so dull," I complained. "I wish something exciting would happen. I wish I could go to England. Or even New England!"

She laughed. "It seems unlikely that you'll get to England today. So instead of wishing for something that may or may not happen, why not pick something, no matter how small it may seem, that you can do to spice up your life today?"

I don't know if it was her use of the word *spice* that brought those recipes to mind, but I dug out the old box and picked out a recipe for English trifle. The results were so delicious that the next night I baked some Scottish shortbread. And that weekend, I cooked up a New England boiled dinner.

The funny thing is I eventually did get to England—about four years after that phone conversation with my friend. But if I'd waited to feel excited about my life till then, I'd have missed out on more than a hundred new recipes that I cooked over those four years.

> *Dear God, I don't want to put my life on hold,*
> *saying, "I wish I had...." What can I do today*
> *to make some small dreams reality?*
> —LINDA NEUKRUG

MAY 23

For who hath despised the day of small things?
—ZECHARIAH 4:10 (KJV)

About two years after my husband died, my granddaughter Jamie announced one day, "Nanny, you need a husband. I'm going to ask Jesus to send you one."

"Okay, Jamie," I said. Jamie was only three and a half. She didn't really understand that prayer—and romance—don't work that way. The next day she told me with uncontained enthusiasm that she had talked with Jesus and He told her He was sending me a husband who would look like Grady (Jamie's pet name for my late husband).

Two years later, someone entered my life quite suddenly—without warning. We wrote and talked by phone for two months before I saw pictures of him. Jamie and I stared at the photographs in stunned silence. This professor/minister/farmer from Oklahoma bore an amazing resemblance to the husband I'd lost four years before.

When Gene Acuff arrived in Atlanta from Oklahoma, Jamie went straight into his arms. "I knew you'd come," she said softly, arms still tight around his neck. Jamie beamed throughout the entire ceremony when Gene and I were married shortly thereafter.

Oh, Father, teach me not to scoff
at small beginnings and small prayers.
—MARION BOND WEST

May 24

Gray hair is a crown of glory.
—Proverbs 16:31 (NASB)

*S*ometime back, I read an article on why hair turns gray: it is related to the body's production of something called melanocyte. But experience tells me that gray hair is mostly caused by children. Not other people's children, but your own.

Actually, my first gray hair and our son Brock's first step were a simultaneous occurrence. That exact moment also represents a milestone in my faith walk. That's when my prayer life began in earnest.

Keri, our daughter, on the other hand, didn't contribute much to the "snow on the mountain" until she decided it was time to be a teenager. Less dramatic, but just as heart-stopping, her antics came in spurts, always with the same effect on her mother's tresses: Phone rings. "Hello." "Mama, let me speak to Dad. *Now*!" Or worse: Phone rings. "Hello." "Mrs. Kidd"—Keri's boyfriend's voice— "let me speak to Dr. Kidd. *Now*!"

As mothers, we certainly don't want children to be afraid. We want them to develop confidence, believe in themselves. So we pray, and we gray, and we look forward. Which brings me to my final point: what grays my hair builds my faith. I guess that's why a wise man once said, "Gray hair is a crown of glory."

Father, I look past every fear and put my faith
in You. You are truly a mother's glory!

—Pam Kidd

MAY 25

So Abraham called that place The Lord Will Provide.
—GENESIS 22:14

The day after our son's wedding in Seattle, Washington, Lynn, our daughter Kendall and I flew home to Colorado. We were exhausted but filled with wonderful memories...and a few questions about how life would be different for our family on this side of the milestone.

"Does this mean I can no longer call Derek and leave dumb messages on his answering machine?" Kendall asked, tears suddenly filling her eyes.

"Of course you can," I assured her, but her question touched off a few of my own. *How will my relationship with Derek be different? How will I be a good mother-in-law? What will the holidays be like?*

In my heart, I knew this was another familiar lesson in learning to let go, which always reminds me of the story of Abraham and Isaac, so I shared it with Kendall. "The Bible tells the story of Abraham, who was called to surrender or 'let go' of his son Isaac on Mount Moriah. What a struggle that must have been! He knew what he was letting go of—the son God had promised him—but he didn't know what, if anything, God had in store for him. When he got to the place of surrender, he found that God had provided and had given him back even more than he had surrendered.

"Maybe that's how you feel now, Kendall. You know that you're losing your childhood relationship with your brother, but you don't know what you'll get in its place. That's where our faith comes in. We have to let go of the way things were in order to make room for the way they will be, and trust God to provide."

As I finished talking, I looked over at Kendall. She had fallen asleep. I could hardly blame her. Besides, the story was more for me than for her, and as I started to doze off, I began looking forward to the exciting new relationships we had ahead of us as a family.

Father, when we let go of something,
You fill our emptiness with something even better.
—CAROL KUYKENDALL

MAY 26

Praise his name in the dance. —PSALM 149:3 (KJV)

It was a paralyzing moment: a skunk had walked in through the patio door and was ambling its way across the kitchen. "Don't move," our daughter Katrelya whispered. "Stay quiet." I blanched, petrified at the thought of how we would cope if it let loose with its spray.

Slowly moving with the grace of a shadow, Katrelya went through the patio door, raced around the side of the house, then opened the back door so the skunk would have an exit. Sure enough, after crunching a dish of cat chow, Mr. Skunk raised his head, sniffed the air, and lumbered out.

A family of skunks is raising their young in the woodpile across our fence, under a large Chinese elm in our neighbor's yard. We are becoming wise in the ways of skunks and are constantly amazed by their intelligence and amused by their unusual antics.

"Turn out the lights," I said to Katrelya on a late summer night as she came to the dining table to join me in a bedtime cup of tea. "Look—what's that moving about the bushes?" We both crept outside and peered into the darkness.

"It's skunks," she said. "Two huge skunks with their tails up and spread out like fans." Mesmerized, we watched. They were dancing, tumbling, and chasing each other in what was probably a mating ritual as beautiful as an orchestrated ballet. Within moments they were gone, out of our range of vision.

"Wow," I mused, "I never thought skunks could be so graceful and lovely."

"Not only that," our daughter answered, "they make sweet pets, too."

"Don't even think about it!" I gasped.

"De-scented?" she asked.

"Never!" I said.

In all our forty years of living in the foothills, close to wildlife, we had never seen the likes of this: skunks, the much maligned, dancing in the moonlight.

For the blessings of "all creatures, great and small,"
I give You thanks, dear Lord.

—FAY ANGUS

MAY 27

The patient in spirit is better than the proud in spirit.
—ECCLESIASTES 7:8 (KJV)

*W*hen my grandson Bob received his college degree, our family attended the graduation. After the usual round of congratulations and hugs from friends and family, we gathered at a restaurant for lunch.

We had placed our orders when I said to Bob, "We are so proud to be here to see you receive your bachelor's degree."

"Then start planning for the time when I get my master's degree, Grandmom," he said.

"And you're going to start that next fall?" I asked.

"Yes, I am." His voice was almost hard with determination. "I'll have to work to pay for it, but I already have a job here at the college."

"That's great!" I exclaimed. "What will you be doing?"

He straightened his shoulders a bit and fixed his eyes on my face as he answered, "I'll be moving furniture, emptying trash, mopping floors, painting walls, and—"

I interrupted him to ask, "You'll be doing custodial work?"

"Yes. Are you ashamed of me, Grandmom?"

"Oh, no!" I reached over to clasp his hand in mine. "I'm very proud of you. Not every young man your age would be willing to do that kind of work to get his education."

Bob moved into my outstretched arms and we hugged each other, both already looking forward to that next graduation day.

Dear Lord, bless those who work
hard to make the most of the gift of life.
—DRUE DUKE

MAY 28

"If you have faith as small as a mustard seed...nothing
will be impossible for you." —MATTHEW 17:20

I grew up in the church, but my friend Stacey didn't. Now, as a young woman, she was awakening to the whole spiritual side of life. It was exciting for me, but a bit frightening too. Her faith was so young and tender—I was afraid that one great trial would send her reeling.

Then her dog Arkus got sick—very sick. Stacey was devastated. She took Arkus to the vet, and when they hooked up Arkus to IVs and other machines, Stacey spent whole afternoons lying beside her, praying.

Late one evening Stacey stopped by my house in tears. "I don't want Arkus to die! She's my best friend!" Silently, I considered the facts. Arkus was twelve years old. She had a severe digestive problem. The vet had not been encouraging. So I talked to Stacey about how there is a time for everything, about how much joy Arkus had given her over the years, about how God was a God of love and could give us peace no matter what happened. Then Stacey went her way—and kept praying that Arkus would be well again.

Two weeks later, my back door opened and in romped Arkus, complete with shaved areas where the IVs had been. Stacey glowed as she said, "See, God healed her! I knew He would!"

Mature faith is wonderful, but maybe it takes a new believer to remind us that all things are possible—for herself, for me, and for a much-loved pooch.

Thank You, Father, for the exuberance of newfound trust—
and for Your love for all Your creatures!
—MARY LOU CARNEY

MAY 29

*So I commend the enjoyment of life, because nothing is better
for a man under the sun.* —ECCLESIASTES 8:15

I rushed home from work to babysit Indy and Noah, my two grandsons. I hadn't seen them much lately. I was juggling my job, school, housework, and gardening. There was no time for anything else.

I was still in my business suit and heels when they arrived. Four-year-old Indy grabbed my hand, ready to run to the pond to feed the ducks.

"Grandma," he said excitedly, "go get your play clothes on!"

"Oh, Indy," I laughed, "I don't have any play clothes."

He looked at me wide-eyed. "What do you wear when you play?" It was the third time that week the issue of play had come up. When a deliveryman hustled to my door with a package, I joked that he was as busy as I was. He smiled and said that the key to life is to remember to find time to play too. I responded with a blank stare.

It came up again two days later at a seminar. When asked to create a personal schedule that included time for me to do something just for fun, I came up empty-handed.

The following Saturday afternoon when the boys came over, I wore my newly labeled play clothes—jogging pants, tie-dyed T-shirt, and tennis shoes. I took their little hands in mine and we ran to the backyard, not to weed the garden, not to rake the leaves, and not to do homework at the patio table, but simply to play. Now that's an accomplishment!

> *Father, Indy, Noah, and I are lying here on the grass and
> watching the sun set across the pond. We just wanted to say
> thanks for a really fun day and a beautiful pink sky tonight.*

—MELODY BONNETTE

*"Let me inherit a double portion
of your spirit," Elisha replied.* —2 KINGS 2:9

*W*e were at a school picnic when my dad began watching an Arizona Diamondbacks baseball game on his tiny three-inch television. My nephew Christopher peered over his shoulder and with the double-edged sword of innocence and boldness typical of an eight-year-old said, "Papa, can I have that when you die?" My dad had to laugh at his honesty.

I thought of that story recently when I ran across Elisha's reply to Elijah in the Old Testament. Before God takes Elijah up to heaven in a fiery chariot, Elijah asks Elisha what he might do for him. Elisha longs not for material wealth but for an inheritance of the great prophet's spirit. My first thought was, *Now that's what I'd like to inherit from my dad, a large measure of the indomitable spirit that keeps him working tirelessly for the causes he believes in.*

But then came the question: What kind of spirit might my children inherit from me? I remembered the promises my husband Paul and I made when our children were baptized, and I wondered how faithful I've been to those promises and what spirit I convey. I have taught them the Lord's Prayer. *Do I show a spirit of forgiveness?* I bring them to church. *Do I show a spirit of community?* I've placed the Scriptures in their hands. *Do I show the spirit of compassion Jesus taught?*

Every day I have the opportunity to pass on so much more to my children—and to everyone I encounter—than a few material gifts. And going through the motions of worship and church life isn't enough. I need to show the gift of God's Spirit as it lives and works in me. That's a priceless inheritance.

*Great God, give me as large a portion of
Your Spirit as You think I can handle,
and help me share it with everyone I meet.*

—GINA BRIDGEMAN

MAY 31

This one thing I do, forgetting those things which are behind,
and reaching forth unto those things which are before.
—PHILIPPIANS 3:13 (KJV)

My grandson Drake and I were sitting on the family room floor, looking at books, when suddenly he jumped up and ran to the kitchen. He patted the table and said, "Eat. Yesterday." Then he walked around, touching each chair where a family member sat. "Mama. Baby Brock. Me." I smiled. Yes, we all ate together last Sunday. But to Drake, it was yesterday. The past is a new concept to his two-year-old mind, and everything that's not of-the-moment is "yesterday."

Sometimes I'm a bit too much like Drake. It seems as though every hurt, every slight, every unkind word spoken to me happened yesterday. I keep it fresh—and painful—by revisiting it often. I don't let time do its healing work by putting the past behind me.

Soon Drake will learn the difference between yesterday and the many other layers of the past. I'm going to work hard to learn that too.

You are the God of all my yesterdays and
all my tomorrows. Give me grace today
to place both those things in Your hands.
—MARY LOU CARNEY

June

JUNE 1

"This day shall be for you a memorial day."
—EXODUS 12:14 (RSV)

From the time I was a girl of twelve, I enjoyed summer fishing trips with my father in his fourteen-foot aluminum boat *The Charu*. Dad always sat in the stern handling the motor controls, but whenever I had a trout on my line, he jumped up beside me ready with the net. He'd help unhook the slippery fish and then pass me bait for the next cast. When Dad died, my son Phil was just two and not yet under the spell of hook and line. It wasn't long, however, before he was out trolling with his dad in that same dependable boat.

By last summer Phil had grown to a boy of twelve...and one evening he took me fishing. Suddenly I felt that old familiar tug, and hollered as I always used to, "I've got one!" Phil was right there to grab the line and swing a fat *kokanee* into the boat. "That's a beauty, Mom," he whistled. And, just like Dad, Phil unhooked the wriggling fish and passed me more bait.

We cruised awhile longer without catching anything—or so it appeared. But for me, the evening had been an unexpected cast backward in time, and the childhood memory I had hooked was a beauty. As we headed for shore, I looked at Phil manning the controls, squinting into the setting sun, and I prayed, "Help me, Lord, to fill his net with a good catch. Among his memories let there be some real beauties."

*Dear Lord, guide me by Your understanding to stock
my days with tomorrow's prizewinning memories.*
—CAROL KNAPP

JUNE 2

I have set watchmen upon thy walls. —ISAIAH 62:6 (KJV)

Our dog Jessif is a control freak. She has to know that my husband Keith is sitting at his desk before she'll eat her dinner. She has to be on alert to guard the house, even though she barks as if barking leaves a bad taste in her mouth. (She barks and then runs her tongue over her teeth and makes faces before she barks again.)

Maybe she is the way she is because she was taken from her mother too young. She has been with us since she was about one month old, so tiny that she fit into my two hands and had to be carried down the back steps to the yard. Maybe she feels responsible for us.

She knows she has to stay awake in order to be a guard, so she is more resistant to sleeping than any other dog I've ever known. I love watching her fight sleep. Her eyes start closing and her head begins to droop, and she pulls herself back from the edge of sleep as if she's ashamed to have been found failing in her duty. I always pretend not to have seen her struggle, especially when she eventually loses, as she always does.

Then I love watching her sleep. She is, as Keith always says, force at rest. It makes me feel that I have a chance to guard her for a change. Sometimes I think God gave us dogs to show us His vigilance...and to give us a chance to emulate it.

Dear God, You are the force that never rests.
Be ever watchful over me.
—RHODA BLECKER

June 3

The desire accomplished is sweet to the soul.
—Proverbs 13:19 (KJV)

When I graduated from high school, I had to accept that there was no money for further education. But through the next twenty years of marriage and children I never lost the dream. Finally, at age thirty-nine, I was able to enroll in college. For eight grueling but exciting years, I lived for the day I would be through with college and get my degree.

The day I finished my last exam, I walked out of the classroom into the bright May sunlight and looked around expectantly. *I've made it!* I thought. *There should be fireworks, a brass band, and flags flying! I made my dream come true.* But the campus was deserted and quiet, as it always is during exams, and there was no one to share my victory.

Feeling strangely depressed, I walked slowly toward my car. And then I recognized the let-down feeling—it was all over. I'd had it before—particularly when my older daughter entered kindergarten, even though I'd been nudging her toward that milestone from the day she was born. Both times I was grieving because the goal had finally been reached. It was a kind of ending, and I felt strangely alone.

I was still feeling depressed when I opened the front door—and was overwhelmed by a banner proclaiming, Way to go, mom. we're proud of you. My two daughters put a black construction paper graduation cap on me while my husband John gave me a big kiss and led me to the table where a rather lopsided cake was waiting. Here was my celebration! I didn't need a brass band. I had something better: a family who had gone with me through the eight years, and who had made it possible. "Thanks," I told them. "*We* made it!"

> *Dear Lord, help me always to look in the right place*
> *for appreciation and applause. Thank You for the*
> *people in my life, but most of all, thanks because*
> *You are always there cheering me on.*
> —Bonnie Lukes

June 4

"My Father is the gardener." —John 15:1

I like gardens—but not *gardening*. I am good at planting, usually in a rush of adrenaline brought on by seed catalogs with blossoms bursting off the page. But when the blush of the moment fades, I tend to forget about my flowers. And as time goes by, weeds grow and my garden begins to look, well...ragged.

My friend Desila, on the other hand, likes gardening. Her beds are beautiful, her blossoms huge and richly colored. So I had to laugh the other day when she showed up with something for my flowerbed—a flat gray stone that read: MY GARDEN WAS AT ITS BEST LAST WEEK. SORRY YOU MISSED IT.

I think the rock was meant to motivate me to take better care of my flowers. But it's done more than that. It's made me think about the way people perceive my actions, too. That moment when I'm short-tempered with a waitress, the times my driving gets too aggressive, the laugh I have at the expense of someone else. These things don't occur often—but when they do, I want to say, "Wait! I looked better last week when I was doing church volunteer work. When I was letting that hassled mother in front of me in the grocery store line. You should have seen me when...."

My well-placed stone reminds me that life, like gardens, requires ongoing care. And you never know who's looking to see just how well you're blooming!

Master Gardener, weed from my life all that
is ugly and selfish. Let me grow strong and
tall in the beauty of Your love.

—Mary Lou Carney

JUNE 5

He that believeth and is baptized shall be saved.
—MARK 16:16 (KJV)

*O*n a balmy Sunday in early June, my husband Robert and I attended St. Luke's Episcopal Church, my former church home in Kearney, Nebraska, where we had the great joy of seeing my little granddaughter Saralisa baptized into the family of Christ.

As we stood at the baptismal font behind Saralisa and my daughter Karen, and heard Father Park speak those precious words, "I baptize you, Saralisa Christine, in the name of the Father and of the Son and of the Holy Spirit," tears of joy started flowing down my cheeks. Then I looked up and saw Anita, Beth, and Verna, members of the prayer group I belonged to when I lived in Kearney, beaming smiles at me. We had prayed for this moment, and our prayers were now being answered in the most lovely way. How beautiful Saralisa and Karen looked, happy in their new church home.

I think I hadn't realized until that moment how valuable my membership in this church family had been to me and, yes, how much I missed my friends there. I even felt the presence of my dear friend and prayer partner Carolmae, who had died shortly before I moved away. And a deep truth rang in my heart like a bell: those who are baptized into Christ's family can never be separated.

I will return to St. Luke's many times in the years to come, both in person and in thought. And I know, too, that Carolmae will keep her promise to "meet me at the river."

Lord Christ, thank You for this family that bears Your name,
this family that is our true and lasting home.
—MARILYN MORGAN KING

June 6

*W*hump! Tim's landing was perfect, just below my rib cage, an accidental Heimlich maneuver. As I struggled to catch my breath, he hopped onto my pillow, looking annoyed that I had ruined a perfectly good sleeping spot. I glared at him and rolled over. I still had another hour before my alarm was set to go off, and I intended to enjoy it.

I had just gotten back to sleep when Nickel launched her attack, sticking a paw in my ear. A shake of my comforter sent both cats scrambling. A moment later, I heard the toilet flush.

Not again! I had asked the cats very nicely not to drink out of the commode, but when they refused to listen, I closed the lid. Now, every few days, they have voiced their protests with toilet-flushing sprees. I abandoned my last hour of sleep and marched to the bathroom. There they posed, completely still, jet-black bookends. Tim was perched on the tank, looking angelic. Nickel faced me, her ear-probing paw poised on the handle, waiting for me to make the first move.

I struck quickly, scooping one cat in either arm, and dashed for the bedroom. I dropped the cats on the bed and hopped up myself. Then I pulled the comforter up over my head, trapping the three of us in a striped, downy tent. Slowly, Tim climbed into my lap and reached up with one paw to bat my nose. I scratched his nose. He pawed my stomach, so I tickled his. Satisfied, he curled up in my lap and began to purr. Nickel slithered into my lap and used Tim as a chaise longue, stretching out so I could tickle her stomach, too.

Quite suddenly, I opened one eye to the muted but insistent beeping of my alarm. I was curled in a ball around my two roommates.

*Father in heaven, thank You for my extended
"feline family." They are my friends and guardians
and my foot-warmers, too. What a special gift!*
—KJERSTIN WILLIAMS

June 7

"Show me the path where I should go, O Lord; point out the right road for me to walk." —PSALM 25:4 (TLB)

Four quotes in bright colors and varying sizes are taped to my kitchen cabinets. The first quote, on a piece of shocking-pink paper, says in huge black letters, GET OVER IT. STOP WHINING AND START WINNING. That quote wakes me up every morning and reminds me to hold no grudges and maintain a positive attitude all day long.

Quote number two is on the cabinet over the counter that holds seventy jars of tea. It says, IF YOU'RE COLD, TEA WILL WARM YOU. IF YOU'RE HEATED, IT WILL COOL YOU. IF YOU'RE DEPRESSED, IT WILL CHEER YOU. IF YOU'RE EXCITED, IT WILL CALM YOU.—BRITISH PRIME MINISTER WILLIAM GLADSTONE. That quote reminds me to be hospitable and invite my friends over for tea often. I do, and my little tea parties have enriched my life immeasurably over the years.

The next quote, the one taped to my kitchen cabinet just to the right of the kitchen sink, spells out four of the most important sentences I can say: I AM PROUD OF YOU. WHAT IS YOUR OPINION? I LOVE YOU. THANK YOU. Those four sentences nudge me to be a more affirming, affectionate, appreciative, and positive person. I tried to punctuate my conversations with those four sentences when my children were growing up.

The last quote, to the left of the kitchen sink, typed on bright yellow paper, proclaims, IF YOU HAD FAITH EVEN AS TINY AS A MUSTARD SEED, YOU COULD SAY TO THIS MOUNTAIN, "MOVE!" AND IT WOULD GO FAR AWAY. NOTHING IS IMPOSSIBLE.—MATTHEW 17:20 (TLB). That's the one that gives me constant hope, unlimited encouragement, and a daily dose of comfort, no matter what I'm trying to accomplish.

So there you have it—a whole philosophy of life on my kitchen cabinets.

Father, for the wisdom of others and the soothing comfort of Your Word, I thank You.
—PATRICIA LORENZ

The Lord will perfect that which concerns me.
—PSALM 138:8 (NKJV)

I sat down at my computer this morning to write an important letter, a task that I'd been putting off. But the words didn't come easily, so I decided to clean my keyboard instead (another procrastination technique). I got some cotton swabs from the bathroom, some cleaning solution from the kitchen, and I went to work wiping off each key.

That's when I noticed that the question mark key was much dirtier than the exclamation mark key. Had I been doing more questioning than exclaiming lately? How about since I woke up this morning? I easily remembered several questions:

Why did I eat two muffins? Why is my friend experiencing more than her fair share of difficult circumstances? Why do I still worry about our children, even though they're grown and gone? What should I say in this letter? Why do I procrastinate so much?

How about exclamations? Had I uttered any words of conviction?

My mind went totally blank. But then I spotted some, right there above my desk; a bunch of God's promises that I'd taken from the Bible and written on sticky notes so they would permeate my mind when I sat there.

I can do all things in Him who strengthens me (Philippians 4:13).

For nothing is impossible with God (Luke 1:37).

The joy of the Lord is my strength (Nehemiah 8:10).

God is with me always (Matthew 28:20).

God knows the plans He has for me...to give me hope and a future (Jeremiah 29:11).

Amazing how these one-line promises could become exclamation answers to most of my questions.

I looked down at my clean keyboard. *The question mark and exclamation point are at opposite ends*, I thought, *but for today, at least, I've connected them.* Now, back to that letter!

Father, may every question today lead me
to an exclamation of Your promises!

—CAROL KUYKENDALL

JUNE 9

Thou hast put gladness in my heart. —PSALM 4:7 (KJV)

June was family time in our vacation cabin at Mammoth Lakes in California. For two glorious weeks, we became part of the history of the rustic log cabin built by settlers in 1908. All the furniture, beds included, was made of massive logs. We put our feet up on the iron rail that fronted a huge rock fireplace and sipped hot chocolate to the rhythmic creak of rough-hewn rockers. No phone, no television, just us and the children, and then just us. Now that my husband John was gone, it would be just me.

"It won't be 'just you,'" my son Ian insisted. "Let's all go. You can fish with the kids, Mom, and I'll teach them to tie hooks at the very same table where Dad taught me."

Apprehensive and sad, I went.

Driving up the highway into the Inyo National Forest was like entering a warm embrace. The snow-capped mountains and dancing aspen were still home away from home. As we stepped into the cabin and my son gave me a teary-eyed hug, I once again felt the comfort of John's arms around me.

We pulled out the photo album. The grandchildren giggled over stories— the dog falling through the iced-over lake, a lightning storm that zapped our power, the bear we met on the climb to the top of the falls. We cozied up in the same rockers and hiked the same trails, absorbed in the nostalgia of *then*. But it was *now*. Time to move on to new adventures.

Traditions kept. Traditions created. Then and now, both better than good.

For tears and sadness turned to joy
and gladness, thank You, Lord.

—FAY ANGUS

June 10

Let us draw near with a true heart in full assurance of faith. —Hebrews 10:22 (KJV)

Some days anxiety looms up out of the blue and snatches me. Sometimes I can't even describe my fear. It could be anything: my mother is having tests for an ulcer; I haven't allowed enough time for groceries so I'm stuck in line, late for my next appointment; the car keeps stalling; a friend hasn't called in a while, so I'm convinced he's angry with me.

During these frightening episodes, only one thing is sure to help: prayer. Not reciting familiar words or reading the Psalms or talking; my "anxiety prayer" has no words at all. I curl up in the corner of my sofa, facing the pretty stone gazebo on the small square of green separating me from Connecticut's Stonington Harbor. I close my eyes and imagine myself opening the sliding glass door. God stands in front of the gazebo, His arms open to me. I start walking, then running, to Him. He lifts me like the terrified child I am and swings me around through the air like the loving Father He is. Then He sits in the gazebo facing the water, holding me in His comforting arms until my breathing slows and my anxiety lessens. I feel His love, forgiveness, and grace just as surely as I hear the gentle waves and tinkling wind chimes.

I stay there with Him as long as I need to. I don't beg Him for help or tell Him my troubles. He knows. And when I open my eyes to my familiar living room, I'm always calm.

Father, never let me forget that You are just that: loving, forgiving, and comforting.
—Marci Alborghetti

JUNE 11

For with thee is the fountain of life:
in thy light shall we see light. —PSALM 36:9 (KJV)

This is my favorite time of night," my mother said. "Dark enough so you can see the fireflies, light enough so you can catch them. Do you know what lightning bugs are, Solomon?"

My two-year-old looked confused. "I don't think he does," I said. Outside, the moon showed through the clouds in a dim yellow haze.

Crickets chirped. Stray sparks glistened in the field next door. I held Solomon's hand and pointed to the sparks. "Those are lightning bugs!"

"Look at them all!" Mom said.

The sparks of light twinkled above the tall grass. There must have been a hundred of them.

"Well," Mom said, "what are you waiting for? Go catch them!" Barefoot, I crept over the dew-covered lawn to the field. Arms outstretched, I reached for flashes, grasping at the air. Years disappeared, and I felt the same excitement I'd felt nearly thirty years earlier. The same yard, the same glorious feeling, being with my mom beneath the stars chasing sparks of light. In the darkness, I followed the flashes and then I had one, a tiny little lightning bug safely caught in my hands.

"Look, your mom's got one!" my mother said.

Solomon cheered. "Yeah! Mama's got a light! Mama's got a light!"

Bright yellow twinkled from the creases of my hands.

"That is a firefly, Solomon," my mother said.

"Mommy lights up," he said.

Beneath the stars, we *oohed* and *ahhed* as our hands lit up, catching fireflies until it got too dark to see. Later that night, as I lay in bed, I felt as if I'd completed a circle: I'd recaptured a favorite childhood memory and made it stronger and brighter by sharing it with my son.

Dear God, thank You for letting me see
Your light through the eyes of my son.
—SABRA CIANCANELLI

JUNE 12

Say to those with fearful hearts, "Be strong, do not fear."
—ISAIAH 35:4

At work, when they needed someone to dress up as a bear for Saturday story time, guess who volunteered? Yes, anything to distract me from the phone call I knew I had to make to apologize to a friend for an unsolicited criticism. While I struggled to don the heavy fake-fur costume, the long feet—that is, paws—and the hairy hands with four-inch nails, I had visions of how happy the children would be to see me.

While I yanked and pulled on the enormous head, I glowed. Maybe some kids would even ask for my "paw-tograph"! Plus, I'd be postponing that dreaded call!

As I lumbered through the store, I could see that out of the twenty or so children who were there, only two or three appeared actually happy to see me. The others? They scattered in terror. Some cried. Some wailed. Some leapt into their parents' arms for safety. I guess a six-foot-tall bear was five more feet than they'd bargained for.

Since bears aren't supposed to speak, I could only watch silently and couldn't say what I wanted to: "I came to make you happy! I won't hurt! Come up to me, please!" But even if I could have given voice to my words, they wouldn't have been heard over the shrieks and tears.

Inside my hot furry cage, I had to laugh, although ruefully. Wasn't I that way too many times with God? A difficult phone call to mend a friendship, my former fear of driving—maybe God was handing me those challenges as loving gifts. And there I was screaming, "No! Go away!"

As I made my way to the backroom to pull off my furry head, I knew that as soon as I yanked off my paws, I'd be dialing my friend's phone number to make that overdue apology.

Thank You, God, for putting loving challenges in my life.
Help me not to run from them screaming!
—LINDA NEUKRUG

June 13

Call upon Me, and I will answer. —Psalm 91:15 (NKJV)

My mind was on my daughter Amy Jo and her four-week-old baby. Brock was golden-haired and healthy and constantly hungry. Every hour he needed to eat. Plus, he cried a lot! So I prayed for little Brock. I prayed that he would sleep that night, that he would rest and be at peace, that his little stomach would stay full beyond those sixty short minutes. Amy Jo's husband was away on business and she was exhausted beyond words. As I prayed, I visualized an angel—complete with giant wings and flowing robe— standing beside Brock's crib, comforting him and singing him back to sleep.

Later, as I climbed into bed, Amy Jo called. "Can you come over? I just need someone else to hold the baby and let me get a few minutes sleep." Gladly, I went.

After Amy Jo nursed Brock, she handed him to me and shuffled off to bed. "Wake me up when he starts crying," she said over her shoulder.

So I began rocking Brock. After a while, I laid him in his crib and patted his stomach. The minutes slipped by and turned into hours. For three hours Brock slept—and so did Amy Jo. Every time he stirred, I prayed and hummed hymns until he was quiet. "That's the most sleep I've gotten in the last month!" Amy Jo said happily when I put Brock into her arms.

As I drove home, the blackness of night giving way to the first hint of dawn, I realized just how miraculously my prayer had been answered. Brock was attended to by an angel that night...an angel named *Nana*.

How doubly generous, God, to let me
be part of Your answer to my prayers!
—Mary Lou Carney

JUNE 14

Can any hide himself in secret places that I shall not see him? saith the Lord. Do not I fill heaven and earth?
—JEREMIAH 23:24 (KJV)

The fog was unusually thick for a mid-June morning in Tennessee. In the forest behind our home, a late-night rain had saturated the canopy of tall trees. Now the dripping leaves combined with the fog to mimic a resplendent rain forest. The branches of one tree, completely dead, were filled with hundreds of mist-coated spiderwebs, intricately spun to mesh perfectly with the tree's limbs. Normally invisible, they had been revealed by the misty fog.

"It makes you realize," my husband David said, "how many unseen things are woven around us every day of the week. Then out of the blue, some unexpected circumstance, like the fog on the spiderwebs, brings us new vision."

Later, over breakfast, I recalled a painful time when our family had been the target of a barrage of hurtful acts.

"You know, we would never have had any idea how many people loved us if that hadn't happened," I said. "Like the fog this morning showing us things we hadn't seen before."

"Yep," David answered. "Can you imagine God, who sees the unseen world of everything, somehow weaving all their workings together according to His plan?"

"Nice of Him to send the fog this morning," I answered. "And it's nice to be reminded that He's got us covered."

Father, thank You for these glimpses of Your omnipotence.
—PAM KIDD

JUNE 15

Blessed is he whose transgression is forgiven.
—PSALM 32:1 (KJV)

W hen I was a child, my parents had a hard-and-fast rule about what films I could see. I was never permitted to attend a movie until it had been checked out in *Parents* magazine. If the magazine listed it as being suitable for my age group, then I could go; if the magazine objected to the material, then I could not. It was that simple.

One Saturday afternoon, while my parents were away on a trip and my grandmother was taking care of me, a horror double feature was appearing at the theater. I had looked up the pictures and knew that both were deemed unsuitable for me. I also knew that Grandma was unaware of our movie rule, so ever-so-sweetly I asked her if I could go to the movies with two friends. She said yes.

Off I went, skipping all the way to the theater, where for three hours I shuddered and screamed along with the other kids as zombies came out of graves and a man turned into a werewolf at midnight. Afterward, I skipped home to dinner.

But my carefree attitude changed to worry when my parents returned. *What if Grandma mentions the movies? What if one of my friends tattles? What if...?* Finally, when I could bear the what-ifs no longer, I confessed my guilt to my parents.

My father seemed surprised. "What movies did you see?"

"*Wolf Man of Paris* and *The Valley of the Zombies*," I replied. He seemed flustered, but my mother was more in control.

"Anybody brave enough both to see them and tell us about it is a good child."

She hugged me, and my father put an arm around my shoulder and said three wonderful words, "We forgive you."

Those words are with me still. They are the same with my heavenly Father who forgives me my trespasses when I am sorry.

> *Dear Lord, let me never forget the*
> *things that I learned as a child.*
> —ELEANOR SASS

JUNE 16

Put your hope in God. —PSALM 42:5

*W*hat if this happens again?"

That's the fearful question I carried around in my heart after my husband Lynn suffered a cerebral hemorrhage that threatened his life and required two brain surgeries before he recovered earlier this year. It's the same question many of us ask after something fearful happens in our lives.

As I remember back to the terrible day that terrorists attacked our country, I ask myself:

What if terrorists strike again?

What if another plane gets hijacked?

What if something like this happens to me or someone I love?

As I ask myself these questions, I remember what I kept repeating when similar what-if questions plagued me after Lynn's brush with death. For every what-if question, God gave me an even-if answer:

Even if... I have to face my worst fear, God is still in control.

Even if... things don't turn out the way I want, God's love is still sufficient.

Even if... _____ God's promises are still true.

(*Write your fear in the blank.*)

> For every what-if fear, Father,
> remind me of your even-if promise.

—CAROL KUYKENDALL

Then shalt thou call, and the Lord shall answer; thou shalt cry, and he shall say, Here I am. —ISAIAH 58:9 (KJV)

Yesterday I stood in a shopping mall dressing room, forcing myself to try on bathing suits to replace my dilapidated tank suit that had finally disintegrated. How had my once-girlish figure gone from lithesome to lumbering so fast?

Trying to wriggle out of a spandex suit for a "mature figure," I bounced against the wall, and someone in the next dressing room asked if I was okay. *I'm not okay*, I wanted to wail. *I'm older, heavier, and way more insecure and scared than I ever thought I'd be at this stage of my life.*

I left the store without buying anything, feeling sad and upset. But then, as I looked at the sun glinting off a runaway balloon soaring over the parking lot, a conversation went back and forth in my head.

"I'm older," a woeful voice said.

Another voice answered right back, *Yup, you are.*

"I don't know what the future will bring."

Nobody does.

"My health could fail."

It might.

"I'll run out of energy."

Could happen.

"I can't stand to live with this anxiety."

Don't have to.

"But I'm stuck! I'll always be inadequate and anxious!"

No, you won't. You can change. You can accept that life changes and trust that I'll always be present to help you.

Me whining, the "other voice" answering. The voice of God.

Dear God, help me to be aware that You're always "talking back to me." And help me actually to listen.

—MARY ANN O'ROARK

JUNE 18

I devoted myself to study. —ECCLESIASTES 1:13

I had—at the tender age of fifty—enrolled in a master of religion program. Now I was struggling to find time for all the reading and research and writing for my class on the Gospel of Luke and the Acts of the Apostles.

It was 5:00 a.m., and I sat on the floor of my family room, surrounded by reference books. Some were left over from my undergraduate days; some had been bought as I taught church classes over the years. But most of them had come to me when Mother died six years ago.

How she loved the Bible! She would spend hours "running references" on a certain word or Scripture. Many times when I visited her, I'd find her sitting at the dining room table surrounded by books and legal pads covered with purple ink. *She would be so proud that I've gone back to school*, I thought, *especially to study religion. Too bad she isn't here.*

The words in front of me blurred. I swallowed back my tears and reached for the book closest at hand. It fell open to a page where a yellow bookmark rested. I looked at the bookmark: "My Darling Daughter," the heading said. I looked closer; it was a poem. *A poem for me. Why is it here in this book? Why hadn't Mother given it to me?*

The last lines of the poem seemed to come from Mother's own lips: "You are a shining example of what every mother wishes her daughter was/And I am so very proud of you." And then, in purple ink, she had signed it: "Mother."

I smiled and settled in to read, knowing that God would help me get everything done. And Mother would be proud.

Even though our loved ones are with You, God, thank You for
those moments when they seem so very close at hand.
—MARY LOU CARNEY

JUNE 19

Our Father who art in heaven. —MATTHEW 6:9 (RSV)

When I first learned the Lord's Prayer, "heaven," to my young ear, had a faraway sound. It was a remote, fairy-tale kind of place where very good people went after they died. A Father "in heaven" wasn't much help right now!

Since then I've come to feel just the opposite. heaven, to me, means a reality closer and truer than anything I can see and touch. It means this commonplace earthly life is caught up in God's eternal plan.

The Dutch evangelist Corrie ten Boom had a visual aid that expressed this well. Corrie had arrived for a visit, and my thirteen-year-old daughter Liz and I were helping her unpack. From the bottom of Corrie's suitcase, Liz lifted a folded cloth with some very amateurish-looking needlework on it. Uneven stitches, mismatched colors, loose threads, snarls.

"What are you making?" Liz asked curiously.

"Oh, that's not mine," Corrie said. "That's the work of the greatest weaver of all."

I probably looked as dubious as Liz did.

"But you're seeing it from the wrong side!" Corrie went on. Shaking the cloth open with a flourish, she turned it around to display a magnificent crown embroidered in red, purple, and gold. "You have to look at things from heaven's viewpoint!"

heaven's viewpoint...when I pray to my Father in heaven, I speak to the One who can make something beautiful of the tangled threads of a lifetime. I am asking Him to help me see the perplexities of daily life "from heaven's side."

Our Father in heaven, give me eternity's
perspective on the small activities of this day.

—ELIZABETH SHERRILL

JUNE 20

If possible, so far as it depends upon you,
live peaceably with all. —ROMANS 12:18 (RSV)

*E*very mother dreams of her children living harmoniously under one roof, but what happens when a sister and brother rub each other like sandpaper? The mother is the one who ends up raw and hurting. And what if something wonderful happens to cause the sister and brother to become a team, if only for a few precious minutes? Then it is healing salve to a mother's heart.

My son Philip had invited me to the school playground for a private launching of his model rocket. Brenda wanted to watch, too, but Phil wasn't having his moment of glory ruined by any little sister. She tagged along anyway. He went to work setting up his equipment in the field. The fluorescent orange rocket thrust upward through the weeds like an exotic flower. Brenda had turned dejectedly toward home when Phil mumbled, "I guess she can stay."

The three of us watched the rocket swoosh into the clouds and drop a few seconds later into the trees. Who do you think struggled through the thick undergrowth and spotted a flash of orange high in the branches of a birch? Brenda. Who dragged a long pole to her brother so he could dislodge the rocket from the tree? Brenda. And who waited on the ground braving swarms of mosquitoes until it had been safely retrieved? Brenda.

It would be an overstatement to say that Philip thanked his sister profusely and the two of them remained friends happily ever after. Yet for a brief time they had needed each other. For me, watching at the edge of the woods, it was enough. We had launched more than a rocket in the schoolyard that summer afternoon.

Father, help us to see the grain of caring,
humor, and helpfulness beneath the sandpaper
finish in those who rub us the wrong way.

—CAROL KNAPP

JUNE 21

Love does not demand its own way. It is not
irritable or touchy.... Love is very patient and kind....
—1 CORINTHIANS 13:5, 4 (TLB)

*S*ure enough, he was right on cue! I watched from the kitchen window as, with some effort, he uncurled his lanky frame from the flowerbeds where he had spent the last hour pulling weeds. He checked his watch. *Any time now*, I could almost hear him think, as only wives can.

He unlatched the garden gate and walked briskly to the mailbox, its bright red flag waiting to be lowered. Resentment bubbled up within me. For the twenty-seven years of our married life, each afternoon *I* had gotten the mail. It was the highlight of my day. A three o'clock cup of tea, then sorting, sifting, and stacking—bills underneath, periodicals and catalogs on the side, the open-me-first priority of personal letters right on top. But since his retirement, daily *he* had been getting the mail. With irritation I watched him thumb through it, then lay it on a rock until he had finished putting away his tools, unaware of my cooling cup of tea and impatient waiting.

"He's invading my space, unsettling my schedule!" I complained to a friend.

She smiled. "Have you thought that for all those years *you* have had the pleasure of the mail—and maybe now *he* is entitled?"

Her reply brought me and my complaint into focus. This most honorable man, who had spent more than half a lifetime working hard to provide a comfortable living for the children and myself—this dedicated man, who served his Lord with joy and gladness—indeed, he was entitled!

My love gift to him: *John-who-gets-the-mail, you are entitled*!

Those we love the most, Lord, we so often
take for granted. Help us to join our lives,
one to the other, with acts of loving-kindness.

—FAY ANGUS

JUNE 22

"Even to your old age and gray hairs I am he,
I am he who will sustain you." —ISAIAH 46:4

With a brush and a blow-dryer as my weapons, I've been waging a yearlong war against middle age. So far, middle age is winning, as hormones have their way with my head, both inside and out. A cowlick has suddenly developed a mind of its own, a couple of spots are thinning, and what little body my hair once had has lain down and died. Every morning as I stand in front of the mirror, I get so frustrated that I don't know whether to throw something or cry.

It's just hair, for crying out loud. It doesn't really matter, I tell myself. So what *is* the matter? One day it comes to me: This isn't about a head of willful hair; it's about a life that I can't control. It's feeling that things that seem to come so easily to others—friendships, nicer homes, professional success—don't seem to come to me at all. It's silly, because they do, of course, and they will, but try to tell that to someone in a midlife crisis.

Finally, even though this isn't really a hair issue, God sent me one little thought about my hair that helped me win the skirmish: *Just let it do what it wants to do.* Suddenly, I found the courage to do something I've wanted to for a long time—have my hair cut really, really short. Now I wash it, gel it, and... let it do what it wants to do. No more battles. No more frustration. In fact, my carefree hair reminds me every day to quit trying to control my life, and to let God do with it what He wants.

Father, help me to be satisfied with
You and what You bring my way.
—LUCILE ALLEN

JUNE 23

And I will strengthen the house. —ZECHARIAH 10:6

On a sun-bright day one June, my son Paul and his six children suddenly appeared at my house. They needed a place to stay, a listening ear, and someone to cook and care for them, for...well, we didn't know how long. Can you imagine the sense of panic that swooped over this sixty-five-year-old grandmother who had grown used to living alone, loves peace and quiet, and cooks as little as possible? It had been a long time since so much mothering had been asked of me. Was I up to it? I felt overwhelmed, the way I do when my normally neat garden has become overgrown. But, of course, I invited them in, managed to scrounge up a meal, and we talked and talked until the sun went down.

Then Paul helped me open the sofa bed, put sheets on the guest bed, roll out my sleeping bag, carry blankets and pillows from the basement, and fix a "crib" for baby Joseph in the inflatable kiddie wading pool. When everyone was finally bedded down and I entered my own bedroom, closing the door behind me, I was too tired to pray anything but "Dear God, help!"

The visit stretched on for ten days. At times I thought I'd never make it, and I longed for my lost privacy. There were moments of irritation when our individual needs bumped up against each other in our now-crowded living space. And most nights, I fell into bed in exhaustion. But I'm still amazed at several things. Within a day or two, a power greater than mine took over as I swung into action as the maternal figure in a busy household, a role I hadn't held for many years. Though I was tired at night, I slept well and woke refreshed. I became reacquainted, on a deep personal level, with my son, and discovered again that Paul has the *sweetest* soul this side of heaven. My grandchildren, who have lived most of their lives in Colorado, have become real people for me in a deep new way.

Paul and the children are back in their own home now. All is well. And Grandma has discovered something: By the grace of God, weeds did not take over my inner garden. In fact, hearts have sprouted up anew all over the place!

My trustworthy God, help me to remember, always, that You
will empower me in any challenge in which love is the labor.
—MARILYN MORGAN KING

June 24

Love always protects, always trusts, always hopes, always perseveres. Love never fails.—1 Corinthians 13:6–8

"Come look what I found!" my niece Carol calls from the back bedroom. We all cluster around a tiny white box she is holding. She lifts the lid to reveal two small circles of gold nestled on white cotton. Mother's and Daddy's wedding rings. It has been twenty years since Daddy's death, since Mother slipped that ring off his finger before closing the casket. But Mother's ring comes as a surprise to us all.

"I didn't even know she had a wedding ring!" my sister says, picking up the tiny, frail band. "I never saw her wear it." We never saw Mother wear any jewelry. My sister places it back in the box and reaches for Daddy's. "I'll take this one," she says, slipping it on her index finger. "You take Mom's."

The sliver of gold feels cold and solid in my palm. Mother's marriage. I knew it had not been an easy one, yet she had remained faithful to Daddy and to the vow she'd taken when she was just seventeen years old. I look at my own wedding band—thick gold with circles of diamonds. "This ring represents love," the minister had said at our ceremony twenty-six years ago. "It has no beginning and no end." Nice words, but I had soon learned that feelings weren't enough. It took commitment. The kind my mother had had. That last month, when Daddy was dying of cancer, Mother hardly left his side, even to eat and sleep. Love? Certainly. But more than that. She had made a decision to do what she said she would do. "Till death do us part." It was a lesson I could use to make my good marriage even more secure.

I slip Mother's ring on the finger next to my own gold band. It fits just fine.

Dear Father, in a world of quick fixes and fickle promises, thank You for Your never-changing commitment to us. Empower me to apply that same steadfastness to my own relationships.

—Mary Lou Carney

The Lord, your God, is in your midst.
—ZEPHANIAH 3:17 (RSV)

*N*ot long ago I received an e-mail from my brother Steve, who does a great job of keeping us out here in Arizona up to date on his family back in Michigan. After filling me in on some news about his job, he began the report on his family with this hastily typed sentence: "Everything is god around here." I'm sure he meant to type *good*, but after I finished reading his letter I couldn't get that little typing mistake out of my mind.

Everything is God around here. How often can I report that about my life? Sunday mornings for sure, with teaching Sunday school and both my husband Paul and me singing in choir. But I thought about some other recent days. Yesterday I spent an hour catching up on the newspaper, yet I'm still behind in my reading through the Old Testament. I seem to be able to schedule a monthly night out with my friends but can't make it to a regular Bible study. And while I don't like admitting it, today I passed along a bit of e-mail gossip when I could have better spent that time adding a name or two to my church's e-mail prayer chain.

Everything is God around here. I say that phrase in my mind almost every day now, then take inventory to see how my life is measuring up. No surprise, there's always room for improvement. But that little reminder has made a big difference, continually making me aware that every day, God is ready to be invited into each moment of my life.

Come, Lord, and be a part of
everything I think, say, do, and feel.
—GINA BRIDGEMAN

JUNE 26

Who has gathered up the wind in the hollow
*of his hands?" —*PROVERBS 30:4

I watched the strong winds move across the water on my backyard pond. A storm was approaching and the wind gusts were close to twenty miles an hour.

"It's so easy to see the wind on the water now," I mused. Not so when I was a teenager vacationing in Florida. I spent the summer sunning, water-skiing, and learning how to sail from a tanned blond instructor named Robby. I remember sitting in his small two-person Sunfish when he said, "You've got to maneuver the boat into the wind. Look for the breeze on the water and tack toward it." He pointed ahead to a darkening rippled area. "The wind on the water looks a bit like fish feeding below the surface."

I squinted into the sun, looking out across the water for some sign that the wind was approaching. I shook my head, frustrated. "I don't see it."

A few minutes later the wind filled our sails. Robby trimmed them and turned toward me. "We can't see the wind, but we can see its effect on the water," he said. "It's a little like noticing God in our life. We can't really see Him, but we can see His effect."

Looking out into my backyard now, I watched my grown children and young grandchildren attempt to fly a kite in the breeze. I watched the wind race across the pond, reach the kite, and lift it high. My grandbabies, their soft, wispy hair blowing in all directions, ran after the kite. My children and their spouses cheered, and Misty, my oldest daughter, video camera in hand, documented it all. I joined along in the cheers, not just for the kite high in the air, but for the ability to see the effect of God's gracious love on my family and me.

Powerful Creator, may I always see
Your presence in my life.
—MELODY BONNETTE

The Lord seeth not as man seeth; for man looketh on the
outward appearance, but the Lord looketh on the heart.
—1 SAMUEL 16:7 (KJV)

I t was the first warm day of spring, and my children and I headed toward the playground to exercise our winter-weary bodies. Mary, who was crawling the previous fall, now explored eagerly, deftly climbing stairs and whizzing down the baby slide. Her famous smile (famous at least in our neighborhood) grew wider and wider. I smiled, too. I love to see my kids happy. After about ten minutes, she moved over to the big kids' equipment. Up she scrambled, tiny legs stretching mightily to get up waist-high steps. Down she came on the five foot-slide. She did it many times.

Then, in a flash, Mary was at the monkey bars. I watched from a short distance away, knowing she could not get up higher than the first rung. Mary grinned at me, face peering over the second rung. Then, just as it occurred to me that she could slip and bash her mouth, she did. Hard.

I raced over. She was bleeding and her lip was a mess, but it didn't bother her much. In less than a minute she wriggled out of my arms and ran off to play some more.

Some time later, Mary came over for a hug and smiled gloriously, just for me. I stared in horror. Her two upper front teeth were chipped. Not badly, but each had an obvious ding.

My heart sank. My precious girl had a noticeable flaw. I mentally ran through the accidents that would have been worse, but still my foolish, worldly heart said, *Why, oh why, did it have to be her beautiful smile?*

Being closer to God than I, Mary did not share my vanity. She grinned through her imperfections, showering me with the same love she'd always exuded, and headed for the slide once more.

Father, You love me in spite of my imperfections.
Help me also to see through the flaws of
others as You see through mine.
—JULIA ATTAWAY

JUNE 28

To this end we always pray for you.
—2 THESSALONIANS 1:11 (RSV)

*W*hen I discovered gardening (and combined it with my Scottish heritage of thrift), I accidentally discovered a special way to pray for my children. Instead of throwing out their old boots, I turned them into planting pots. Several pairs now sit cheerfully on the steps around my deck and door. Pansies, chrysanthemums, lobelia, marigolds, impatiens.

Here are Phil's size-thirteen hiking boots. *Dear God, help Phil at the university today. Keep his mind alert for the quiz on Friday.* I come to his old high-tops. For some reason I remember when he'd folded his six-foot-four-inch frame into two plastic laundry baskets. *Thank You for Phil's silliness!* Heather's boots have curled up at the toes from the rain; they look like elf shoes. *Help Heather in her job hunt. Guide her to something meaningful and worthy of her intelligence.*

I'm almost done...but someone's missing. My youngest, Blake, won't give me his boots. He wears them full of holes and falling apart. One pair he painted silver. He wore these shoes to emcee his sister's wedding last year, dancing the Macarena on the tabletops. *Thank You for Blake, who keeps us laughing. Please be with him today in the callbacks for his school play!*

I put away my watering can and prayed:

> *Be with all my children, God. Help them*
> *to be everything You've meant them to be. Fulfill*
> *in them every good resolve and work of faith by*
> *Your power, so that Your name may be glorified.*
> —BRENDA WILBEE

*Therefore all things whatsoever ye would that men should do
to you, do ye even so to them.* —MATTHEW 7:12

When I was in college, I worked as a waitress in a large, busy restaurant. The owners trained the staff well, but they were not very tolerant of mistakes, and on every table there were cards for the customers to write down their comments about the food and service. Most customers didn't bother with them.

One evening, however, I brought a couple the wrong soup, and they became furious. They said they were going to complain to the manager about me, and reached for one of the cards. I fought hard to hold back my tears because I was afraid I would lose my job, but I did my best to be courteous.

Another couple at the next table must have heard the remarks, because when I took their order, they smiled and told me to take my time bringing their food because they weren't in a hurry. That gave me time to pull myself together.

Later, as we were closing, the restaurant manager said he had two comment cards for me. One accused me of being careless and stupid. The other described me as thoughtful and efficient, and said I had been attentive in spite of a difficult encounter at another table. "This second card saved your job," the manager told me.

Ever since then I have made an effort to thank people who do their jobs well, no matter what those jobs may be. I try to be specific about what they have done well. Sometimes I put my gratitude in letters. I don't know whether my efforts have saved anyone's job or made a difference in anyone's life, but they mean something to me. I know how it feels to be appreciated for something I've done, and I just like to pass on the feeling.

*Dear Lord Jesus, You are so quick to applaud me,
for even my smallest accomplishments.
Help me to be like You with others.*
—PHYLLIS HOBE

JUNE 30

For there is nothing covered that will not be revealed, nor hidden that will not be known. —LUKE 12:2 (NKJV)

God seemed far away one morning as I stood wearily washing last night's dinner dishes. Granny knelt in the garden beyond my window, pushing the point of a trowel into hardened earth. It had been the third season of little rain and, as was her custom, she discussed the problem with God.

"This California drought is getting frightening, Lord," she told Him. "We need Your help before everything dries up!"

Just then my four-year-old son barreled out through the back door.

"Who are you talking to, Granny?" he asked, skidding to a stop.

"I'm asking my Father for rain," she said.

My son's eyes darted around the yard puzzled. "But you don't have a father," he protested. "Anyway nobody can make it rain."

"I have a heavenly Father, Timmy. And He can do anything," she answered firmly.

"Where is He?" Timmy said. "I don't *see* anybody!"

"Shut your eyes tight," she ordered. He did, his freckled face crinkling with effort. "Now, can you see the sunshine?"

"No. It's all dark."

"Do you think the sun is gone because you can't see it?"

"No!" His eyes popped open and he laughed. "There's the sun!"

A grimy little finger pointed at the sky. She nodded.

"Our heavenly Father is like the sun," she explained gently. "Even when our eyes are closed, we know it's shining. And one day we'll open our eyes and there He'll be!"

I looked up at the sky and smiled, warmed by soapy water and sunshine and Granny's faith.

How wonderful it will be, Lord,
the day I open my eyes and see You!
—DORIS HAASE

July

JULY 1

Remember me, O my God, concerning this, and wipe not out
my good deeds that I have done. —NEHEMIAH 13:14 (KJV)

Some of my grandchildren were almost grown before it dawned on me that I'd made huge mistakes as a mother. As I watched my children raise their own children and had some honest, often painful, discussions with them, I realized I probably could have qualified for Unmother of the Year. My children were very specific:

"You were always working."

"You locked us out of the house during the summer and told us to drink out of the hose."

"You didn't smile much."

"You almost never seemed happy."

"We never got to have sleep-over company."

"You said no most of the time."

Recently, I saw an unforgettable picture in the newspaper: A mother, her face all aglow, followed her young daughter into a garden to gather tomatoes. One look at the child's expression said it all: "I've got the best mother in the world!" I made copies of the picture and mailed them to my children, writing, "I wish you had memories like this."

The first response came in today's mail in a hastily scrawled letter I'll always keep: "In bed two nights ago, I remembered the day you taught me 'Annabelle Lee.' I remember knowing even then that I loved the strings of words that moved my heart. You taught me to love words, to put them together like sewing an outfit. Maybe the best memory ever was when we could go downtown to the Athens library on a Sunday afternoon. Nothing could be better than that! Libraries, books, words—you taught me to appreciate the written word. And lately, you've taught me to have fun! Thanks, friend o' mine!"

> *Lord, even though we're all adults,*
> *I pray it's not too late for You to show me*
> *how to make more memories with my children.*
> —MARION BOND WEST

JULY 2

So the Lord said to him, "What is that in your hand?"
He said, "A rod." —EXODUS 4:2 (NKJV)

*W*hat's that in your hand?"

The pastor kept asking this question in his sermon this morning. His text was Exodus 4:2 on God's question to Moses, who held a staff in his hands. And his message was about giving God whatever we hold in our hands, because God uses what we offer to help us change and grow—and to help others through our offerings.

The pastor's question reminded me of a game we often play with children. We put a piece of candy in one hand, and nothing in the other, and then offer both closed hands to the child, asking, "What's in my hand?" And we push the candy hand out a little and pull the empty hand back, because we're eager to give the child what's in the candy hand.

I sometimes play the same game with God. I eagerly offer Him what I want to give out of my fullness: the little envelope of money I brought to church for the offering, or my free hour once a week, or the abilities I think of as my strengths. But what about the things in my "empty hand": the weaknesses I'd rather hide, or my fears or recent mistakes. They need to be offered to God for His use as well.

When the offering plate came by, I opened both hands, and along with my little envelope of money, I gave some offerings out of my emptiness—my pride, impatience, my struggle with quick criticism—with this prayer:

> *Lord, I pray You will use the offerings from both my hands,*
> *out of my fullness and my emptiness, to change*
> *me and to change others for Your glory.*

—CAROL KUYKENDALL

JULY 3

They have cheered me greatly and have been a wonderful encouragement to me. —1 CORINTHIANS 16:18 (TLB)

*O*ne evening after a stressful day, when I still had six things left on my to-do list, I collapsed in the big green chair in my family room and picked up the photo album I'd started in sixth grade. It brought back a flood of memories of the fourteen years I was taught by the Sisters of Loretto.

I remembered the nuns going for rides in my dad's airboat with their long black habits tied down to keep them out of the propeller. In the winter, Dad bolted water-skis on the bottom of the airboat and took them out on the frozen Rock River. Bundled up, the nuns rode sleds, saucers, and toboggans behind the boat, screaming with delight. Once, when a freak storm left the entire school playground covered with smooth ice, the sisters let us bring our skates to school and extended our normal recess time so we could skate.

I remembered the sisters holding the ends of our long jump ropes so we could do Double Dutch, or letting us beat them in dodge ball. Of course, they also had us read books, write stories, learn science, and memorize our times tables and the Baltimore Catechism. But it was the fun we had with those nuns that stayed with me. They must have had dozens of things on their to-do lists, but they knew how to relax.

I closed the album, determined to take a page from their book. Now, for at least an hour every day, I take an adult recess: I bike or walk along the shore of Lake Michigan, enjoy my favorite hobby of painting jars, treat myself to the $1.99 breakfast special at my favorite restaurant, read a book for pleasure, or simply take sidewalk chalk and draw flowers on the driveway.

Thanks, Lord, for a world where fun is so easy to come by.
—PATRICIA LORENZ

July 4

First of all, then, I urge that supplications, prayers, intercessions, and thanksgivings be made for all men.
—1 Timothy 2:1 (RSV)

Lord, please help us get back in touch with our son."

That had been my daily prayer for at least six months.

Although Eric and his family lived only forty miles away and we did see them at occasional family gatherings on Sunday afternoons, Eric had become a stranger. Morose, silent, he would slump into a chair and stare into space, ignoring the family chatter. Larry and I knew he worked hard six days a week and was exhausted on Sundays, but the silence seemed to go beyond fatigue. If we could just talk to him alone. But it never seemed to work out.

Then came the time for the annual Fourth of July family get-together at our cabin in the Colorado mountains, one of my favorite family events of the year. I bought food and began cooking. But one by one, I got phone calls from eleven different family members explaining why they couldn't come: unexpected work deadlines; other commitments; car trouble; summer school. Disappointment filled my chest with an ache akin to flu. "Why, God?" I asked.

I found out why when only one guest showed up at our reunion: Eric. For three days, Larry, Eric, and I worked, played, and talked together in the serenity of the high country. Eric shared concerns about his job, his finances, his children. By the end of the visit, Larry and I both felt closer to our son than we had felt in years.

A prayer. God's answer, far exceeding anything I had dreamed of.

Father, as I pray today,
I place my trust in Your greater vision.
—Madge Harrah

JULY 5

*Shall I come to you with a rod, or with love in a spirit
of gentleness?* —1 CORINTHIANS 4:21 (RSV)

*W*e were visiting my husband Paul's parents in Ohio, and Grandma thought we'd enjoy watching the Fourth of July parade in a neighboring town. But when we arrived, the main street was empty. She had misread the time of the parade in the newspaper, and we had missed it. All we could do was turn around and head home. My daughter Maria didn't realize what had happened until Grandpa turned the car onto their street.

"We're going home?" Maria asked. "But what about the parade?"

"I goofed," Grandma answered, sounding sad and a little embarrassed.

Nobody said anything. I knew that whatever happened next to fill the silence would set the mood for the entire day. *Help me say the right thing*, I prayed. Then an idea that hadn't even popped into my head yet popped out of my mouth: "Let's have our own parade."

Everyone jumped on the idea. "I'll drive the lawn mower, with Maria in the cart in back," said my twelve-year-old son Ross, running off. "I'll push Dan," Paul said, helping his big brother out of the car and into his wheelchair. "We need music," Paul's brother Tom said, heading to the garage and returning with an old plastic horn, a metal bucket, and some sticks. "I'll get the camera," Grandpa said, while Grandma ran into the house and returned with a toy piano and a huge smile. Tom's wife Ann brought their dog Randy out on a leash, and I grabbed the big American flag from the front porch to carry myself. We marched our horn-blowing, bucket-banging parade around the neighborhood, laughing and waving, bringing neighbors out to cheer and laugh with us.

I can't always control what happens, but I can control how I react when things don't turn out right. By bringing love instead of scorn, and with the help of God's joyful Spirit, I can do more than make the best of it—1 can have a parade.

*Lord, help me to think first,
then speak with Your wisdom,
Your joy, and Your love.*

—GINA BRIDGEMAN

JULY 6

*Many, O Lord my God, are the wonders which You have
done, and Your thoughts toward us.* —PSALM 40:5 (NASB)

It was summer in Minnesota, and the birds were nibbling at the feeder—only not at ours. Seven-year-old Hannah, visiting Grandma and Grandpa, decided to hang an invader—a fine mesh bag filled with more seed—from the post. I had doubts about the idea, but it seemed essential to her that we try. Instead of eating from the bag, the birds were frightened by it and stayed away. Several days later, with Hannah's permission, I took it down.

Two weeks later, back home in Alaska, where I'd accompanied her, Hannah was about to don a lavender sundress on a cool rainy day. "Hey, Hannah," I suggested, "why don't you try the little purple shirt with the heart buttons under your sun dress. It would look cute ... and keep you warm."

Hannah had her own ideas—and they didn't include wearing that shirt. Then I remembered the birdseed bag we had tested at my house. I kindly reminded her that I'd tried her idea then and was asking her to try mine now.

Hannah popped on the shirt and dress, glanced in the mirror, exclaimed, "Grandma, it looks great!" and skipped off to play.

We had learned from each other. We had each tried an idea important to the other. One was successful; one was not. But we had cared for one another enough to be a team and extend the gift of giving our ideas a chance.

Isn't this what our gracious God asks, that I care for Him enough to open my life to His ideas? Ideas that *always* work!

*Dear God, from a far-flung universe to a Savior born among
us to life without end, Your ideas are spectacular!*

—CAROL KNAPP

July 7

And this is my prayer...that you may be able to discern what is best and may be pure and blameless until the day of Christ. —PHILIPPIANS 1:9, 10

When I have a decision to make, I say a prayer that a friend shared with me years ago: "God, either shut the door real tight or open the door real wide. That way the answer will be clear." God's answer has never been so clear as it was one spring night not long ago.

I'd had a tiring day at school. The senior play was that night, and I'd promised my students I'd go. I arrived at the gym just in time to squeeze into my seat in the second row. The curtain opened. As tired as I was, I couldn't help but smile. My students were singing and performing as I'd never seen.

The lights came on at intermission. Suppressing a yawn, I looked at my watch. *If I left now I could be home and in bed in an hour.* "Lord," I prayed silently, "I really want to leave. Please open the door real wide or shut it real tight, so I'll know what to do."

I got up, walked to the side door that led to the parking lot, and pushed the handle. The door wouldn't open. I tried again. It wouldn't budge. I reached my seat again and sat down. *Guess I found my answer,* I thought.

The play ended, and within minutes I heard my name called. My students hurried over, all talking at once.

"I knew you'd be waiting!"

"I saw you right when I got onstage!"

"Miss B, my mom couldn't make it. I knew you'd be here to take her place!"

I gathered them in my arms, scratchy costumes, sweaty bodies, and all. "I can't think of any place I'd rather be!"

Thank You, Lord, for the wisdom of locked doors.

—MELODY BONNETTE

JULY 8

Be strong and of a good courage, fear not...
for the Lord thy God, he it is that doth go with thee.
—DEUTERONOMY 31:6 (KJV)

*W*hen I was growing up in eastern North Carolina, my grandmother had a huge wisteria bush in her front yard. During hot summer days, the bees buzzed thick and swiftly around the luscious lavender blossoms, setting here and there to feast on the sweet nectar. I was terrified of the bees and stayed well away, often running up on the porch if I thought they were after me.

Then one memorable day, Grandmother marched right up to the bush among the swarming bees. She selected the most perfect clusters, breaking them easily with her experienced hands. I watched in horror, terrified she'd be stung. But the bees darted here and there, all around Grandmother's head, and not one stung her.

Years later, I came to understand that Grandmother had not taken dominion over the bees; she had taken dominion over her fear. And although it hasn't been easy, her example has helped me take control of my own fear.

Last week, as I sat under a shade tree reading, a large, brown wasp soared from the sky in a circle, then gently touched down on my arm. I remained very still, waiting until it had rested, then it took flight and was gone. Somehow I think Grandmother would have been proud of me.

Father, all kinds of things cause me fear,
but in Your presence I find courage.
—LIBBIE ADAMS

JULY 9

"There is no one besides You, nor is there any
rock like our God." —1 SAMUEL 2:2 (NASB)

ifty years of marriage!

The family insisted we mark this milestone with a special celebration. Soon the e-mails were floating back and forth as plans were made to rent two cottages at the lake and have a family reunion.

Two families planned to fly, and the third would be making a three-day drive. "The locals" (ourselves and our oldest son's family) would be figuring out what to put where and where to put whom. Finally all eighteen of us were settled in for a week's worth of visiting and eating and laughing and swimming and boating.

Our anniversary gift was unique. One son had found a big rock weighing between one hundred and two hundred pounds, and together with his brothers had heaved, hoisted, levered, and wrestled it into position. At that point their wives took over, painting our names with a gold *50* on the top of the rock. A green trailing vine with each person's name written on a leaf was then painted around the edges.

The rock now sits in a prominent place in our flower garden. Every time I pass it, the rock brings back fond memories of our celebration. And it reminds me that over the course of fifty years, when the rains descended and the floods came, when the winds blew and burst against us, our marriage did not fall because it was built upon the Rock of Ages.

Thank You, Lord, for being the solid
foundation of our marriage.

—ALMA BARKMAN

JULY 10

All discipline for the moment seems not to be joyful,
but sorrowful; yet to those who have been trained by it,
afterwards it yields the peaceful fruit of righteousness.
—HEBREWS 12:11 (NASB)

*W*hen God's answer to an urgent but selfish prayer turned out to be an unmistakable *no*, I begged Him to tell me why. All I seemed to hear was, *Remember the peach tree?* But no memory surfaced until spring arrived and the Georgia fruit trees began to blossom.

I'd been about nine and I had talked back to my mother. Mostly, I was a goody-two-shoes and I wasn't used to being punished. But when I saw Mother's face, I took off running.

She ran right after me. I sprinted out the back door and down the seventeen wooden steps. She was right on my heels. I fled through the backyard and ducked into a tiny hole in the hedge that separated our yard from our neighbor's. To my horror, she squeezed through the hole and the chase continued. I ran right through the middle of the leisurely Sunday-afternoon croquet game in the Fowlers' backyard. As I hopped over the wooden balls, the game stopped like a freeze-frame in a movie.

Mother was just inches behind me when I saw the old peach tree that I often climbed with my friends. I scrambled up it and jumped several feet through the air to the hot tin roof of a garage, feeling safe at last. But there came Mother right up the tree, climbing almost effortlessly. I stared in terror as she sailed through the air like Peter Pan and stood facing me, only slightly out of breath. Our neighbors watched silently and attentively.

"Would you like me to give you your discipline up here or back at home?" Mother asked. I climbed meekly down the peach tree and we walked home together as the croquet game started up again.

> *My Abba, thank You for the times You have*
> *pursued me relentlessly and corrected me.*
> —MARION BOND WEST

July 11

Everyone who has this hope in him purifies
himself, just as he is pure. —1 John 3:3

During my last years at college, I spent days in front of my computer, working on my senior thesis. Outlines turned into drafts, drafts transformed into revisions, revisions into new revisions, and, before I knew it, November had turned into April. Somehow in the midst of all that work I found myself slipping away from having time with God. Sure, I still went to Bible study, but I kept thinking of all the other things I needed to do before I could get back in God's good graces: catch up on my Bible reading, update my prayer list, clean my room so I'd be more focused in prayer.

I spoke with a friend from home. "I have to go," she said only a few minutes into the conversation. "The housekeeper is coming tomorrow, and I have to get this place straightened up." I hung up, laughing to myself. *Who would clean house before allowing a housekeeper inside?*

As crazy as that sounds, that is just what I was doing with God. He wants to talk, even if I haven't called in a while or if the pages of my Bible have become a little dusty. All I have to do is take the first step. He'll cover the rest.

Lord, turn my feet toward Your path and help
me remember that I don't need a perfect heart
to talk to You, only a willing one.

—Ashley Johnson

JULY 12

Be still, and know that I am God. —PSALM 46:10 (KJV)

Every summer our family trundles up to the High Sierra of California and spends two weeks tucked into a log cabin beside a rushing stream. We call it our "wilderness experience."

Here we can run in fields splattered with Indian paintbrush and buttercups, gather cones from the towering ponderosa pines, and listen to the call of the whippoorwill in the twilight. Here our children learned to fish. Here, also, we stopped frozen in our tracks the morning we saw the huge wet paw prints of a bear dripped across the patio to our front door!

Away from alarm clocks, telephones, TV, and all the pressure points of the calendar, we have no schedule. We get up when we wake up. We eat when we are hungry. We go to bed when we are tired. We talk less and listen more—to the sounds of the woods, twigs snapping under foot, squirrels chattering in the trees, the clatter of rain on a sloping tin roof. The Chinese call it "the pause that lets the soul catch up with the body."

Spiritually, our wilderness experience has taught us the importance of bringing that "catch-up pause" down from the mountain so that our body and soul keep sync one with the other. Daily, now, we pause in the frantic busyness of our lives and take a few moments to cultivate an inward stillness. The poet Longfellow called it an "inward healing"—a time to listen to the voice of God speaking through the quiet.

Take that quiet now, and in your inward stillness may you come into the peace of inward healing.

> *We take a silence, Lord, where our lips and hearts are still*
> *and we no longer entertain our own imperfect thoughts. We*
> *wait quietly to hear Your voice and know Your will in the*
> *silence of our spirits, that we may do Your will and do that*
> *only. (Adapted from Henry Wadsworth Longfellow)*
>
> —FAY ANGUS

July 13

I have made you and I will carry you;
I will sustain you and I will rescue you.
—Isaiah 46:4

*S*everal years ago, on a trip to China, my husband Robert learned that the Chinese think of life in twelve-year segments. Age sixty is considered a complete lifetime, and the sixty-first birthday represents the beginning of a new life. Worldly responsibilities are complete, so it's an ideal time to develop the life of the spirit.

Of course, we're living longer now, so many of us are still quite young at sixty and continue our earlier responsibilities. But now that I'm in my seventies, I've consciously chosen to accept my elderhood. I'm beginning a new life in which I'm free to make spiritual growth my top priority. I consider it to be the most valuable stage of life. Sure, I have plenty of aches and pains and other physical nuisances, but in prayer and meditation I sometimes glimpse a reality that is so vast and so glorious that those minor physical ailments shrink into insignificance.

So today this elder with the graying hair and thinning bones would like to leave two thoughts with you. If you're in the earlier life stages, think of each failure as a stepping-stone to wisdom. And if, like me, you're in your autumn years, you have fully lived your wisdom and your foolishness. It's now time to harvest the spiritual wonder of your life.

Awaken my spirit, Holy One. As my body weakens,
may my spirit grow stronger in You.
—Marilyn Morgan King

JULY 14

*I am come that they might have life, and that they might
have it more abundantly.* —JOHN 10:10 (KJV)

On a sweltering summer day, I stagger through my New York City
apartment door, dripping perspiration and dropping shopping bags.
Cans of cat food tumble across the floor, a lemon rolls under a bookcase. My
shoulder aches, my knee hurts, and I trip over the broom I forgot to put away.
Flooded with fatigue and self-pity, I wonder, *Why is life so hard? Why is the
weather so hot? And where on earth is the can opener, so I can feed the cats wailing
around my ankles?*

The message button blinks on my answering machine. *Now what?* Grumpily,
I press the button and hear my sister-in-law's cheerful voice, singing a Mister
Rogers song. "It's such a good feeling to know you're alive—"

Jennifer was diagnosed with Parkinson's disease more than ten years ago,
when she was in her early fifties. Since then, she's dealt with physical challenges
I can barely begin to imagine. Jennifer has gone through long hours of surgery,
rigorous therapy, difficult dental work, and has gradually lost a lot of her
mobility and independence. It would be understandable if she had become
irritable and angry, lashed out in frustration, or dissolved into self-pity.

Instead, she's moved to a new house, gone to exercise classes, cultivated
friends at church, and supervised and cuddled six grandchildren—and leaves
singing messages on my answering machine.

Jennifer is not in denial about anything; she's just one of the most
commonsense, up-front, positive people I know. No wonder we all adore her.

Once again I press the button on my answering machine. When she sings
"... when you wake up ready to say, 'I think I'll make a snappy day....'" I'm up for
making one too. I mop my brow, feed the cats, and look out my window at the
blue of the Hudson River.

It's such a good feeling to know you're alive. Now I'll return Jennifer's call.

> *Dear God, thanks for the people who remind me
> "it's such a good feeling to know we're alive."*
> —MARY ANN O'ROARK

JULY 15

So that your trust may be in the Lord, I have taught you
today, even you. —PROVERBS 22:19 (NASB)

"Mom, I'm losing my voice!" Elizabeth croaked. It was Tuesday. Her next performance of *The Velveteen Rabbit*—in which she had the lead—wasn't until Saturday. Chances were that her voice would recover in time.

Wednesday came and Elizabeth's voice disappeared entirely. That night I got up three times to turn on the shower for steam, in the hopes of lessening the barking cough no syrup could soothe.

On Thursday, Elizabeth barely spoke at all and drank lots of licorice tea, and I began heavy-duty prayers. I again got up at night to keep her room steamy.

On Friday, Elizabeth chatted with some friends for ten minutes after math class. She came home squeaking. I called our pediatrician, who prescribed a heavy-duty cough suppressant.

That night I was in a quandary. I knew without a shred of doubt that if God wanted to, He could cure Elizabeth's laryngitis. Elizabeth knew it too. The question that weighed on me was *What if He doesn't want to? What if He has some other idea in mind?* I wrestled with what to say to my eleven-year-old. Simply saying "Trust in God" seemed as if I were promising that He would wave His magic wand and all would be well. Yet, "We'll pray, but we have to accept God's will" seemed feeble and convoluted. I ended up saying nothing.

On Saturday morning, Elizabeth got up, wordlessly waved hello, and ate her breakfast. We made a trip to the pharmacy for throat lozenges.

Sitting in the audience that afternoon, I was stunned by how good Elizabeth was. Her voice cracked in one of her sad solo songs, but the effect was simply to make the audience teary. I sent up a silent thank You to God. Evidently my daughter had approached Him with the same confidence she had put into her performance.

Father, whatever the situation, give me confidence in You.

—JULIA ATTAWAY

JULY 16

Through him and for his name's sake, we received grace.
—ROMANS 1:5

*T*his has been a summer of babies for our family. In July my niece and her husband arrived from Birmingham, Alabama, with their newborn Finn and his fourteen-month-old brother Aiden. While they were here, my first granddaughter was born, Isabelle Grace. Next came my niece Scarlet's baby, Lillian. They, along with my grandsons Drake and Brock, are sure to put the "din" in family dinners for years to come!

My daughter-in-law Stacy has already begun to play baby-friendly versions of hymns for her wee one. "Isabelle's favorite song is 'Amazing Grace,'" she told me recently. "She always gets quiet when it comes on."

When I hold a newborn and look into those eyes, I can't keep from believing in a divine Creator and in His grace—unmerited favor—from the minute we're born. Maybe Isabelle Grace, so fresh from those mysterious realms, knows this in a way we don't...or can't.

Grace. What's so amazing about it? Everything! How blessed I am that my new granddaughter will help me remember that every day.

I praise You, Father, for the miracle of new life and for life
renewed through Your tender and constant care.
—MARY LOU CARNEY

July 17

"My grace is sufficient for you, for my power is made perfect in weakness." —2 Corinthians 12:9 (RSV)

*T*onight, while picking blackberries across the street, I remembered a conversation I'd had with my daughter three years before. I'd wanted to rip out the vines and plant something prettier. "But I like the wild look," Heather had objected. "You don't have to tame everything!"

I've come to realize she's right. Some things *are* better left wild. In nature, and *human* nature as well. It's important that I do my best to meet the many expectations around me. But there are times I need not rise to each challenge. Some things aren't worth it. Sometimes the energy just isn't there. Sometimes I need just to "let the weeds grow," let things run a little wild and not worry about taming everything.

As with blackberries, in time such honesty can produce its own fruit. An "I don't know" gives people a chance to share what *they* know. When I get to the "end of my rope," letting go allows others to step in and help. Admitting to a cranky day enables friends to be more gracious and forgiving—and teaches me patience whenever I'm part of someone else's cranky day.

Across the street grow plump, sweet fruit, a reminder that whenever I'm honest about my imperfection, good things can and do grow.

God, You created all things—the cultivated garden and
thorny thicket. Out of both, You always bring Your fruit.

—Brenda Wilbee

JULY 18

Blessed are the dead which die in the Lord...
their works do follow them. —REVELATION 14:13 (KJV)

*D*uring one of my weekend visits to my ninety-four-year-old father's retirement home in Pennsylvania, Daddy kept gamely trying to stay upright, independent, and awake. The afternoon that I left to drive back to New Jersey we had a time of prayer as we usually did. Daddy, as always, asked for a safe trip for me, and then added, "Lord, please help me to catch up on my work. I've gotten so far behind."

I chuckled a bit to myself as I drove home, wondering, *What work is he talking about?*

In the next weeks, I discovered what he meant. He was behind in his prayer schedule. For him, prayer was his work. Every day, every week, he had gone through his overflowing loose-leaf notebook filled with letters and prayer requests from friends, missionaries, and missions around the world. As he prayed over every person, every request, he would mark the date.

One reason Daddy had been willing to give up his independence and move to the retirement home was to have more time to pray. But now, he didn't have the energy to go through the book or even to read the new letters that came. Yet as his strength waned and his tongue thickened, he would phone friends to find out how they were and what he could pray for as he sat immobilized.

"How much your dad's prayers and interest in us have meant" was the comment that came again and again after his death. "He was a true prayer warrior."

What a legacy!

> *Lord, thank You for those who have prayed for us over the*
> *years. May we take up the work they have laid down.*
> —MARY RUTH HOWES

JULY 19

My soul yearns for you in the night;
in the morning my spirit longs for you. —ISAIAH 26:9

*W*ill you pray with me?" an attractive young woman asked timidly during a break at a women's retreat where we'd been talking about turning our "I can'ts" into "I cans." We found a quiet corner, and her words tumbled out, describing a life filled with difficulties. She was a single mom with four children, working full-time at a job with some pressing problems, and the man in her life had just broken their engagement. "I can't figure out what to do," she admitted, wiping away tears. "I feel so lonely and overwhelmed."

My heart ached for her, and we spent the next several minutes praying together, asking God to show us some "I cans" in the midst of her "I can'ts." When we finished, I took out a piece of paper, wrote "I CAN" across the top, and handed it to her. "Let's think together," I suggested, and soon she had these ideas written down on the paper:

Three ways I CAN ask another person to help me:
Spend time with me.
Spend time with my children.
Pray for me.
Three people I CAN ask for help:
Mom
Sandy
Cindy
Three ways I CAN have fun:
Go to the movies.
Go out to eat.
Attend special events.
As she tucked her "I CAN" list into her Bible, I prayed...

Lord, with You, we can turn our
"I CAN'TS into "I CANS!" Thank You.

—CAROL KUYKENDALL

JULY 20

*Turning around, Jesus saw them following
and asked, "What do you want?"* —JOHN 1:38

My grandsons Ryan and David played in a baseball tournament two counties over one scorching July Saturday last year. David's game ended about one o'clock, and Ryan didn't play until four. My daughter-in-law Patricia offered to take the younger kids swimming. Mark had his swimsuit, but I hadn't brought anything for Caleb and Olivia.

My husband and I tried two stores without success. "Everyone's sold out," one clerk told me. I was dreading three hours with two hot, cranky, and disappointed children when I spotted an OPEN sign on a resale shop. Five minutes later Caleb had three-dollar black trunks. Ten more minutes of rummaging through bins yielded a purple tank that would fit Olivia.

"Do you like it?" I asked her. She nodded.

"Will you wear it swimming?"

"No," she said softly.

"Why not?" I demanded. "Purple is your favorite color!"

"Because I don't want to go swimming!" Olivia said. "I want you and me to play in the park!"

So we did. We played on the swings, the spring horses, and the merry-go-round. And I thought about the many times that I was sure I had all the answers to other people's problems. In reality, I hadn't even asked the right questions.

*Remind me, Lord, that it's vital to ask,
and answer, the right questions.*
—PENNEY SCHWAB

Blessed are you who weep now, for you shall laugh.
—Luke 6:21 (NKJV)

*W*hile watering my husband Gene's three beloved tomato plants, I discovered that some of the tomatoes were missing. To my horror, I spotted Lovey, one of our dogs, chewing on a tomato! Just then, Red Dog came trotting up proudly holding a nice-sized tomato in her mouth. "*No!*" I screamed, but both dogs continued devouring their newfound treats.

When Gene came out later to admire his tomatoes, he stooped down for a closer look. "Marion! Who's been picking the tomatoes?"

Looking in the other direction, I mumbled, "The dogs."

"What?"

"Just the green ones." I tried to smile.

Not even a hint of a smile from my husband. I quickly explained, "Well, they do look exactly like the green tennis balls we throw for them to retrieve, and they probably figured...."

"What are you going to do about it?" he said.

Right then Lovey came up to offer Gene a tomato she'd dug up from its hiding place, and I sashayed back into the house and considered bolting all the doors. A few moments later in the kitchen, our eyes met for what seemed like forever. "Normal dogs don't eat tomatoes off the vines," he explained grimly.

Don't laugh, Marion. This is serious business. "I know, I know...." I thought I glimpsed a hint of laughter in Gene's eyes. I ventured a half smile, and so did he. I snickered. Then my husband started laughing out loud, and I fell over onto the kitchen counter, laughing helplessly.

Father, one of Your most remarkable
gifts is laughter—especially in marriage.
—Marion Bond West

JULY 22

But though God has planted eternity in the hearts of men,
even so, man cannot see the whole scope of God's work from
beginning to end. —ECCLESIASTES 3:11 (TLB)

I'd never ridden a four-wheeler before. I climbed up onto the back and held on tightly to my twelve-year-old son Thomas's stomach. "Mom, just relax. You'll be fine."

"Are you sure you know what you're doing?"

"Yes, ma'am." He clicked the gear with his foot.

"Is your helmet fastened right?"

"Yes, Mom. Let's go. You'll like it."

He drove me around our wooded property. *Ah, Thomas knows me pretty well. He's not going fast.* He reached ahead and carefully pushed back tree branches so they wouldn't slap us. As Thomas headed down hill, he drove slowly as though leading an old horse down a rocky cliff. He wound around and stopped at the little creek. We didn't talk—we didn't need to.

I relaxed and thought back over the past year. So many changes: My grandparents had both died; our middle daughter left for college. Thomas seemed to be taking charge, riding me around, leading the way. I began to trust his skills. I admired his confidence and kindness.

My thoughts raced ahead. Years ahead.

One day I'll be really old, Thomas will be grown and even have children of his own. I don't want anything else to change. Talk to me, God.

A truth came just as gently as the leaf floating down the creek. When the end comes, there will be a place prepared especially for me, a perfect place. I will love my new home even more than the majesty of these woods. No fear. Like Thomas, my Shepherd will be right beside me.

Oh, Lord, You know the outcome.
You won't leave me. It's going to be good, isn't it?
—JULIE GARMON

July 23

Let your requests be made
known unto God. —Philippians 4:6 (kjv)

*M*y husband Bob and I celebrated our golden wedding anniversary last June. For days our mailbox was filled with beautiful cards, bringing congratulations and words of love. I saved the cards for our scrapbook and cut their colorful envelopes into small pieces to fit face down in the notepaper holder on my desk.

Now when I need to make a shopping list or jot down a telephone number, I reach for one of these pretty slips. On the reverse of the one I choose, I find the return address of a friend, and at once my heart is warmed with special thoughts. I pause a moment to speak with God about that friend. Another friend has an afflicted child; another, an aged parent. I know of two who are facing financial burdens. Then there are the happy grandparents and the man who has been promoted in his job.

Each one has a special need for my prayer, be it asking for aid or voicing thanksgiving.

From time to time all of us can use a nudge to pray for others. These little pieces of paper do the nudging for me!

heavenly Father, heed our prayers,
especially as we seek Your blessings for others.
—Drue Duke

JULY 24

*"The gardener...cuts off every branch in me
that bears no fruit."* —JOHN 15:1–2

The half-mile narrow trail around Lake George in the high Sierra to our favorite fishing hole is beautiful but treacherous. Laden down with fishing gear and haversacks, my husband and I walked carefully beside flaming red fireweed and gold California poppies, digging our heels into the crumbly shale to keep from sliding down the steep bank.

"Hold on to a branch to steady yourself as you come down!" John called up as he waited for me at the water's edge. Stepping down from a large rock, I grabbed for a branch and was gingerly groping for a foothold when I slipped. Suddenly, I was falling, and, with an ominous snap, the branch I was holding on to broke. I skidded down the rocky bank and would have plummeted into the lake had John not been there to catch me.

"Are you hurt, honey?" Yes, I was hurt.

I limped painfully back to our van for the bumpy ride to the local hospital. X-rays showed that I had cracked my tailbone, not seriously, but enough to cause discomfort for several weeks.

"For heaven's sake, lovey," John said, "you should have known better than to hold on to deadwood."

Unable to fish with John for the remainder of our vacation, I had lots of time to think about what he had said. I discovered that I had held on to deadwood not only by the lake, but in the rest of my life, too. The "if only I had" of regrets and guilt. Resentments. A grudge held on to for years and years. "Lord," I prayed, "help me to let go of the deadwood in my heart."

Now I've learned to reach for living branches that will not let me down. On the lakeside trail, they're branches growing green. In my heart, they're faith and forgiveness.

Dear Lord, help me to prune the deadwood from my life.

—FAY ANGUS

For God does speak—now one way, now another
*—though man may not perceive it. —*JOB 33:14

*P*lease, God, just let there be a parking space for me!" That had been my morning prayer for weeks, ever since I started physical therapy for my arthritis. The drive from downtown meant I couldn't get to school until nearly noon, and parking was scarce. After a twenty-minute hunt, I realized there wasn't a spot to be had. I headed home, dreading having to cancel my meeting with my research adviser, angry I would miss my classes.

At home, I sat in the car for a few moments, wondering what to do. The therapy was helping, but the schedule was interfering with my work. My health was improving, but at what cost? *Would I have to drop out of school? Would I ever make progress in my research at this rate?* Then my gaze settled on my bicycle, a dusty blue cruiser, unused since I moved off campus the previous year. A crazy idea began to take form. Shaking my head, I muttered, "I can't ride that thing all the way to school!" I shuffled toward the bike, still stiff from the morning's workout. The tires were a little soft, but everything seemed in working order, even the lights. I dusted off the seat and rolled it out to the driveway. *Maybe once around the block*, I thought. I pushed off, and before I knew it, I had looped the block twice. I grabbed my backpack from the car and pushed off again, this time to school.

God's answer to my parking space prayer that day was "No." Instead, He led me to something better. In the two years since I started commuting by bike, my health has improved by leaps and bounds, in part thanks to medicine and exercise, but also by the grace of God, who gave me hope I might make it to school on that dusty blue bicycle after all.

Thank You, God, for Your wise
and generous answers to my prayers.
—KJERSTIN WILLIAMS

JULY 26

The memory of the just is blessed. —PROVERBS 10:7 (KJV)

My bachelor son Phil and I were rolling down an Alaskan highway during my summer visit. "I'll have to clean this messy handprint off your side window, so I can see the scenery better," I said.

There was a pause before Phil replied. "Actually, Sarah made that a long time ago...and I was leaving it for a memory." Sarah, three at the time, is my granddaughter and Phil's niece.

I was speechless over his display of tenderness. Here was a guy driving a big four-wheel-drive pickup truck that he likes to keep shined, and its accessory package included five tagalong sticky fingerprints.

Months later, back home in Minnesota, my three-year-old grandson Clay, playing with my loon collection, added a stubby beak to those already broken. He mixed up the birds on the shelf to suit himself, even stacking a smaller one in the hollowed back of a larger one.

I won't rearrange the loons or repair its stunted beak. Thanks to Phil, I don't see damage or disorder; I see imagination—and a dear little face engrossed in play. I'm leaving those loons just as they are...for a memory.

Jesus, by Your grace, may the prints
I leave behind be the keeping kind.

—CAROL KNAPP

JULY 27

The wisdom from above is first pure,
then peaceable, gentle, reasonable, full of mercy
and good fruits. —JAMES 3:17 (NASB)

*M*ore than fifteen years ago, I went through an emotionally draining period. I spent a good deal of time alone in my basement office, struggling to come to grips with things. Then one day the postman rang the doorbell to deliver a small parcel. I recognized our daughter's handwriting on the label and wondered what had prompted her to send me a gift. Inside, nestled in some crumpled tissue paper, was a pewter pear.

As I lifted the pear's lid, a gentle breeze blew through the open window, scattering the contents of the pear across the kitchen floor. Scrambling to retrieve the snippets of colored paper, I noticed our daughter had printed out a different Bible promise on each one. There must have been several dozen all told. I could just imagine her in her pajamas, sitting cross-legged on her bed with her Bible in her lap, painstakingly printing out each promise she found. I phoned her that evening to thank her.

"That's your prayer pear, Mom. I found it in a secondhand shop and decided to fill it with some encouraging verses. And you know what? I think I benefited just as much as you will."

Thank You, Lord, that the
fruit of Your Spirit blesses the one who manifests it
just as much as the one who is refreshed by it.

—ALMA BARKMAN

"Go and look toward the sea," he told his servant.
And he went up and looked. "There is nothing there,"
he said. Seven times Elijah said, "Go back." The seventh time
the servant reported, "A cloud as small as a man's hand
is rising from the sea." —1 KINGS 18:43, 44

*M*y sister's coming home next week!" The excitement in my cousin Lajuana's voice kicks her east Texas twang into high gear.

My daughter Lanea, Lajuana, and I pray by phone together just about every night. We begin by sharing what the Lord has done for each of us that day, things for which we're grateful. It might be an unexpected blessing or an answer to prayer.

"We talked about the Lord. And you won't believe it, but she's been encouraging people and telling them that they have to have faith!"

Some of the things we pray for are easy to believe, but of all the prayers we have prayed, the one for Lajuana's sister has been about the most difficult. The fiftysomething grandmother had no desire for any kind of spiritual connection; she was serving time in jail for drug abuse and theft, and there was a history of family strife between the sisters. I prayed year after year for her, with no answer, no obvious sign, no miracles in sight. I prayed without much hope. I think I was afraid to hope.

"We talked and laughed for hours and hours!" I can hear the smile in Lajuana's voice.

I'm speechless, something that never happens when I talk to my cousin. As I listen, I'm overjoyed. There's new hope rising in me, and I begin mentally to scan my list of "lost cause" prayers, eager for signs of God's faithful answers.

God, even when the answer seems to be impossible
or a long way off, give me the courage to keep praying.
—SHARON FOSTER

July 29

*Thy faithfulness endures
to all generations.*
—Psalm 119:90 (RSV)

Last July, I helped host a reunion of my mother's family, the Bantas. Though Mother died in 1976, three of her brothers and sisters were there, as well as four later generations. My grandparents have a total of seventy-six descendants at this time. I couldn't help marveling at the fact that all of these people existed because of two people who fell in love and married ninety-nine years ago.

As my cousins and I talked, we discovered that we'd raised our families based on similar values (for example, going to Sunday school and church was not negotiable), and some of the same faults (our sense of reserve caused a cut-off of hugs and kisses at adolescence), and that these patterns had repeated through the generations.

Recently, as I was babysitting my granddaughter Saralisa (a typical, try-my-wings two-year-old), she started pulling books out of my bookcases onto the floor. I jumped up, about to scold her, when I remembered my grandparents' home library. So I sat down on the floor with her, told her how special books are, showed her each one, let her hold them, and encouraged her to help me put them back. The last one to go back was my grandmother's family Bible. I held it close to my heart, and then let Saralisa hug it before we placed it back on the shelf.

Saralisa now has her own little space on the bottom shelf, with a few of her books, including a children's Bible storybook. And she leaves my books alone. Thanks, Grandmother Banta!

*Help me always to remember, Lord,
to interact with those I love as if the future
depended on it. Because, of course, it does.*
—Marilyn Morgan King

Make sure that nobody pays back wrong for wrong,
but always try to be kind to each other
and to everyone else. —1 THESSALONIANS 5:15

On my desk sits one of my all-time favorite pictures of me with my older sister and two younger brothers. There we are, four adults in midlife, with our arms around one another, each wearing an expression that reflects our childhood personalities. The picture is proof that we're still comfortable enough to be ourselves when we're together.

It also reminds me that family matters. "You can argue all you want here at home," Mom used to tell us, "but when you go out in the world, you stick together." After she died, I wondered if that legacy of loyalty would last without her at the hub of our wheel, connecting us and keeping our circle intact.

I recently heard a woman complain that visiting family is just too much trouble, what with all the packing, all the travel, all the emotional baggage and hassles. "So we stopped doing it," she said simply. My picture represents the opposite choice. In spite of the hassles, in spite of the distance or our differences or the missing hub, my siblings and I haven't given up our bond. We make the effort to get together. At the bottom of the picture, I've taped this quote by Kurt Vonnegut:

"Be nice to your siblings. They're your best link to your past and the people most likely to stick with you in the future."

The picture on my desk reminds me that family matters, and in each other, we not only have a common history, but a hopeful future.

Lord, thank You for my unique circle called family.

—CAROL KUYKENDALL

Whatever your hand finds to do, do it with all your might.
—Ecclesiastes 9:10

Right after my kids returned to school, I volunteered to alphabetize and photocopy more than five hundred forms that parents had filled out to create an emergency phone calling system for grades pre-kindergarten through twelve. Thousands of pieces of paper and several days later, my feet hurt and my back ached from standing at the copying machine, and still the job wasn't finished. As the machine whirred nonstop, I thought about all the people who have such jobs, particularly those whose often unnoticed hard work makes my day easier.

The thought returned the following Sunday morning when an usher handed me a church bulletin, thirteen pages of not just hymns and the order of service, but announcements and a calendar—everything I needed to know for the week ahead. A prayer suddenly rose up in me: *God bless the hands that created this.* A few days later, I awoke early and suddenly remembered I'd volunteered to bring food for a school meeting. I quickly dressed and raced to a nearby bagel shop, where someone had been up since 4:00 a.m. making bagels. *God bless the hands that created these,* I silently prayed as I carried a fresh dozen out the door.

So many people toil anonymously to contribute to the smooth rhythm of modern life. I'm offering a prayer of blessing and thanks for all those who make getting through every day a little easier.

*Lord, strengthen and inspire those who may work unseen,
but certainly are not unknown to You.*
—Gina Bridgeman

August

August 1

Do not hide your face from me. —Psalm 27:9

I'd brought my three-year-old granddaughter to the beach. Lugging blanket, umbrella, plastic pail and shovel, a thermos of lemonade, and a picnic basket, I found an inviting stretch of sand and gratefully laid down our gear. For me it was a welcome break from weeks of pressure, finishing one demanding assignment and launching another.

For a blissful hour we were absorbed in constructing an improbable castle with an elaborate canal conducting seawater to our moat. We ate our lunch and were collecting shells to beautify the castle walls when I noticed one of our sandwich wrappers blowing away.

"We don't want to mess up the pretty beach," I said as I started after it. *This will be a little environmental lesson for her.*

I hadn't gone thirty yards when a wail stopped me. "What's the matter, honey?" I called back.

"I couldn't see you!"

"But...I'm right here!"

"I couldn't see your *face*."

Wrapper and ecological education abandoned, I went back to where a little girl stood with a bucketful of shells and eyes full of tears. *My face*! I thought. She'd seen what I was *doing*, but that wasn't enough. She needed my face turned toward her, telling her, "I see you. I'm attending to you. I care."

Maybe, I thought as we alternated slipper shells with scallop shells on the grand gateway to our castle, *that's my trouble, too. Maybe I've been so busy asking what God wants me to do that I've failed first of all to seek His face, to start each day with a relationship, to ask to hear not His orders, but just that He loves me.*

Your face, Lord, I will seek (Psalm 27:8).

—Elizabeth sherrill

AUGUST 2

The light that shines through the darkness—
and the darkness can never extinguish it. —JOHN 1:5 (TLB)

The lure of the Blue Ridge Mountain breezes was just too tempting, so instead of heading for bed as midnight approached, I let myself out onto the long gray deck and sank into a plastic Adirondack chair. Slowly my eyes adjusted and the stars above me became clear and clearer. For often-hazy August, the sky was unusually dark and the stars unusually bright. I sighed in pure pleasure: after years of living in dense Maryland woods, the open sky here in Virginia is a new joy for me.

Like a child discovering the stars for the first time, I began to play with ideas: *Gee, what if all that is really a great black velvet drape and the stars are pinholes where heaven shines through!*

Suddenly, out of the corner of my eye, I became aware of a flickering.

Somewhere beyond the black mound of Massanutten Mountain was a thunderstorm. I watched the flashes and flickers silhouetting the ridge for quite a while, but heard no thunder. *Strange, I watched the TV forecast at eleven o'clock and there were no storms.*

Curious, I crossed the deck, entered my office, and called up the Virginia weather radar on my computer. There was only one storm anywhere in the three-state area, a large red-orange blob covering Cape Charles—the point where Chesapeake Bay meets the sea at Hampton Roads—a five-hour drive away from us. The night was so clear that the darkness could not hold back the lightning; it bridged the ridges and lit up my deck 170 miles away.

As I called Bill to come see the silent display, I thought of how many times the Lord's light had bridged the dark valleys in my life to bring His peace and His presence. Watching lightning moving out to sea—beyond two mountain ranges, the long Piedmont and the Tidewater—I knew I was seeing a parable in action: darkness cannot extinguish light.

Lord, bring Your light over the ridges
and into the valleys of my life.
—ROBERTA ROGERS

AUGUST 3

The simplicity that is in Christ.
—2 CORINTHIANS 11:3 (KJV)

*D*uring my early morning walks I inevitably became bored as I huffed and puffed. A jogging friend explained that she fought the boredom by praying for her neighbors as she passed their homes.

Approaching Bobby and E.J.'s house the next morning, I asked God to do something simple for my friends of more than forty years. E.J. had been diagnosed with Alzheimer's and ALS (Lou Gehrig's disease). Bobby, his wife of almost fifty-seven years, cared for him at home with astounding love and patience. "Lord, give them laughter," I prayed. "Let E.J. remember something funny today."

Every morning as I passed their house, I prayed for Bobby and E.J. Then one day Bobby confided to me, "I just want him to go to heaven from our home, not some facility." It didn't look likely. Just to get E.J. to eat, Bobby had to feed him, one spoonful at a time. I wasn't sure how long she could handle it alone.

One day E.J. waved to me from their open front door, smiling. "Thank You, Lord," I prayed. "He's still at home. Content and kind—just much leaner."

The sun was barely up one sultry summer morning when I passed Bobby and E.J.'s house, unable to think of what to pray for. Finally I said, "Lord, do something brand-new for E.J. today."

After I got home, I checked my phone messages. One had been left early that morning. "Marion, Bobby wanted you to know that E.J. left this life from his beloved recliner in the bedroom around six thirty. She's okay, and she knows he is too."

Father, You stand ready to answer even the simplest,
most hurried prayers in Your magnificent way!
—MARION BOND WEST

AUGUST 4

Where two or three are gathered together in my name,
there am I in the midst of them. —MATTHEW 18:20 (KJV)

I remember often going to my husband Norman's office whenever he needed to talk through a sermon or a speech. "Lord," he'd say, "we have this problem. You know what it is without our telling. Please guide us in the right direction. Make us receptive to Your will. We thank You for this help that You are now giving us."

Then we'd sit quietly for a while. We never concentrated on the specific problem or on possible solutions. Instead, we tried to make our minds quiet and open. Sometimes, I'd think of some appropriate phrase from the Bible, like "In returning and rest shall ye be saved; in quietness and in confidence shall be your strength" (Isaiah 30:15 KJV) and focus on that. After a while, one of us would say to the other, "It seems to me this is the way to deal with this." Or, "I believe we've been on the wrong track with this one. Perhaps we should handle it this way." It was uncanny how often the same conviction came to both of us and how often a clear line of action would open up where things were obscure before.

If you're facing a problem or a decision in your life, why not ask a friend or loved one to be your partner in prayer?

Lord, thank You for the guidance You give me through
quiet prayer with my brothers and sisters in Christ.
—RUTH STAFFORD PEALE

Let us therefore follow after the things
which make for peace. —ROMANS 14:19 (KJV)

I was pretty proud of myself when I took my car in for an oil change last week. *Now that's off my mind*, I thought.

And it was—until on the drive home from work the next evening, dark gray smoke started pouring out from under the hood of my car.

"Hey, lady," another driver shouted at me, "your car's burning up!" I was already swinging over to the side of the road. "I see it, I see it!" I muttered.

When I popped open the hood, I saw that the oil cap was missing. The mechanic had forgotten to put it back on. I drove the rest of the way home—1 had no idea that wasn't a good idea—and worked myself into a state of anxiety.

They'll tell me it's my fault, I thought. *They'll tell me they can't fix it. I'm probably ruining the engine by driving it. I'll have to take them to court.* By the time my imaginary fears had the judge holding me in contempt for not checking my car before I got into it, I knew that I had to pray. *God, thank You for keeping me safe. Now please keep me sane! I need Your help to deal with this situation calmly.*

The next morning, at eight o'clock sharp, I called the oil-change place. One hour later, a young man in a blue uniform showed up at my front door and I got a sincere apology, a thorough engine checkup, and a coupon for a free oil change.

"I was afraid the manager would fire me on the spot," the mechanic said as he cleaned up. "I sure would like to thank you for being so calm about this."

I smiled as I remembered my panic and anger and fear. "I had to ask for some help staying calm," I admitted. "And I appear to have gotten it."

Today, Lord, let me come to You with my worries.

—LINDA NEUKRUG

AUGUST 6

Must you also muddy the rest
with your feet? —EZEKIEL 34:18

It was a hot afternoon, and my eight-year-old son Zeb ran off to play with his friends Mike and Devin. What walked into the kitchen a couple hours later was a body Zeb's size covered with mud. In his ears, his nose, his hair, around his eyes, the stuff was all over him.

Although my mouth dropped open, words momentarily failed me. When I found my voice, I asked in amazement, "What did you *do*?"

"Oh, we were just playing in some mud," Zeb answered with classic understatement.

I wasn't sure if I should lecture him or laugh. So I drew him a bath instead, hoping the wisdom for an appropriate response would come to me soon.

As the tub was filling, Zeb said, "Mike was in big trouble when his mom saw him."

"What did she say?" I asked, feeling a kinship with Mike's mom.

"'You get in here *right now*!'"

I stifled a laugh as I found myself appreciating Mike's mom in a new way.

Devin was being cared for by his grandma that day, and I asked how she had responded to the awful sight. Zeb smiled with the memory as he told me, "She said, 'Wow! You're a *masterpiece*!'"

And suddenly it was my heart's prayer that, before he's fully grown, I'll be young enough to respond to my son's childhood as wisely and as lightly as Devin's grandma. At least, occasionally.

Father, please bless our parenting so that the children
You've entrusted to us will grow from the love in our lectures
and the lightness in our laughter.

—ELLYN BAUMANN

We have different gifts, according to the grace given us.
—ROMANS 12:6

O n our daughter Lindsay's wedding day, her father and I escorted her across a mountain meadow in Yosemite National Park toward a handmade wooden cross that stood in a mound of wildflowers. There, in the midst of God's spectacular creation, in front of family and friends, Lindsay and Jeff Waymire repeated their vows. Her pastor from Solana Beach, California, officiated, her sister Kendall sang, her brother Derek stood on the bride's side, and a fawn pranced around the edges of the wedding party as if to honor Lindsay's love of animals.

Everything was "*soooo* Lindsay," people told us at the reception afterward. Their observations were an answer to our prayers. We've always wanted our children to be "*soooo* themselves," by knowing who they are, and then having the courage and confidence to *be* who they are. That process puts each person in the family on a life journey of self-discovery.

Our family photo albums are filled with reminders of Lindsay's steps in that journey: her unique hairstyles and unusual clothing combinations, the attempts at playing various musical instruments and dabbling in sports, going off to camp by herself. In some pictures I see self-consciousness; in others, the fierce determination to do life her way, even if that wasn't always our way.

One of the challenges of parenting is to hold a child loosely, so she has the freedom to outgrow childhood roles and expectations, as she stretches beyond the family mold to create her own mold. But it's a mutual journey of growth that requires an exchange of grace and encouragement between parent and child. And when both have the freedom to keep being "*soooo* themselves," that relationship grows into an adult-to-adult friendship. That's why being yourself matters.

Father, may we hold each other loosely,
so we can encourage each other to keep becoming
the people You've created us to be.
—CAROL KUYKENDALL

AUGUST 8

"Lord, teach us to pray." —LUKE 11:1 (KJV)

*I*t was beastly hot and smotheringly humid, no one had slept well, and some last-minute changes to our plans had made John and Elizabeth extra cranky. In short, we were in for a rough day. All of that was basically irrelevant: my college roommate was having a medical procedure done that morning, and I'd promised I would come stay with her for the afternoon. I fervently hoped that none of my kids would have a meltdown while I was gone. With some trepidation, I packed up snacks and ice water and delivered my children to the various friends who were going to care for them for the day.

Once I was on the subway, I took a few moments to send up a prayer: *Lord, please watch over my kids and help them stay calm if they get upset*. My mind wandered, and I decided that my prayer was somehow off-target. Was I praying that John wouldn't give Louise a hard time? Or that Elizabeth's emotional fragility would dissipate once she got in the sprinkler and cooled off? What *was* it that I was really trying to say? What was it that mattered?

I didn't want my kids to be distraught. But like any mom, I'm generally happier when my children don't embarrass me. I decided that part of what I'd been asking God to do was to make my kids behave so my pride wouldn't be wounded. My mixed motives made for a sloppy, inarticulate prayer.

I decided to pray for something simple and pure instead: *Lord, send Your grace to my children to keep them close to You*.

Ah! It all fell in place. The real problem wasn't how anyone felt. The real problem—the only problem—was our relationship with God. Freed from the dam of confusion over what was important, the words of my prayer flowed forth. It wasn't going to be a rough day after all.

Lord, I don't always have the right words.
Teach me to pray for the things that are important.

—JULIA ATTAWAY

August 9

*Write it on a tablet for them...that for the days to come
it may be an everlasting witness.* —ISAIAH 30:8

"Look, a garage sale!" My daughter Amy Jo pointed to a brightly painted sign. I kept my foot on the accelerator. I had a dozen errands yet to run, and a garage sale was definitely not on my to-do list.

But when we finally came upon it, even I was impressed with the line of cars stopped to shop for bargains. We parked and got out. Tables covered the yard, laden with old records, baby clothes, even a lava lamp. In the middle of one table was an oversized, spiral-bound book. Amy Jo reached for it. "Look," she said, waving the book over her head, "it's a 'Grandma Remembers' book! Can we get it?"

I thought about Mother. Although she loved to write, her eyesight was failing. And after her stroke a few years ago, she simply wasn't as sharp as she had once been. Still, she had stories to tell and memories to share. And because she was seventy-four, I wasn't sure just how much longer she could share them in person.

"Come on," Amy Jo pleaded. "It's only a dollar, and I know Grandma will love doing it!"

So we bought it. Little did we know just how valuable that book would become to us. For Mother spent the last year of her life pouring out her past, leaving a legacy in longhand. A legacy laced with God's wisdom.

For memories preserved, I thank you, Lord.
—MARY LOU CARNEY

For where your treasure is, there will your heart be also.
—MATTHEW 6:21 (KJV)

I'm curled up in the big old chair by the fireplace in the cabin next door to our house, with my notebook on my lap. It's my time to be alone with God for a day, so I've come to this place made sacred by years of prayers.

It will be a day of gratitude for the richness in my life—my beloved husband Robert, my children, grandchildren, and now four new little great-grandchildren; my longtime friends in Nebraska and the newer ones in Colorado; for the many caring readers who write me letters of encouragement, as well as those who are appreciative but don't write. I thank God for the ponderosa pine that seems to bow to me as I look out the front window; the blue spruce I watched my grandfather plant in the 1930s that now towers over the house; for the crispness of morning and the cool night breeze, for potatoes and milk and carrots and cheese; for shimmering aspens that wave to me, and the creek across the road that is God's music; for the living art of white clouds changing form against a lucid blue sky; for...

As I continue my list of treasures, the words stop. I find myself in wordless prayerfulness that will be with me throughout the day as I write in my journal, do a bit of dusting, fix and eat lunch, and just rest in the silence and love of God.

I invite you to find twenty or thirty minutes sometime before the sun sets on this day to sit in a quiet place, kick off your shoes and your cares, and join me in gratitude in companionship with our special friend Jesus.

*Holy Friend, we've come here to thank You
for* _____. *(FILL IN THE BLANK)*
—MARILYN MORGAN KING

AUGUST 11

Judge not, that ye be not judged. —MATTHEW 7:1 (KJV)

*E*very autumn I get aggravated all over again. Each day on my walk, I pass a yard with a beautiful little pear tree. It's the only tree in the whole front yard, all the more noticeable for its loneliness. No taller than an average man, this little tree is literally bent over with the weight of luscious, shining fruit. Every day I walk by, hoping to see its owners gathering this bounty, taking advantage of the wondrous resource God has given them right in their own front yard. And every year, the fruit ripens, falls, and rots on the grass.

I'd be satisfied if the owners would hang a sign on the tree saying, PLEASE HELP YOURSELF to hungry passersby. At least that way there wouldn't be all that waste, and the poor little pear tree wouldn't labor all year for naught.

One day last week I went walking by the tree, fuming at its inconsiderate, wasteful owners, when I had one of those light-bulb-over-the head moments. *What am I so angry about?* I thought. *I've allowed my anger to spoil one of the most beautiful parts of my walk. I'm so annoyed with the homeowners for wasting the resources God gave them, that I'm wasting those He's given me!*

Maybe I was the one who needed to wear a sign around my neck saying PLEASE HELP YOURSELF. Just as a reminder.

*Father, help me be less critical of others
and more aware of my own need to change.*

—MARCI ALBORGHETTI

AUGUST 12

[God] is able to do exceeding abundantly above all that we ask or think. —EPHESIANS 3:20 (KJV)

"Please pray that I can find the right place for my mother," my friend Denise asked when she had to move her mother from the house in Brooklyn where she'd lived for thirty-six years to an assisted-living facility.

"The problem," she told me, "is Muffy."

Muffy was a Brittany spaniel. "Mom's had so many losses—Dad, my brother, most of her friends. Muffy is her lifeline!"

And that created a dilemma. Some of the places Denise visited had a no-pets rule. At last Denise located an attractive retirement community where, she was assured, the dog would be welcomed by all concerned. Over a strenuous weekend, Denise got her mother and belongings moved to her new home, only to have the aides refuse to enter the apartment with the dog there. Denise was frantic, taking weeks off from work to provide her mother's daily care.

What about those prayers? I wondered. *Why had faith and effort resulted in such a wrong choice?*

But as it turned out, they hadn't.

Bringing Muffy back from his morning walk one day, Denise noticed a man helping his wife from a car into a wheelchair beside a pile of suitcases. Seeing the dog, their faces lit up. "A Brittany spaniel!" the man exulted. "We haven't seen one since ours died last year. Looked just like this one!"

"Does he live here?" the wife asked hopefully. "Would you bring him to visit us now and again?"

It even "happened" that the apartment they were moving into was directly across the hall from Denise's mother—and the man handled his wife's care himself. Muffy lives with them now, and Denise's mother visits the dog and her new friends every day.

Father, I'd forgotten that Your answers to prayer always encompass more than just the needs I know of.

—ELIZABETH SHERRILL

*Praying always with all prayer and supplication
in the Spirit.* —EPHESIANS 6:18 (KJV)

I hadn't paid much attention to them before, but now I notice them everywhere I travel—flowers placed along the side of the road in memory of loved ones who lost their lives in accidents there. One afternoon as I approached my exit on the interstate, I watched transfixed as a couple knelt on the ground at the roadside and set up three crosses covered with colorful silk flowers.

Dear God, did they lose children? Siblings? Friends? That weekend, I noticed several more memorials on the highway as I traveled to Cincinnati. And so I began a new habit of prayer. Whenever I come across one of those makeshift memorials, I pray for the rest of the day for all who've been touched by the tragedy it commemorates.

I've discovered since then that such opportunities for prayer are everywhere if I look closely, like the Christmas tree in my neighbors' bay window that stayed lit until their son came home from Iraq. And if I keep alert for the signs of need that are all around me, I can come closer to following Paul's instruction to pray always.

Father, keep my heart in a continual state of prayer.
—ROBERTA MESSNER

The lines are fallen unto me in pleasant places;
yea, I have a goodly heritage. —PSALM 16:6 (KJV)

Last summer I spent two nights in Red Wing, Minnesota, the sleepy Midwestern town where my mother grew up in the 1920s and '30s. My room in the historic St. James Hotel overlooked Levee Park, which hugs a bend in the Mississippi River.

My mother had often talked about her grandmother's visits to Red Wing. Grandmother Helene would sit for hours near the river's edge in Levee Park, staring across the water. She had emigrated from Norway's breathtaking fjord country to the prairie of South Dakota, and I suppose she never lost her longing for the sparkle and dance of water.

On my last morning in Red Wing, I was able to sit down on a bench in Levee Park, Bible in hand, for some solitary reflection. A young man approached me and asked if he could play his trumpet at a nearby picnic table. "Fine with me," I told him, "if you'll play a tune for me." Perhaps he had noticed my open Bible, because as the rich round notes rolled from his horn and sailed out across the water, I heard the old hymn "Blessed Assurance."

The young trumpeter knew nothing about my great-grandmother Helene or her faith in Christ. But his song evoked for me the image of a short, plump lady, her hair caught in a neat white bun, with a faraway look in her eyes as she gazed at the river in this very place and offered her prayers to the Lord.

I felt a deep peace. "Blessed assurance, Jesus is mine." My great-grandmother Helene knew it to be true and, some seventy years later, so did I.

Loving God, may the praises of my Savior
come through me to my children's children's children.

—CAROL KNAPP

AUGUST 15

*He will teach the ways that are right and best
to those who humbly turn to him.* —PSALM 25:9 (TLB)

*W*henever we visit my husband's parents near Lake Erie, my daughter Maria spends hours digging at the beach, piling up mounds of wet sand, and building tunnels and castles. A princess lives in one and her friends in another. Their activities keep Maria busy for a long time.

Lake Erie waves aren't huge, but they're big enough to wipe out a tiny shorefront village. "Start building a little farther away from the water," I told Maria one time, but she assured me everything would be okay. But soon the waves got bigger. "Mommy, Mommy, oh no!" she cried as water lapped the edges of the princess's castle. "Do something, Mommy!" But I couldn't keep the next wave from washing away Maria's afternoon of work. I hugged her tightly and told her we would build another castle together. Still, it hurt, especially since I'd told her not to build so close to the water.

I thought later that Maria's cries to me are similar to my own cries to God when I go my own way, forgetting His gentle guidance. I'm reminded of a work project that I took on, thinking I'd make some quick money, even though in prayer I'd felt a nudge to decline. But I confidently said *yes*, and then regretted it when the job caused a lot of aggravation. Of course, I ran to God in prayer to fix my mess. Thankfully, He didn't scold me and say, "I told you so." He wrapped His loving arms around me and gave me the strength to finish the job.

*Open my ears, loving God, so that in prayer
I might not only speak but also listen.*

—GINA BRIDGEMAN

August 16

The wolf also shall dwell with the lamb...
and a little child shall lead them. —Isaiah 11:6 (KJV)

*W*hen he was three, my grandson Caleb loved to play "wolf." He would stand in the corner of the playroom and build a tower of cardboard blocks around himself. I would crawl back and forth in front of the tower, growling, "I'm a big, bad wolf! I'm going to eat you up!" Every time Caleb tried to come out, I'd snap my teeth. Finally he'd burst through the blocks and run into the living room, laughing all the way.

One Saturday, after my knees ached from prowling and I'd growled myself hoarse, I changed the rules. I sat down and pretended to cry. "I'm a big, bad wolf! No one likes me! No one will play with me! Won't anyone be my friend?"

Caleb's laughter stopped abruptly. For a moment I thought he would burst into tears. Then he grinned. "Me!" he shouted, tapping his chest. "Me! I will be the wolf's friend!" And he launched himself into my arms.

A silly game? Yes, but one that demonstrated a profound truth: love can often turn a growling wolf into a gentle friend.

Lord Jesus, thank You for the
transforming power of Your Love.
—Penney Schwab

*Now He was telling them a parable to show
that at all times they ought to pray and
not to lose heart.* —LUKE 18:1 (NASB)

"Time to give up praying," I told myself sadly. My prayers were for someone I loved very much. But after ten years, they were still unanswered.

Later that afternoon, a letter to the editor in the local paper caught my eye. "Time to take down the 'Annie Lost Dog' posters. Annie is back home!" Overjoyed, I could hardly believe the amazing news. I'd prayed for Annie for nearly a year because her stubborn owner refused to take his ad out of the paper. The ad explained that Annie was very shy and lost in unfamiliar surroundings. The owner seemed quite desperate. He'd been visiting his daughter in Athens, Georgia, when Annie ran away.

A few days later a full-length story ran in the Athens *Banner-Herald* with a picture of the black Labrador-retriever mix and her happy owner, who said he simply refused to believe his dog wouldn't be found. He'd returned to Athens on weekends, walking the streets calling "Annie" late into the night and sitting outside his daughter's home in thirteen-degree weather hoping to get a glimpse of his pet. When the daughter begged her father to relinquish his hope of finding the dog and begin the grieving process, he intensified his prayers.

Ten full months after her disappearance, Annie was discovered, still wearing her identification tags, twenty-five miles from Athens. "I especially want to encourage others who have lost pets not to give up hope," Annie's ecstatic owner said.

The last five words seemed to leap off the newspaper and land right in my heart. Laying the paper aside, I resumed my ten-year prayer.

*Father, I praise You for caring about fallen sparrows,
lost dogs, and sons who've gone astray.*
—MARION BOND WEST

AUGUST 18

Here a little, there a little. —ISAIAH 28:10 (NKJV)

Augent sun shimmered on the stalks of corn, their thick blades rising like endless green walls. My hoe made hollow sounds in the dirt; sweat trickled down my nose. When I reached the end of the row, I went to sit beside Grandma, who was breaking beans in the shade of the snowball bush.

"I'll never get done!" I pouted.

"'Course you will," she said, her hands methodically snapping bean after bean.

I watched her for a minute and then asked, "Grandma, how many beans have you broken in your life?"

She laughed, piling her apron with yet another batch to break.

"Three or four million, I reckon."

"Seems like I have about that many hills of corn to hoe," I grumbled, rubbing the calluses forming on my palms.

Grandma stopped her work and laid her hand lightly on my knee. "It's all in how you look at it, child. I never think about the bushels and bushels of beans that need breaking. I just think about the next bean. And then the next. One bean at a time is all I have to break." Her eyes were bright behind her bifocals. "By the yard it's hard; by the inch it's a cinch!"

I remember Grandma's advice—when I have four pies to bake for the church bazaar, when my daughter Amy Jo volunteers me to type her class's literary magazine, when every window in my house needs washing, when I pledge to read the entire Bible in a year, when weeds threaten to repopulate my petunia patch. *By the yard it's hard; by the inch it's a cinch.* Then little by little, one by one, I find I can finish my tasks—just as I did those corn rows so long ago.

> *Sometimes I feel so overwhelmed, Father, by the things*
> *I must do. Give me discretion in my commitments.*
> *Today, teach me to take small bites of responsibility—*
> *to do the inch, and see it's a cinch.*
> —MARY LOU CARNEY

Call unto Me, and I will answer thee,
and show thee great and mighty things, which thou
knowest not. —JEREMIAH 33:3 (KJV)

*M*r. May was a short, jolly little man who had a used-furniture shop in our town. He told me once of a day in summer when the sky turned black as patent leather as a storm boomed up in the southwest. The bottom of the cloud seemed to squeeze together and the top spread out until it looked like a great cobra weaving toward him. "It sounded like a hundred jets taking off," he said, his brown eyes narrowing. "I didn't have a cellar to run to; I just sat in my little house and talked pretty earnest to the Lord. I said, 'God help me! I know You can do it!' About that time that funnel just sucked up my house and took off with it, twirling it like a top. It carried us for an eighth of a mile and put us down. The walls of the house all fell flat, and I walked out. Didn't have a scratch."

"The Lord was certainly with you," I marveled.

"If He was, He was a-goin' some," Mr. May reflected.

Like Mr. May, I often cry out for God's instant attention. I may have been busy, happy, forgetting God for hours at a time. Then, suddenly, an urgent phone call; an impending head-on collision; a child's scream; a doctor's report …and I call, "God, help!" No apologies for neglecting Him; no praise for His past goodness; no thanks for His loving me; for being there, listening. I just call, remembering His assurance when Abraham questioned His power and He answered, "Is there any thing too hard for me?" (Jeremiah 32:27 KJV)

May everything that has breath praise You,
God, for Your love and mercy.

—ZONA B. DAVIS

Lo, he passes by me, and I see him not; he moves on,
but I do not perceive him. —Job 9:11 (RSV)

We were putting on a French farce in one of the many theater classes I took when I was a playwriting major in college. I had been part of the crew that built and changed the sets, so I was in the wings when I heard whispers from another part of the backstage area as the second act began.

The entire act hinged on an incriminating letter, which three actors moved from place to place with split-second timing to keep a fourth actor from finding it. We were close to the point where the first actor had to move the letter for the first time, and the props people had just discovered that they had forgotten the letter. The set was closed on three sides, so there was no way to sneak it into place. "What will happen when Denny reaches for it and it isn't there?" the prop person moaned. We crowded downstage, just behind the curtain, to see what was going on.

Denny walked to the fireplace, where the letter was supposed to be waiting beneath a candlestick, hesitated for a moment, then grasped the air firmly, turned, and passed the nonexistent letter to the actress who was to hide it in the bookcase, without missing a line. She caught on instantly, took the nothing, and hid it just as she was supposed to. Throughout the rest of the act, the "letter" changed hands five more times, with everyone cooperating in the illusion that it was really there.

Between the second and third acts, the stage manager went out front to mingle with the audience. When he returned, he was shaking his head. "No one even noticed that the letter wasn't there," he said wonderingly.

Denny had changed into his third-act costume and overheard the remark. "Not so odd," he said. "We all just believed that it was there, so it was."

It was the first time in my life I ever found a practical demonstration of the presence of things invisible, and I never forgot it.

Dear God, keep my spirit alive to the reality
of the things my eyes cannot see.
—Rhoda Blecker

You saw me before I was born and scheduled each day
of my life before I began to breathe. —PSALM 139:16 (TLB)

Holding our new little grandson, delighting in the wonder of tiny hands, button-nose, and eyes blinking in the unaccustomed light of a bright new world, my heart skipped a beat as I thought, *If only my mother could have seen him.*

Just two years before, I had held Mother's frail body in my arms and whispered the gentle reassurance, "Don't be afraid, Mummy darling. You are going right from my arms into the arms of Jesus. He is waiting for you, and when you see Him tell Him how much I love Him."

With a quiet little "Oh!" as though surprised by some angelic light, she went limp in my arms and into the presence of her Lord.

Life taken. Now I was holding *life given.*

I was reminded of the story I'd heard of another new baby. "Come," said the young father, taking his four-year-old daughter by the hand and leading her to the nursery, where they had just tucked in her brand-new baby brother. "Come and say hello!"

The little girl pulled back. "I want to see him all by myself."

Both parents looked at each other, eyebrows raised. "You mean no one else in the room with you?" they asked with some concern.

She nodded, curls bouncing in agreement.

With some hesitation, they let her into the nursery alone, watching and listening carefully from around the corner of the doorway. Standing on tiptoe, leaning over the bassinet, she patted the baby. "Tell me...tell me quick," she whispered, "what does God look like? I've forgotten!"

Father, it is in the sacred moments of birth and death
that we feel Your presence most deeply. Thank You that You
are with me in my ordinary moments, too.

—FAY ANGUS

*Except ye...become as little children, ye shall not enter
into the kingdom of heaven.* —MATTHEW 18:3 (KJV)

*M*y eight-year-old granddaughter Saralisa spent some time with us last year. The first thing she wanted me to do was to go to the creek with her. It's just across the road from our house, so hand in hand, we danced and skipped our way there.

Oh, the sound of the flowing water! It's the most beautiful music I know. I sat on the bank as Saralisa took off her shoes and socks and stepped into the cool stream. The morning sun was shining in golden patches, causing the mica at the bottom of the clear water to sparkle like pure gold. Saralisa had brought along a small skillet with which she "panned for gold," just as her grandmother had done more than sixty years ago.

Suddenly, I was a child again! With only a little hesitation, I took off my shoes and socks and joined in the fun. Of course we both knew it wasn't real gold, but that didn't matter one bit. Our true gold was in the pine-scented mountain air, the sunshine, that inimitable sound, and the feel of the cool water over our bare feet.

Thank You, God! I thought to myself. *For this moment in all eternity, this seventy-two-year-old grandmother is a child again. Time, like an artist on the brink of creation, stands still. And ringing down the centuries, I hear those precious words, "And God saw every thing that he had made, and, behold, it was very good"* (*Genesis 1:31* KJV).

> *Dear God, may I make time to be a child today, letting in
> all the wonders of Your great creation!*
> —MARILYN MORGAN KING

When he hath tried me,
I shall come forth as gold.
—JOB 23:10 (KJV)

We've talked about "rolling with the punches" in our family since the kids were toddlers. When things don't turn out the way you want or expect, go with the flow. If faced with circumstances you can't control or change, don't complain. Make the best of it, which minimizes the impact of the blow.

When you go to a birthday party and get the smallest piece of cake, you still say "thank you" in a nice (not grumpy) voice. When the soccer coach asks you to play goalie, you play goalie, and only your mother knows that's your most unfavorite position to play. When it's cleanup time, you help clean up, even when you know the other guy made most of the mess.

Joseph in Genesis knew how to roll with the punches. He kept finding himself in the midst of difficulties he didn't choose. He was pushed into a deep pit and then sold into slavery by his brothers; he was falsely accused by Potiphar's wife and thrown into prison. But instead of being bitter, Joseph rolled with the punches, making the best of bad situations, and God used his circumstances for good, especially within his own family.

Much of life involves getting used to things not turning out the way we want or expect, or doing what we don't feel like doing. And a lot of it happens within a family, where we have a choice: to complain until everyone is miserable, or to roll with the punches and trust God, which minimizes the blow. Both responses are contagious in a family. That's why rolling with the punches matters.

Father, teach me to minimize the blows of life
by rolling with the punches.
—CAROL KUYKENDALL

Let us then approach the throne of grace
with confidence. —HEBREWS 4:16

*M*y grandson Cameron loves to play soldier, so for his ninth birthday his mother, my daughter Jenny, decided to give him a military-themed party. The invitations were draft notices and my son-in-law designed an obstacle course for the ten boys who were to attend. My oldest son Ted, who'd served as an Airborne Ranger, painted camouflage on the boys' faces, and they ate MREs in the field. (For us civilians, that's meals ready to eat.) The party was a huge success.

Later that summer, Cameron spent an entire day outside arranging his toy soldiers. When he'd finished, he insisted his mother take a picture, just in case she happened to meet a general. How or when this was supposed to occur was of little concern to my grandson. He instructed his mother to hand over the picture so that the army could make use of his battle plan.

I enjoyed telling my husband about Cameron's exploits, and I have to admit that we were both impressed. Even at the age of nine, he felt he had something of value to offer others. *We all do,* I thought later, *whether it's a shared recipe or an unexpected birthday card to a shut-in or even what we're convinced is a brilliant business plan.*

So I've made Cameron's message my own: believe in yourself and in God's ability to use your talents as He sees fit.

Lord, thank You for the lesson in self-confidence
that my grandson has taught me.
—DEBBIE MACOMBER

August 25

A time to heal. —Ecclesiastes 3:3

Jamie, my eleven-year-old granddaughter, phoned today and didn't seem to have much to say. Her silence told me that something was wrong. Usually she talks nonstop, laughs often, and asks enthusiastically, "Guess what, Nanny?" Finally, she blurted out, "Nanny, I miss Robbie so much today. I know it's stupid. He's been dead for nearly three years. But I can't stop thinking about him—what he would have looked like."

Robbie was her little brother. He'd lived only twenty-five minutes.

He was a beautiful baby.

She continued, "I mean, why am I so sad *today*?" Her voice broke, and she released her tears into the phone.

How do you explain to a child that grief is a sneaky thing? That you think it's all over and, suddenly, it reappears. That grief doesn't play fair. "I miss him, too, Jamie."

"I do something pretty dumb, but it helps," she sniffed.

"What, Jamie?"

"You won't laugh? Promise?"

"Promise."

"Well, I've discovered that if I write his name, that it helps somehow. I don't know how, but I've been writing it a lot today."

We hung up after a bit, and I sat at the phone and began to print, "Robbie—Robert Clifford Garmon—Robbie, Robbie, Robbie...."

Dear Lord, I had forgotten that steps to healing
are sometimes very simple.
—Marion Bond West

New wine must be poured into
fresh wineskins! —LUKE 5:38 (GNT)

I stood knee-deep in the ocean, my thoughts swirling like the foaming water around me. For some time I had been incubating the idea of going back to school, maybe to become a counselor or therapist. But at forty-one, becoming a student again would mean many changes: new schedules, new demands, new courage. Was I capable of such a demanding challenge?

I squinted my eyes, looking at the sandy bottom below the surface. Something tumbled against my right foot. Was it a murex shell? I bent down and grabbed a fistful of sand. *Aha!* I felt the rough grooves of the murex in my fingertips.

As I studied it in the morning sunlight, I saw two round eyes, peering out at me. The shell had become a home for a hermit crab. I opened my palm wide. Its two large claws cautiously emerged, then its dark eyes, and finally its whole upper body. I remembered reading that hermit crabs twist their bodies into the spiral of empty seashells. As they grow, they shed their shell for a larger one.

I looked at it. How did it know when to find a bigger shell? Was it scary letting go of the old? As I lowered the crab into the water, I wished it well on its journey of living. And I prayed that when the time came, I, too, would have the courage to leave my little space in search of a new one...roomy enough for growth and change.

Lord, please help me to find room for the growth and change
occurring within me. And give me the courage
to take the bold steps required to act.
—TERRY HELWIG

AUGUST 27

*There is a time for everything...a time to be born
and a time to die.* —ECCLESIASTES 3:1–2

I watch out the car window as the scenery zips by: fields of corn and beans, freshly painted red barns, and herds of grazing Holsteins. I've made this trip to the small town where I grew up hundreds of times. But I realize, as I look at my son-in-law driving and my daughter sitting beside him, I've never before made it sitting in the backseat. I was always the one driving—each mile bringing me closer to my mother and my sister, closer to the warm familiarity of going home. But now my sister has retired to Florida and Mother is buried in the small cemetery down the road from where she lived.

Small feet kick against the car seat and the sound of a rattle breaks into my thoughts. I turn to look at my six-month-old grandson Drake. He smiles and bangs the rattle against his leg. I reach for his hand and begin singing silly rhymes.

Later, I stand at Mother's grave, shaded by the branches of a giant tree. The only sounds are the calls of birds high overhead. With Drake in my arms, I kneel to place a bouquet of purple roses (Mother's favorite color) at the base of her headstone. "She would have loved you so very much," I whisper into the soft baby neck. Suddenly, Drake leans forward and his tiny hand pats the warm granite.

And maybe, just maybe, somewhere in the halls of heaven, Mother smiles at the touch of her great-grandson's hand on her shoulder.

*Comfort us, Father, with the continuing blessing
of Your love—in this life and in the one beyond. Let us teach
it to our children and our children's children.*

—MARY LOU CARNEY

And they came, bringing to Him a paralytic,
carried by four men. —MARK 2:3 (NASB)

It's a scary thing to have your son phone, offhandedly chat awhile, then finally give the *real* reason for his call.

"Mom, I have some health problems that will involve some serious surgery. But don't worry."

Of course I worried. *What if something happens to John?* Now, my children may be married and away from home, but they're still my kids. And in situations like this, I turn to God even more than usual.

That's when I recalled the story in Mark of the sick man carried to Jesus by four friends. *Why four?* I wondered. The Gospel doesn't say, but it seems logical that if the man was too sick to make it on his own, he'd need a stretcher and four carriers, one for each corner.

If it worked in biblical times, it should work now, too, I reasoned. So with motherly concern, I looked for four friends of my own—friends who truly believe in prayer—who would agree to carry John on a "prayer stretcher." I think it helps to pray specifically—not just a vague, "Lord, take care of John." So I said, "Mary, will you take the left front corner, please? Sue, right front. Bonnie, left rear. Kathie, right rear." My position? I reasoned that every team needs cheerleaders. I'd be one, encouraging each prayer and giving them updates on John's condition.

For two months, the four stretcher-bearers continued their faithful vigil. When surgery day came, John's wife Marie said, "Neither of us is afraid. We both sense John is being carried on a bed of prayer."

And how does the story in Mark end? When Jesus saw the faith of the four friends, He said to the paralytic, "Get up, take your mat and go home" (Mark 2:11 NIV).

And within a short time, that's just what John did.

Father, You've told us that anything is possible
if we have faith. Please show me how to have that faith—
the faith that moves mountains!

—ISABEL WOLSELEY

AUGUST 29

Come now, and let us reason together,
saith the Lord. —ISAIAH 1:18 (KJV)

"Can we take the ferry?" my daughter Maria asked, as she does every summer when we visit Coronado, California. The ferry crosses San Diego Bay from Coronado to the city's harbor, a fifteen-minute ride.

"Why, what do you want to do when we get over there?" I asked.

She shrugged.

"I don't care about *being* there," she said. "I just want to go there."

Sounds like something Yogi Berra might say, but it makes sense. Everybody knows the best part is the traveling.

I've been keeping a prayer journal for the past few months, and I'm learning that prayer is like that. I've been praying for a friend to forgive me, and I've been disappointed because I haven't seen the desired result. But as I write my concerns and the nudges from God I feel in return, I learn that prayer is more a conversation than a list of demands.

In talking to God about my friend's forgiveness, I've learned a lot about myself. I've discovered I can be a better friend by being more understanding and watching what I say more carefully. As I listen in prayer, I'm also getting to know God better and learning what He wants for my life.

When I review my prayer journal, I see that not all my prayers have been answered yet. But what may be more important is what's happened to me through the asking. My growth is a reminder that prayer is like that ferry ride. As my young daughter well knew, it's not the "being there" that matters, it's the "getting there."

God in heaven, hear my prayers and lead me on a
never-ending journey to know You better.
—GINA BRIDGEMAN

AUGUST 30

That their hearts might be comforted...
to the acknowledgement of the mystery of God, and of
the Father, and of Christ; in whom are hid all the treasures
of wisdom and knowledge. —COLOSSIANS 2:2–3 (KJV)

*S*moke from the Colorado Hayman fire was thick in the air as we drove away from our beloved mountain village, knowing that when we returned our home might be ashes. Already people five miles from us had been evacuated, and the winds were blowing in our direction.

We thought about canceling our trip to Nebraska to celebrate my grandchildren's birthdays, but what good would it do for us to stay here? We couldn't save our home. So we came up with a plan. We loaded my car with all the possessions we felt we couldn't do without and gave the key to a neighbor who offered to drive the car to a safe place if the fire came closer. Then we drove away in my husband's car.

So what did we save? Well, there were some things (such as legal papers) that had to be safe. But beyond that? We carefully packed a painting by my artist daughter; a few special heirlooms we wanted our children to have someday (such as Grandmother Morgan's family Bible); letters from our children and other loved ones; and pictures and scrapbooks. We left sterling silver, crystal, china, computers and other office equipment, TV, jewelry, furniture, and all our clothes except what we'd packed to take to Nebraska.

Fortunately, the wildfires spared our home and village, but we discovered something about ourselves during that "summer of the great fires." What we treasured most had very little monetary value, and yet these items made us rich beyond measure.

Great Creator of all that is, keep me ever aware
that my most valuable possessions are beyond price.
—MARILYN MORGAN KING

"God can do what men can't!" —LUKE 18:27 (TLB)

*M*y mother's letters to me began when I went away to camp for the first time at age eight. In college, I had my own tiny mailbox, and her letters of encouragement filled it regularly. When I was single and working in Atlanta, Georgia, and West Palm Beach, Florida, I counted on Mother's letters, usually typed at her office at the bank. When I married and had children of my own, her letters, full of love and cheer, continued. When I was widowed in my forties—as she had been in her twenties—Mother's letters insisted that I could make it. When love and marriage came to me a second time, her letters kept coming. Now that she was retired, they were no longer typed, but written in her familiar handwriting.

When Mother died at ninety-two, I realized just how much her letters had mattered. Sometimes I'd forget she was gone and for a moment expect to find one in my mailbox.

Then one hot summer day I received a letter from my cousin Sally Jean. Her mother, Aunty Sally, my mother's sister, had moved into a nursing home, and in cleaning out her mother's home Sally Jean had found something she thought I should have: a faded letter typed on Mother's office typewriter.

May 23, 1952, Friday

The nights are wonderful now. There's a fragrance from honeysuckle, newly mowed grass, fresh plowed earth and chinaberry blossoms that makes you just want to stay outside and enjoy it. Looks like rain tomorrow. I'd better go buy groceries.

Oh, one of my customers just came in and brought me some home-ground sausage and sweet potatoes. Wish you were here....

My heart doing flip-flops, I read the rest of Sally Jean's letter: "I found a bunch of letters that Mom saved. I'll be sending them along from time to time ...."

> *Dear heavenly Father, forgive me when I forget*
> *that with You nothing is impossible.*
> —MARION BOND WEST

September

SEPTEMBER 1

How excellent is thy lovingkindness, O God!
Therefore the children of men put their trust under
the shadow of thy wings. —PSALM 36:7 (KJV)

It was a Wednesday in September. Our daughter Tamara was stranded in Anchorage, Alaska, with a newborn and toddlers Zachary and Hannah, while her husband trained at the police academy. I had come to rescue her.

This day I took Zachary and Hannah to play in the park. Soon an older woman meandered by with a young child in tow. She nodded and smiled but didn't seem inclined to chat.

Zachary and I teeter-tottered while the girls sailed down a small slide beneath the watchful eye of the unknown woman. When I twirled my grandchildren on the tire swing, the other child wanted to swing, too, and the woman came over to help. Haltingly, she told me she was from Russia, visiting her daughter and granddaughter Nicole.

"Oh," I exclaimed, "you're a *babushka*!"

She laughed, nodding yes.

I pointed to myself. "Me, too," I said.

When Zachary tired of the swing, I went off with him to play in the sand, leaving the Russian grandmother still twirling the girls. Somehow Hannah slipped off the tire and fell backward onto the ground. The Russian grandmother was bending down anxiously over her when I scooped Hannah into my arms.

"It's all right," I said. "She's not hurt."

That's when the thought hit me: *Here we are, two grandmothers from countries that used to be enemies, playing in the park with our grandchildren, teaching them to get along and watching out for them with equal concern.*

The two of us left the park. We had met only briefly, but it was long enough for me to gain new understanding of a grandmother's mission: to help shape our world's future by sowing seeds of consideration and respect—starting in the park.

heavenly Father, with my grandchildren in tow,
lead me in Your path of loving-kindness.
—CAROL KNAPP

And he wrote them in two tables of stone.
—DEUTERONOMY 5:22 (KJV)

The moment I'd dreaded was finally here. It was time to say good-bye to Derek, our oldest, in a college dormitory fifteen hundred miles from home. For months I had anticipated this scene, wondering what I could say that would appropriately leave him with a feeling of confidence and support. As it turned out, I barely muttered more than a quick "good-bye."

"It's two o'clock," Derek exclaimed as we finished unpacking his belongings in that tiny dorm room. "I'm supposed to be at a meeting right now!" With a quick circle-of-family hug, he was out the door. From his window, I watched him walk away and felt a stabbing sense of separation...and frustration. I hadn't said *anything*. With tears in my eyes, I pulled a sheet of paper from his desk and jotted down three family messages we'd tried to pass on to our children as they grew up: "Remember, Derek: (1) There is *no problem* so big you can't solve it; (2) We *always* love you; and (3) You are *never* alone. Love, Mom." I tucked the note under his pillow.

A few days later, Derek phoned. "Thanks for your note, Mom. I put it on my wall so I can remember what you said when I'm feeling low." After I hung up, I silently thanked God for a lesson I need to remember:

Sometimes a written message—short and sweet—is more appropriate than a spoken word (or lecture) because it gives a person something to hold on to.

I wonder if that's why God wrote the Ten Commandments on two tablets of stone?

Lord, help me know when it's more appropriate
to communicate in writing, and with brevity.
—CAROL KUYKENDALL

SEPTEMBER 3

Do not interpretations belong to God?
—GENESIS 40:8 (KJV)

I was cat-sitting for my friend Mabel Tendler, who has two and a half cats. Well, they're really two indoor cats and an outdoor orange cat who picks up food from several kind neighbors, including Mabel.

"Make sure to feed him," she had reminded me. "I don't want the poor thing to go hungry. Here's his special dish." No sooner did I fill the bowl and set it down than I got a hungry customer. I heard the noise of dry food being crunched, and I turned to see a big Doberman wolfing down the entire bowl of food.

"Hey!" I shouted. "That's not yours! Leave that alone!" He gave me a big doggy leer and ran off with the orange plastic bowl clenched firmly between his teeth.

The orange cat never showed up the whole week I was there. And Mabel's special bowl was gone, and I was responsible! I agonized all week. Would she cry? Would she yell? My mind conjured up Technicolor versions of how upset she'd be that I hadn't carried out her instructions correctly.

Well, Mabel came home, I confessed—and she laughed! "Oh, that happens all the time. Look in the left corner of the yard and you'll see where Dingo left the bowl."

"But what about the orange cat?" I asked. "The poor thing must have gone hungry."

"I think the orange cat mooches off about six neighbors besides me."

"Oh," was all I said, and then I had to laugh, too—at the doom-and-gloom scenario I'd created in my own mind.

God, is there some "cat dish" in my life I've been blowing up out of all proportion? Let me live calmly today and not in a frightening—and imaginary— future.
—LINDA NEUKRUG

SEPTEMBER 4

For you are our glory and joy.
—1 THESSALONIANS 2:20 (NKJV)

While we were growing up, my two sisters Mary and Katy and I journeyed every summer from Denver to North Platte, Nebraska, for a special weeklong visit with our grandparents.

A visit to Grandma and Grandpa's meant at least two or three *breakfasts* of chocolate cake with white icing, as well as noon meals of pot roast with all the trimmings, or chicken and dumplings.

Then there was the apple tree in the backyard—just right for climbing and eating its sour green fruit. "Not too many," Grandma would caution, "or you'll get stomachaches."

We went on downtown errands with Grandpa where he'd introduce us to his friends. "These are my lovely granddaughters from Denver, Ed and Mary Ellen's girls." His gentle pride always showed in his smiling eyes and soft, friendly voice.

Early evenings, we'd amble with Grandma through the wide, tree-lined streets. Once she led us to a new park in town and told us, "I won twenty-five dollars for naming it 'Park Allura.'" That was the prettiest name I'd ever heard for a park.

For that week, we reveled in the treats, the attention, the knowledge that we were loved just for being who we were. My grandparents died some years ago, but their loving example inspired me to pass on those same traits to my child, and one day, hopefully, his children. It's a legacy of love that never runs out. So, "Thank you, Grandma and Grandpa, for being you!"

Father, thank You for loving grandparents, and for Your love
that accepts me as I am. Help me to look on the people
in my life with pride and joy.
—ELLYN BAUMANN

SEPTEMBER 5

And I will bring the blind by a way
that they knew not. —Isaiah 42:16 (KJV)

Some years ago I used to take my German shepherd for long walks in Philadelphia's Fairmount Park. I'd park my car and take one of the trails that went far up into the hills where I could walk Kate off-leash. After a while I got to know the trails by heart.

One day a friend of mine came along with us, and the two of us were so busy talking that we didn't notice where we were. Finally, Pat looked at her watch and said, "Gosh, I have to get back and make dinner! Which way do we go?" That's when I realized we were lost.

We were surrounded by woods and couldn't see far ahead of us. After trying several times to retrace our steps, we lost all sense of direction. "Wait a minute," I said. "If anyone knows the way back, it's Kate."

I looked at Kate, and in a commanding voice I said, "Kate, take us home!"

Kate brushed past us to lead the way. But after a little while both Pat and I knew it wasn't the way we had come. Kate had taken us off the trail and was leading us up and down some pretty steep hills. She was full of confidence and kept looking back at us as if to reassure us. But the farther we went, the more nervous we got.

Then, suddenly, we came out of the woods and into a huge meadow. At the end of the meadow we looked down a slope and saw the parking lot far below us. "We're home!" I shouted and threw my arms around Kate. So did Pat.

"She knew where she was going all the time," Pat said. "It just wasn't the same way we came."

"No," I agreed, "it was a better way."

Since then I've always tried to remember that when I ask God for guidance—and I do it often—1 have to trust Him to know which way is best for me. Even if I haven't gone that way before.

Lead me, dear Jesus, because Your way
is always better than mine.

—Phyllis Hobe

And to know the love of Christ, which passeth knowledge,
that ye might be filled with all the fulness of God.
—EPHESIANS 3:19 (KJV)

*W*hen I was a child, we lived down a dusty dirt road from my paternal grandmother. I loved going to her house to sit with her under the shady pecan trees as she shelled peas or prepared fresh corn from her garden. I was always barefoot, and on scorching summer days I'd hop along on the high spots where the sand was thinner and the heat less intense. Finally, I'd reach the shade of Grandmother's big yard and cool my feet on the green grass.

My grandmother was not a demonstrative person, and at my young age I sometimes wondered whether she really loved me. But then Grandmother would produce a dime from some unseen pocket and my heart would leap. That was my cue to walk to the neighborhood store to buy a soda for both of us. The sand was still unforgiving, but the thought of the cold drink on my parched tongue would have taken me across hot coals. Grandmother may not have smothered me with kisses, but that cold soda on a hot summer day showed that she loved me.

There are times in my life when I feel that God's love is not so evident either, and I wish He would smother me with kisses. But then, just as the heat of the situation seems intolerable, I spot the proverbial dime: It may be a Scripture or a magnificent sunset or a wise word from a friend. Then I know that all I have to do is wait on Him and trust in His love. It never fails. That assurance makes the trip up the hot, dusty road of life worth every bold step.

Father, grant that I may recognize Your love for me,
especially in the small things that often go unnoticed.
—LIBBIE ADAMS

The eyes of all wait upon thee; and thou givest them
their meat in due season. —PSALM 145:15 (KJV)

Every time I spent a day with Grandma Ellen, she offered me a peppermint. She always had a plastic bag of them in her purse. Though I rarely ate them, it seemed as if every time we went to the store she bought another package. If I asked her if she really needed more, she'd just add a bag to her cart and say, "Well, they're on sale."

After Grandma Ellen died, I helped sort through some of her papers. I was working at Grandma's desk when I heard Mom groan. Turning to look, I saw her pull a plastic bag from Grandma's purse. "What in the world am I going to do with all these peppermints?" she asked. A few minutes later, I heard a louder groan. Several more bags of mints waited in a drawer. Mom had found Grandma's stockpile! "How am I going to get rid of them?" she asked.

At church that Sunday, Mom had an idea. A lady sitting in the pew in front of us seemed to be having some trouble with a cough, so Mom tapped her gently on the shoulder and handed her a mint. The woman smiled and unwrapped the mint quietly. Soon her cough was soothed, but the wrapper's crinkling had caught the attention of a small child down the row, so Mom passed a peppermint that way, too. The next week, Mom gave a mint to another coughing friend and two more children. After the service, several ladies enjoyed mints with their coffee in the social hall. Mom left a handful in the Sunday school candy dish.

A couple of months after Mom's "mint ministry" began, we went grocery shopping, and as we approached the candy aisle, I asked Mom if she had given away most of Grandma's mints. She chuckled but didn't answer. Somehow, I wasn't surprised when I saw Mom reach for two bags of mints. She looked at me, grinning, and said, "Well, they're on sale."

Father, thank You for Grandma's peppermints.
Though I don't like to eat them, they're wonderful to share!
—KJERSTIN WILLIAMS

A soft answer turneth away wrath:
but grievous words stir up anger.
—PROVERBS 15:1 (KJV)

*M*y five-year-old grandson Cameron was ready for his first day of kindergarten. I phoned my daughter Jenny after she dropped him off to catch the school bus.

"How did it go?" I asked. I knew Cameron was eager to start school, but both Jenny and I had our worries about our little Cam riding the big scary yellow bus on his own.

"Another boy spat at him," Jenny told me and then went on to explain the circumstances. Both boys were in line waiting for the bus when some kind of disagreement broke out. Apparently the other boy didn't get his way and spat at Cameron.

My heart sank. I asked Jenny how she had handled the situation, since she was standing right there.

"I didn't need to do a thing. Cameron took care of it," Jenny explained. "He looked the boy directly in the eyes and said, 'If you do that, you can't be my friend.' By the time the bus arrived Cameron had a new friend. They had their arms around each other and were the best of buddies."

I was proud of my grandson's response to mistreatment, but at the same time I was reminded of how often I'm tempted to retaliate in kind when I feel wronged. Jesus calls me to live a life of love; my grandson gave me a beautiful example of how.

Dear Lord, help me always to follow Your—
and Cameron's—example and turn aside anger with love.
—DEBBIE MACOMBER

For everything there is a season, and a time
for every matter under heaven.... A time to keep, and
a time to cast away. —ECCLESIASTES 3:1, 6 (RSV)

ot long after I turned fifty and was getting rid of stuff I hadn't used in years, my father told me I was experiencing a new phase in psychological development. "When you hit fifty," he told me, "you seek simplification."

"Is that what I'm doing?" I asked, giving him a sideways glance while debating whether to keep an autographed book from a friend to whom I no longer sent Christmas cards.

In the three years since, I've often experienced this "urge to purge." I've gotten rid of kitchen gadgets, Easter decorations, lawn furniture. When I sold my house, I threw out bookcases, furniture, and dishes I once cherished.

Then I began to worry. Was simplification nothing more than the discovery of meaninglessness in everything I once enjoyed?

Last week, my three-year-old grandson Rome squirmed onto his big beanbag, with blue blankie and thumb, excited to watch his new *Dora* show. Suddenly, out came his thumb. Frowning, he said to his mother, "Mama, I'm not sucking my thumb very well today."

I laughed. Rome was growing up. What used to bring him pleasure and meaning no longer did.

I went home feeling reassured. I'd get over this urge to purge and get on with my own "psychological development" too. I would learn to find pleasure in my new need for simplicity.

Dear God, keep me growing, keep me learning,
keep me loving, keep me focused on You,
whom I will never outgrow.

—BRENDA WILBEE

Praise the Lord...who satisfies your desires
with good things so that your youth is renewed
like the eagle's. —PSALM 103:2, 5

On April 25, at 11:15 a.m., my fiftieth birthday, I brought in the mail and became a senior citizen. It said so right inside the official envelope cradling a letter of welcome and my own personalized senior citizen card. I felt as if I'd swallowed an ice cube. I looked from the mail to the mirror above the hall table. Yep, I looked old.

I flung the card aside. But the label stuck and grew throughout the day, till I was trapped in it. *Senior citizen...gray, grim, grouchy*. When my husband Whitney bounced in the door, holding a brightly wrapped present, I burst into tears. "What's with you?" he asked. Well, he got the whole earful, and he laughed.

Whipping out his wallet, Whitney produced *his* senior citizen card. "I got it four years ago, remember?"

I hadn't.

"Know why you forgot?"

"Why?" I sniffed.

"Because it wasn't a big deal. It's just crossing a time zone."

So we took our senior citizen cards and got a discount at a fine restaurant. And we had a toast to being seniors *together*.

Lord, help me to face each new day with a youthful spirit.

—SHARI SMYTH

September 11

And it shall come to pass, that before they call,
I will answer; and while they are yet speaking, I will hear.
—Isaiah 65:24 (KJV)

*I*f you had been looking for me fifty years ago on any Wednesday evening, you would have found me beside the black rotary dial phone, waiting for it to ring. And it always did.

Those were courtship days, and Leo and I allowed ourselves just one five-minute long-distance call per week. Back then, even the thirty cents it cost was viewed as an extravagance, especially by those who were not yet in a close relationship.

After we married, Leo continued to call me every day during his lunch break. We quickly shared the developments of the day, whether good or bad. As the children came along, a request I frequently heard while they ate their lunch was "When Dad calls, tell him…" or "When Dad calls, ask him…." It was their moment to share some personal achievement or to ask him for some advice, neither of which could possibly wait until he got home.

Sometimes Leo would dial our number and I'd pick up the receiver before the phone even rang. Such instant connections were always a bit of a surprise, considering the split-second timing involved—and yet not really. Over the years I've found that caring and consistency are the basis of all good communication—including prayer.

Lord, make me as receptive to Your voice
as You are to my calling.
—Alma Barkman

*I have fought a good fight, I have
finished my course.* —2 TIMOTHY 4:7

*W*hen our spunky granddaughter Sarah was six months old, the orthopedist placed her left foot in a temporary cast to correct its tendency to turn inward. We all worried about how this setback might affect her. But little Sarah didn't. She crawled and hobbled about wherever she cared to. I can still see her flying down the hall with the cast clumping along behind.

Recalling her tenacity made me re-evaluate a setback of my own. For six months, I've meticulously followed a low-fat diet to lower my cholesterol. Yesterday, I returned to the doctor confident that my cholesterol count would be down considerably. (After all, I hadn't eaten any "good" food for months!) What a disappointment to find it had dropped only slightly. "Oh, forget it!" I wailed. "I might as well give up."

But today, putting pictures in the family album, I studied one of Sarah displaying her cast. *Sarah didn't quit*, I thought, noting the gleam of determination in her eyes.

It was catching, and I decided right then that, like Sarah, I wouldn't be deterred. *No, I'm going to hobble along*. I'll start by giving thanks that my cholesterol count went down, however slightly, instead of up. And despite the "silence" on my prayers for a relative's restored health, I'm going to keep on upholding her in faithful prayer.

Worried about setbacks? With prayer and thanksgiving, you can effect a *comeback*. Every day.

*Father, when I'm tempted to give up,
remind me of the wondrous ways in which You work.*

—BONNIE LUKES

Even the night shall be light about me. —PSALM 139:11 (KJV)

I just couldn't get into my workout that morning. Even the proximity of other early risers jogging or lifting weights didn't motivate me. My mind was on some hard decisions I was having to make at work, decisions that would have dramatic and long-reaching effects on the whole staff. *How can I know the right thing to do?* Finally, I stepped off the treadmill and, pulling on my sweatshirt, headed outside. Maybe the fresh air would help clear my head.

It was still dark as I turned into the subdivision adjacent to the health club. Stars, brilliant in that predawn moment, filled the sky. A tiny sliver of buttercream moon looked down on me. I walked at a brisk pace past brick houses and well-kept lawns, my breath making little puffs in front of me. A few porch lights glowed, but it was actually darker than I thought it would be.

I made my way down the deserted street, mentally chewing (again!) on my problem at work. Then, suddenly, my path was filled with bright light. I looked up. It was a motion-sensitive light on one of the garages. I smiled at the puddle of light as I moved forward.

A few houses farther down the street, it happened again. Light. Just when I needed it. I kept walking, moving forward, waiting for the light to reappear. And it did. Again and again.

Back at my car, I was feeling better. My decisions were not as overwhelming as they seemed. All I had to do was move forward. And trust the light of God's wisdom to guide me at just the right moment.

> *All-knowing Father, direct my decisions.*
> *Purify my intentions. Let me be guided by Your light!*
> —MARY LOU CARNEY

Our mouths were filled with laughter
our tongues with songs of joy. —PSALM 126:2

*N*ervously I knocked at Mary Dell's door for the first time. Our sons were good buddies, and I knew I needed to introduce myself to her.

I remember waiting for someone to answer the doorbell and being too aware of myself that day—what I wore, what I might say. I was depressed, but help was about to reach me in a marvelous way.

As soon as she opened the door, I felt relieved. Mary Dell was refreshingly real—she came to the door wearing big fuzzy slippers, her hair in a messy ponytail, no makeup, wearing one of her husband's raggedy T-shirts and sweatpants covered in bleach stains.

Mary Dell's whimsical bay window was covered with bright markings drawn right on the glass—happy pictures, family jokes, and silly sayings. Their ancient dog Belle traipsed by me and made her way out the door leaving muddy tracks. Mary Dell didn't wipe them up.

"Want to go to the park?" She pulled on her tennis shoes, still wearing the same odd outfit.

"Sure," I said, trying to sound casual. *What will we talk about*?

We walked laps as our sons rode their bikes. I began to feel comfortable talking to Mary Dell. Really talking. She made me laugh about almost everything—even the unknown, the things I couldn't control. And she knew how to laugh at herself—something I'd never learned to do.

Now, when we walk, I smile. And I finally have the freedom to dress in clothes as mismatched as Mary Dell's.

> *Lord, how I thank You for Mary Dell and her gift*
> *of laughter. Surely it came from You.*

—JULIE GARMON

"Then you will know the truth, and the truth
will set you free." —JOHN 8:32

If Mama ain't happy, ain't nobody happy."

This popular ditty lived on a magnet on our refrigerator for years. At first, I liked the message because it affirmed the positive influence I have in our family. But over time, it began to weigh me down. Was I really in charge of everybody's moods? Yikes! What an exhausting responsibility! And what a guilt-producing message for a mom who already had a tendency to accept responsibility for all sorts of things she's not responsible for.

I learned in a parenting class that when I accept responsibilities that aren't mine—when I assume it's up to me to find lost shoes or be sure my children all have their stuff before they go out the door in the morning—I keep others from accepting theirs. And if I'm responsible for keeping my children happy, they won't learn that their choice of mood is up to them.

By the same logic, my mood is my responsibility, and I need to deal with it. Maybe the words on that magnet need to be changed to something like, "If Mama ain't happy, she might need a time-out." So far, nobody's asked me to edit refrigerator magnet messages. I guess that's not my responsibility.

Father, help me to learn what I'm responsible for
and what I'm not, which is a truth that will set me free.

—CAROL KUYKENDALL

September 16

Talk no more so very proudly, let not arrogance
come from your mouth. —1 Samuel 2:3 (RSV)

*S*ome years ago I saw an ad on television for some sort of cosmetic product or shampoo. The ad began with a model saying, "Don't hate me because I'm beautiful."

While I am not beautiful, I never had any inclination to hate her. I thank God—if not every day, then when it occurs to me—that I do not conform to the media's idea of beauty. Believe me, I have enough problems.

When I first came to Los Angeles, I had a roommate who was classically beautiful. She devoted at least half of her energy trying to ensure that she stayed that way, another quarter of it worrying about what it would be like if she lost that beauty, and the last quarter fretting that all men ever saw in her were her looks and that she would never be loved for herself.

I have been blessed with many things. If I were beautiful, too, I think I would have fallen into arrogance, thoughtlessness, and selfishness. But my looks have kept me, not humble, but humble enough. And I know for certain that I am loved for myself.

So I have to be grateful that God knew what He was doing when He decided to give me a roundish body, a narrow forehead, and pouchy eyes. He knew I'd need them to find my way from myself and closer to Him.

Thank You, God, for the imperfections in myself
that remind me of Your care for me.
—Rhoda Blecker

*Rest in the Lord, and wait patiently
for him.* —PSALM 37:7 (KJV)

*W*hen I was sixteen, I fell in love. I had just started dating then, and I was green and starry-eyed. Although I knew in a short while that it wasn't meant to be—the young man was a few years older than I, and we were from different worlds—my heart would have no part of it. I was convinced that I would never again feel the same way about another human being. In my innocence, I prayed that God would somehow correct all the problems in this unlikely relationship and give me the desire of my heart. For two years, I held on to my dream and repeated that prayer, wondering why God wasn't answering me.

At one point, I confessed my despair to my brother-in-law Marion.

"Be patient, Libbie," he said. "You'll probably end up marrying someone you haven't even met yet." That wasn't what I wanted to hear at all.

But by January of the following year, Marion's prediction had come true: I had met the man I've spent thirty-one years with, and who truly is the desire of my heart. And I'm grateful that God loved me enough to say no when I was asking Him for all the wrong things.

It's still true that God doesn't always respond to my prayers in the way I want Him to. But day by day, my experience teaches me that His way is always best.

*Father, help me to trust in Your plan for my life,
even when Your answer is no.*

—LIBBIE ADAMS

*Truly the light is sweet, and a pleasant thing it is
for the eyes to behold the sun.* —ECCLESIASTES 11:7 (KJV)

*D*riving the Southern California freeways during rush hour is a test of true grit and something to be avoided if at all possible. I had deliberately timed my return home from a conference in San Diego to miss the traffic. I was whizzing along, making good time when, suddenly, coming around the turn that feeds 57 North westward onto the 210 freeway, I found myself caught in a hideous backup. *Bother!* I thought. *Now what?*

By the time I had inched my way around the bend and was driving west, I had my answer. The long line of cars had all slowed down and were crawling along so that their drivers could see one of the most magnificent sunsets I have ever experienced. I joined the drivers who had moved their cars over to the right shoulder to stop and catch the wonder, mesmerized by the brilliant light that filled the sky with reds and gold and surreal electric pinks.

It didn't last long, probably no more than five or ten minutes. Then came the gray of dusk. As suddenly as we had been caught up in the glory of a celestial light show, we were once again earthbound. Those of us parked on the shoulder revved our engines, turned our wheels, and jostled our way back into the rush of the traffic.

I didn't think a sunset could get any better than the ones I'd seen over the ocean in Hawaii, but here in midst of the stress-filled California rush-hour traffic, God splashed a canvas across the sky of such dazzling glory that freeway drivers slowed, pulled over, and bestowed the accolade of a pause that, in our best Hollywood tradition, applauded "Bravo!"

*How magnificent is Your handiwork, Lord God of creation!
And how much more will be Your glory
when I see You face-to-face!*

—FAY ANGUS

September 19

A time to laugh. —Ecclesiastes 3:4

I was babysitting three of my grandchildren, and it was time to bathe two-year-old Thomas. I got him and all his toys into the tub and began to wash him, sitting at an angle on the edge so I could continue talking with Jamie and Katie, his sisters. Then before I could catch myself, I lost my balance, slipped backward, and fell into the tub fully clothed!

My granddaughters laughed hysterically. Thomas, observing them for a few seconds, threw his head back and joined in the laughter. As I sat in the warm water with my arms and legs extended, I felt this tremendous laugh making its way out. I leaned against the pink tiles and let it come. The four of us were joined together by our laughter, which lasted for perhaps three minutes and was exhausting and satisfying and unforgettable.

Of course, I wouldn't have laughed in my young motherhood days. I would have resented anything that made me look less than perfect, and would have been in a nasty mood for the rest of the evening, probably not speaking. And we would never have mentioned the incident again.

I'm glad I have finally learned—through experience, age, and God's grace—that there's a time to laugh, even at myself and my humanness.

Father, help me to see the lighter side of things.
—Marion Bond West

Be not thou afraid when one is made rich. —PSALM 49:16 (KJV)

We've worked hard, but money-wise, it's been a tough year. So the phone call was the proverbial straw that broke the camel's back.

"Pam, did you hear about Paige? She just inherited over a million dollars from an aunt she never knew existed!"

Okay, God, I thought after I hung up, *this is a bit hard to understand.* Paige has never had to work, never taken her children to church, never helped with community projects. In fact, her biggest concern seems to be her golf game. *Why her, God?*

After that, my anger came in odd ways: Writing a check for groceries, an unfamiliar bitterness tightened my heart. In a parking lot, my eyes fell on a red convertible and I gritted my teeth in hopelessness.

Finally, late one sleepless night, I went out to sit on the porch. I thought about my life. It's a very good life. I thought of our son Brock's progress in his job, the people he's been able to help, the way he's careful to tithe his money to church. I thought of Keri, focused on becoming a psychotherapist for the right reasons. She's always doing something to make life better for someone else. I thought of my husband David, who never says no when I come up with some idea for a project that will ultimately cost him time or money. The truth is, I am very, very rich in all the things money can't buy. I wouldn't sell a single one of my blessings for a million dollars. "So why am I so angry?" I whispered to the night. And I knew exactly what I needed to do.

God, tonight I am so ashamed. I know that You always find a way to fill my family's needs. Yet, something good happens to my friend and I get angry and afraid. For a long time, I've been telling You that I want to be a person who feels joy in the good fortune of others. First, I'm going to hand my future over to You, Father. Then I'm going to show You the kind of person I want to become.

That night I slept like a baby. The next day I called Paige to tell her how happy I was for her. The words came from a light and joyful heart—and from one very rich friend to another!

Father, You have given me so much. Give me a grateful heart
to share in the joys and sorrows of my neighbors.
—PAM KIDD

Hear my voice when I call, O Lord. —PSALM 27:7

*S*unday morning found me in the Seattle, Washington, airport, waiting to catch a plane back to Chicago. I moved through the crowded boarding area, too restless just to sit and wait. Other travelers checked their watches, read their books, or worked on their laptops. But mostly, they talked on their cell phones.

I caught snatches of conversations as husbands phoned wives, sons checked in with their mothers, sisters caught up on all the news. It seemed as though everyone was talking to his or her family!

Everyone except me. I looked at my new cell phone, cute and snug in the side of my purse. Problem was, I'd forgotten to charge it the night before, and my battery was too low to make any calls. *How could I have been so forgetful?*

I was working myself into a bad mood when I happened to glance out the window. The sky seemed to go on forever, a pale blue broken by patches of angel-hair clouds. On the horizon, stately pine trees poked their heads toward the arching expanse. A wide-winged bird came briefly into view before veering off and soaring out of sight. And like that bird, my spirit began to rise, too. *I don't need a cell phone to communicate*, I thought. So there in the midst of the hubbub of Gate C7, I closed my eyes and began a silent conversation. *Hello, Father. I just thought I'd check in with You....*

A few minutes later, as I boarded the plane, I watched the other passengers stow their cell phones. Smiling, I patted the side of my purse, grateful for the low battery that led to my leisurely preflight conversation with my heavenly Father.

*How good it is, God, to know that I can always
"phone home" and find You waiting for my call!*

—MARY LOU CARNEY

September 22

"As a mother comforts her child,
so will I comfort you." —Isaiah 66:13

My husband Whitney and I had just come home from an overnight trip, and our pet sitter wore a long face. "That wild kitten got in the house," she said. "He's upstairs and won't let me near him. I'm so sorry."

The kitten belonged to a stray named Babe who lived on our porch. She had given birth to him in the woods. He'd never seen a human till the week before, when she brought him home to us. He was as wild as could be, and now he was in the house. I hadn't a clue how to catch him.

I climbed the stairs in dread. There he was, his little yellow face poking around the corner. When he saw me, he hissed and raised his back, unsheathed his claws, and sprang for my face. I ducked just in time. He ran to the bedroom; I ran in after him and closed the door.

The kitten was hunched in a corner under the bed, panting with fear. I thought about ways to trap him. *The butterfly net! If I chase him long enough and tire him out, I can put the net over him. Then I'll cover the net with a towel and....*

But, no. The little guy would never get over the trauma if I used such force. *Think, Shari, think. If you were that kitten, what would take away your terror?* I closed the door softly, went out to the porch, picked up the mother cat, and carried her up to the bedroom. She sniffed at the rug. "Meow," she called. I heard a rustling from under the bed.

The kitten's taut little face appeared, draped with the dust ruffle.

He raced to greet his mother. She washed his ears and talked to him in soft meows. He purred. Ever so gently I nudged them both into the crate I had waiting and carried it downstairs to the porch. When I opened the crate, kitten and mother strolled out.

I bowed my head and said:

Thank You, God, for comfort and comforters.

—Shari Smyth

*I will praise thee; for I am fearfully
and wonderfully made.*
—PSALM 139:14 (KJV)

O ne of my favorite memories of my mother is the celebration of her last birthday. Her worsening emphysema, the result of a childhood lung infection, had mostly confined her to bed by the age of sixty-five. But on this glorious spring day, we surprised her by having a horse-drawn hayrack pull into her driveway, loaded with all of her children and grandchildren carrying balloons and singing "Happy Birthday." We bundled her up, put her on a lawn chair, along with her oxygen tank, and off we went for a ride on country roads at sunset. She'd always loved horses, sunsets, and family celebrations.

In our family, birthdays have always mattered. When our kids were little, we started with balloons at breakfast and candles in the doughnuts on the red-and-white "This Is Your Special Day" plate.

The kids are grown and on their own now, but we're still a birthday family. Though I can't find any Scripture that exactly says this, I believe that God, who gave us our birth dates, intends our annual birthdays to be a time to consider the unique gift of His personal creation of each of us. It's a great time to think about who He created us to be, and where we are in the process of becoming that person. Though we grow up, we never outgrow the opportunity to celebrate that life-shaping gift. That's why birthdays matter.

*Lord, may I use my birthday to
celebrate the person You created me to be.*
—CAROL KUYKENDALL

SEPTEMBER 24

How shall we sing the Lord's song in a strange land?
—PSALM 137:4 (KJV)

One morning, a few months after Robert and I were married, I woke up with an insistent longing I didn't understand. I knew it wasn't dissatisfaction with our marriage. I had never in my life felt so happy and fulfilled. What could possibly be missing?

Rather than try to figure it out, I gave the question to God and went back to sleep. A few days later Robert said something about "community," and it went straight into my heart where the ache was.

When we were first married, we were so busy setting up a household that all we wanted was to be with each other. We kept talking about finding a church and we visited a few, but we didn't feel a real need to belong. Since we prayed together daily, we felt we already were a community of two. But could it be that wholeness in a relationship calls for a third dimension—the dimension of *reaching out together*?

Suddenly I remembered a day when I was about seven years old, when the new music teacher asked each child to sing a line from the songbook so she'd know where to seat us for class. My heart was pounding because I'd been told that I couldn't carry a tune. My singing that day was way off-key, but Miss May was a wise teacher. She placed me in the center of a group of children with good pitch. And I found, to my utter surprise, that in that situation I really could carry a tune.

I think it's like that in a church family. A beautiful chorus is created by all the voices singing together. When one gets off pitch, the influence of the whole can bring that person back into harmony. Robert and I have now found our place as part of a spiritual community, and I've come to see that as we reach out together, our own song becomes more harmonious. It's a big part of what makes our holy love whole.

> *Be the Conductor of our chorus, O God,*
> *and let us always seek to blend our notes with others*
> *into Your perfect harmony.*
> —MARILYN MORGAN KING

I will hear what God the Lord will speak.
—PSALM 85:8 (KJV)

My baby grandson stayed overnight with us the other night. He had to sleep in an adult bed. I was afraid he might wake and crawl to fall from the bed. I found myself listening all night. I'm sure that I woke every time he stirred. If one of my own children has troubles, I hear it immediately in their voices. If one of my husband's machines or motors changes sound in the slightest, he instantly hears it. We hear best what we listen for, what most interests and concerns us.

Sometimes I don't listen intently enough. One rainy day last week I intended to stay in by my warm fire and read a new book. First thing in the morning a thought came to me that I should go visit a neighbor of mine. I certainly did not want to go. I pushed the thought away. Again and again through the morning the thought came back to me: *Go see Millie.* It would not leave my mind. After lunch I kept thinking of her until, finally, I splashed out into the rain and drove to Millie's house. I found her so lonely that she was in tears. That afternoon was a few hours I will always remember. For when I left, she was cheerful again.

Holy Father, help me to listen to the still small voice.
—LUCILLE CAMPBELL

Wisdom is with the aged men, with long life
is understanding. —JOB 12:12 (NASB)

For several years I've participated in a writers' group once a month. I critique their work, answer questions, and offer advice on getting published. I try to encourage the members as much as I can. They're quite prolific; they often send their work to magazine and book editors, and enter contests. Some have seen their prose in print, and others have finished ambitious memoirs they're trying to get published.

Why is this group so special? Every member is over the age of eighty. Their founder is still writing poetry at ninety-five. They inspire me because they all have dreams—of writing a good story, seeing it published, and sharing it with others. And aside from the occasional jokes about fading memory and bifocals, they don't see their age as an obstacle to achieving their dreams. In fact, as each day passes, they continue to use the gifts God has given them. Age is never an issue.

Thanks to these friends, I'm filled with hope when I try to picture myself twice the age I am now. I don't fear growing older because I've seen that enthusiasm and good humor can help keep my spirit young. Also, I know that God will still have work for me. I think of others whom God put to work in their later years: biblical heroes like Noah and Moses, and more recent heroes like Mother Teresa and the Reverend Billy Graham. As my own parents continue to work and volunteer, I see firsthand that God will have plenty for me to do as long as I'm healthy and my spirit is willing to follow where He leads me.

Lord, as my body grows older,
keep me young in heart, mind, and spirit.

—GINA BRIDGEMAN

The memory of the just is blessed. —PROVERBS 10:7 (KJV)

*N*ot long ago I stayed with my four grandchildren, who live in another state, while their parents were away for the weekend. As I loaded them in my car for a trip to the bookstore, video store, then supermarket, the eight-year-old asked, "How old are you, Grandma?"

I told him my age, whereupon for a long moment he pondered my five-and-a-half-decade advantage, and then declared, "Grandma, when I'm your age, you'll be in heaven!"

Since I couldn't argue with that, I only said, "You're right, Nicholas." Then, laying his hand on my arm, he said softly, "But, Grandma, I won't ever forget you."

Of course, being the doting grandmother that I am, that memory brings tears of love every time I think of it. But it also made me wonder just how my grandchildren will remember me. Will they remember the tired grandmother who loses patience at the end of a long day and hurries them off to bed? Or will they remember the fun grandmother who takes them to the playground and packs a picnic for the park?

Now when I have the opportunity to be with my grandchildren, I work at making memories—of a loving grandmother who always has the time to listen to them, to play with them, and to show my love for them.

Dear Lord, help me to leave behind
kind and loving memories.
—PATRICIA PINGRY

*O Lord, open thou my lips: and my mouth shall
shew forth thy praise.* —PSALM 51:15 (KJV)

The letter came on the stationery of a pottery barn in Vermont. "You probably won't remember me," the woman wrote, "but I want to thank you for your part in launching this business."

I read on in bewilderment. A pottery business in Vermont? We'd met, the letter continued, at the Mohonk Mountain House some years ago. I remembered the occasion very well—a Wildflower Weekend at a nature preserve in upstate New York. But there had been eighty or more flower enthusiasts taking part, and I didn't, in fact, recall this particular lady.

She, however, remembered a remark of mine on one of the guided walks. The leader had pointed out a cluster of bluets at the edge of the woods that, unlike their vigorous cousins carpeting the meadow, were stunted and colorless. "They just got started in the wrong place," he said. And I, apparently, had commented, "It's a good thing people can pick up and move."

"Your words were like a shaft of light in a dark place," the woman wrote. Miserable in a desk job in the city, she'd eventually sold her condo, moved to Vermont, and turned her ceramics hobby into a full-time business.

All this, I wondered, *from a throwaway remark I can't remember making*? But, of course, mine was just a tiny piece in a design only God saw whole. The plan for her life was His, that shaft of light on her path, His words to her alone. The significance of my comment was beyond my knowing. What I do know, what this letter tells me, is that the role each of us is given to play in the lives around us is greater than we dream.

*Remind me during the year ahead, Father, that You
can reach out to Your children through
anyone at all...even me.*
—ELIZABETH SHERRILL

*Thou openest thine hand, and satisfiest the desire
of every living thing.* —PSALM 145:16 (KJV)

*D*o you sometimes wonder if the prayers of a mother's heart
are answered?

Recently I've been praying that our twenty-five-year-old daughter Lindsay
would know God's love in a special, tangible way. Two nights ago, she called
from California; her voice broke as she said, "Mom, my bird flew away." Her
bird is a cockatiel that is more than a bird because of the way it responds to
Lindsay. Sometimes she lets it fly around her apartment, and when she whistles,
the bird echoes the sound and lands on her shoulder.

Lindsay said the bird flew out her patio door that afternoon, flopped around
on the roof, and then disappeared into the trees. She blamed herself and spent
three hours scouring the neighborhood, looking up into treetops and whistling.
She saw and heard nothing. "When these birds get stressed, they are apt to keep
getting farther away, and I know it won't be able to survive long outdoors,"
she said.

The next morning, Lindsay got up early and looked again before going to
work. At noon she decided to drive home and try one more time. As she whistled
at the trees around her apartment, a woman appeared and told her she thought
she had heard the bird at the swimming pool several blocks away. Off Lindsay
went, and as she neared the pool, she began whistling. Way in the distance, she
heard a faint echo. Again she whistled. Again the faint echo. She kept following
the sound, which got a little louder, until she came to a tall wrought-iron fence,
and there on the other side, hopping along the ground, was her bird. Lindsay
whistled as she stuck her arm through the wrought-iron fence and the bird
jumped on to it, crawling up to her chest where it snuggled down, whistling
in response.

"I found my bird!" Lindsay told me gleefully when she called later.

The song in my heart is still singing with praise.
—CAROL KUYKENDALL

They that dwell under his shadow shall return...
and grow as the vine. —HOSEA 14:7 (KJV)

W hen my children were small, I was the magical elf of our pumpkin patch. In mid-August, when the pumpkin vines began setting on fruits about the size of apples, I would sneak into the garden with a nail, stick, or barbecue skewer, and scratch each child's name on a baby pumpkin. The scratches made a thin mark, but didn't otherwise damage the fruit. Better yet, the tiny globes remained invisible beneath the broad, scratchy pumpkin leaves and my work went unnoticed.

Over the next few weeks as the pumpkins swelled and turned first ivory, then yellow, then brilliant orange, the scars would grow, too, stretching with the shell and forming a brownish welt. By harvest time each fifteen-pound pumpkin would be personalized with a two-inch-tall name—a source of infinite amazement and speculation.

After the first September cold snap, I would casually suggest, "Maybe we'd better go pick those pumpkins." My four children would rush to the dead garden and easily spot the orange pumpkins glowing like lanterns amid the leaves blackened and shriveled by frost.

"Mom," Tess would suddenly shriek, "it has my *name*!" The enchantment never failed. As the older children caught on, they still let Trina, the youngest, delight in finding her special pumpkin without spoiling my secret. Even when all the children were old enough to solve the mystery, they would remind Mom to "go name the pumpkins" as soon as they first bulged on the vine.

I haven't grown pumpkins for years now and half of my children have left home. Very often I wonder whether my relationship with God has made any difference in their lives. *Did I pass on my faith really and truly? Did I make an impact?* Then I pause to consider the faint etchings on those tiny pumpkins—and know that in God's good time, for my children, too, there will indeed be a joyful harvest.

Lord of creation, thank You for the miracle
of growth, in my garden and in myself.
—GAIL THORELL SCHILLING

October

OCTOBER 1

*T*he road ahead was dark and deserted. My car's wipers whined as they pushed a mixture of snow and ice back and forth across the windshield. I grasped the steering wheel with white knuckles and prayed silently. My daughter Keri and I were driving toward Birmingham, Alabama, where she was to participate in a scholarship competition the next morning. Winter storms are an oddity in the South, and I was terrified. I didn't want Keri to know.

She sat silently beside me, eyes straight ahead.

"If you want, you can turn on the radio," I said. Static followed, then a jumble of voices and music, and finally Elton John filled the car with a love song.

My heart melted, thinking of the child beside me. Then, in the midst of my anguished prayers for all the dark unknowns, the presence of God filled my heart with a confident knowing. "Keri," I said, "someday we'll remember this moment and everything I'm about to say will already be true. You are going to get a good scholarship. You are going to excel in college. Someone very wonderful is going to fall in love with you, and all the scattered, confusing pieces of your life will fit perfectly together. I know this because God has put it in my heart to say this to you.

"Someday we'll be dancing at your wedding, and we'll remember this night, and we'll laugh with happiness. Who knows? I might even get Elton John to sing this very song as you walk out onto the floor for the first dance!"

Five years later, I pick up the phone. Keri gives me a glowing report of her first class in graduate school. She speaks of the teenage girls she will be counseling and offers an update on her boyfriend, who attends another graduate school nearby. "Mama, have you written to Elton John yet?" she says with a chuckle. And with those words she tells me everything a mother needs to know.

*Dear God, in my scariest moments, You point me
to the place where, in Your time, You fit the pieces of my life
together into a perfect whole. Thank You.*

—PAM KIDD

Always seek after that which is good for one another
and for all people. —1 THESSALONIANS 5:15 (NASB)

When I rediscovered that wonderful childhood poem "The Cupboard," by Walter de la Mare, in an old poetry book, I had no idea what fun it would become for my five-year-old grandson Caleb and me. We were visiting my son in his new home. Phil had, to a child's mind, a "portal to another kingdom" in his kitchen—a tall white cupboard in which he stockpiled just about every kind of candy there is.

Caleb would have cleaned him out if I hadn't declared, "I am in charge of the cupboard."

"I have a small fat grandmama," I quoted,
"With a very slippery knee,
And she's Keeper of the Cupboard,
With the key, key, key.
And when I'm very good, my dear,
As good as good can be,
There's Banbury Cakes, and Lollipops
For me, me, me."

I even had a small key with which I pretended to open the cupboard door.

Caleb, catching the spirit, eyes gleaming, recited, "When I'm very good... as good as good can be," every time he thought he should have a treat. Inserting the names of the goodies in Phil's stash, he'd say, "There's cherry twists and jelly beans for me, me, me."

Engaging our imaginations, Caleb and I created a great memory with that poem and my son's candy cupboard. The poem focused us on kindness and goodness in our daily interactions, because the secret of the cupboard isn't the key or the candy...the secret is in what *really* opens the cupboard door.

Jesus, Your goodness and kindness, imparted to me,
open eternal treasures to which You hold the key.

—CAROL KNAPP

OCTOBER 3

Being reviled, we bless —1 CORINTHIANS 4:12 (KJV)

*W*hen our teenage grandchildren were small, our visits to their home always brought a chorus of "Can we go home with you?" or "Can we come and stay the night!" We loved having them.

At bedtime, Marinell, the youngest of the three, liked to snuggle down in the big, extra-long bed that had been her father's and listen to me read a story. When her eyelids became heavy, we said our prayers and then I would wind up the little plush puppy that played "Lullaby" as she drifted off to sleep.

One night when saying her prayers, she said, "God bless Mama, God bless Daddy; God bless Paul Mark; God bless Grandma and Grandpa."

"You left out Stokes," I told her.

"I'm not going to 'God bless him.'"

Surprised, I asked, "Why not?"

"Because he wouldn't let me have the marbles."

"But we must forgive our enemies," I reminded her.

"He's not my enemy, he's my brother," she said firmly.

"Then *I'll* ask God to bless him," I told her. "God bless all brothers."

As I tucked her in, I heard a small voice murmur, "God bless Stokes."

Later, after I had kissed Marinell good night and left the room, I thought of the lesson: were I to look at all people as my *brothers* and no one as my *enemies*, there would be far more thanks and blessings in my prayers.

heavenly Father, remind me that peace does not begin
with other people, but with myself.
—ZONA B. DAVIS

OCTOBER 4

Charm can be deceptive and beauty doesn't last,
but a woman who fears and reverences God shall be
greatly praised. —PROVERBS 31:30 (TLB)

It was early fall, and my morning prayer routine was starting to slip by the wayside. Sort of the way my personal appearance had slipped since I quit my job at the radio station to stay home and work.

Just before my forty-ninth birthday, my sister Catherine arrived for a weekend. She plopped a gift bag filled with eight little presents on my lap. "Happy birthday! Here's to a new you!" she said, her eyes twinkling.

I opened box after box. Lipstick, eyeliner, blush, eye shadows, little brushes to apply them all, and a case to keep them in.

While I was thinking to myself that I liked my "plain Jane" look, she whisked me into the bathroom and applied touches of highlighter, shadow, and liner to my eyes. When Catherine finished my makeover, I couldn't believe my eyes. They looked bigger, brighter. *Nice.* I liked it all...the blush, the lipstick, the whole look.

"It takes a little time every morning, but if you do it every day it'll become a habit," she advised.

After Catherine's visit, I thought about my other "habit" that I'd let slip. Daily prayer. I thought, *What if I combined my prayer time with my makeup time?*

The next day, as I added a touch of eye shadow, I prayed, "Lord, please let these eyes of mine see the needs of others and respond accordingly."

With the blush brush in hand I said, "Lord, my cheeks are pretty full. Help me to watch the fat grams today and exercise. Keep these cheeks smiling, Lord. Help me to see the good in others and to pass out smiles by the truckload."

Finally, the lipstick. "Lord, help me to use my mouth and the words that come out of it to Your glory. Help me to speak only with kindness."

My makeup routine is now a habit. So are my morning "makeup" prayers.

Thanks, Lord, for all the daily reminders
to come to You in prayer. Thanks, also, for a sister
who wants me to be the best I can be!

—PATRICIA LORENZ

OCTOBER 5

For we know not what we should pray for as we ought:
but the Spirit itself maketh intercession for us with groanings
which cannot be uttered. —ROMANS 8:26 (KJV)

I was a young teen then, thoroughly uninterested in house chores. The ironing board wobbled and groaned as I drove the iron into the shirt collar one more time. It crinkled even more.

"Your trouble is that you're working too hard," Grandma said, taking the iron. "Let the heat do the work, not all that pushing and pressing." Almost effortlessly, she ironed the collar smooth.

That happened a long time ago, but I thought of it again on a recent hectic day. I had run to the window for the hundredth time to check my toddler, then back to folding laundry. Could I get Breton to piano lessons and back in time to babysit? And what about the PTA? By afternoon, stress weighed heavily on me like an overloaded backpack.

Suddenly I could see Grandma taking the iron: "All that pushing and pressing!" I should be letting the Holy Spirit do the work! Wasn't that what "casting all your care upon him" (1 Peter 5:7 KJV) was about?

Sure enough, as I made time to pray for help, I found that the still small voice was present: "Your husband would be willing to help with the driving. Don't be so worried about telling the PTA 'no' this time." Before I knew it, my day's work was done, and I even had time to relax that evening with my family.

Are you working too hard today? Remember Grandma's words: "Let the heat do the work."

> *Lord, help me remember that Your burden*
> *is light when carried in the Spirit.*
>
> —KATHIE KANIA

Behold, you are beautiful, my love; behold,
you are beautiful. —SONG OF SOLOMON 1:15 (RSV)

*V*isiting our grandson's school for the first time, I was startled to discover that his second-grade teacher had a disfiguring birthmark covering nearly half her face. A dark purple discoloration spread from her left ear across her cheek and lower lip to her jaw line.

Warm and welcoming, the woman herself had obviously come to terms long since with the burden of an unusual appearance. It was I who felt awkward, conscious of the effort to neither look away nor stare. *If it was hard for me as an adult, how*, I wondered, *did our seven-year-old grandchild handle it?*

I found out when he got home from school that afternoon. "Your teacher seems like a very nice lady," I ventured.

The youngster nodded. "She doesn't look like other teachers," he said.

I nodded, waiting to hear how he would handle the situation. "Yes," he went on, "even when we're noisy, she has a smiley face."

It was said in a child's piping voice, but the message I heard was God's. *I don't look at your blemishes either*, I heard Him say. *I look at you with the eyes of love.*

Let me see through Your eyes, Father,
the beauty in each person I meet today.

—ELIZABETH SHERRILL

OCTOBER 7

"Bring the whole tithe into the storehouse...
and see if I will not throw open the floodgates of heaven
and pour out so much blessing that you will not have
room enough for it." —MALACHI 3:10

*S*aturday morning I sit at the kitchen table with my five-year-old daughter Elizabeth, a pile of dimes, her piggy bank (actually a wrinkled brown dog), and a box of church envelopes. We are disbursing her first allowance, a hefty one dollar!

"Why are you giving me ten dimes, Mom?"

"Well, this is how your grandpa did it with me."

I remember Saturday mornings years ago, another kitchen table, pile of nickels, my own bank, and a question: "But why do we put a nickel in the bank and give a nickel to church, Daddy?"

"Because we give God one-tenth of what we earn, and we save one-tenth." Then Dad stacked the coins to show how 10 percent of fifty cents is a nickel.

The clink of a coin in the bank followed, then the solemn sealing of the church envelope and Dad's proclamation, "Now you have forty cents left to spend however you want!" *Forty cents*! An enormous sum in those days of penny candy and nickel soda pops. I'd pick up the nickels and dash off on my bike to the corner root beer stand.

As Elizabeth seals her church envelope, puts Wrinkles back on the shelf, and runs to show Daddy her bulging coin purse, I smile and am encouraged. Alex and I are to tackle revising our budget this week. Our expenses are increasing, but our income is not. Still, I'm reminded of Dad's good math. God's timeless formula works in any age. If we give to God first, what is left will be enough.

Help me to give unselfishly to You, Lord,
and to trust Your promise to provide.

—MARY BROWN

OCTOBER 8

A fool takes no pleasure in understanding, but only in expressing his opinion. —PROVERBS 18:2 (RSV)

One of the biggest surprises I've uncovered in my family history research is that John Ross, my maternal great-grandfather, was fifty-four years old when his only child, my grandfather, was born.

"How strange," I remember saying when my mom and I made the discovery. I even rechecked the dates to be sure we hadn't made a mistake. "Imagine becoming a father when most of his friends must have been grandfathers," I said.

"I'll bet there's an interesting story there," Mom added.

Continuing to research, I learned that my great-grandmother Mary was John's second wife, more than twenty years younger. His first wife had died young, and when he married my great-grandmother, both longed to have children even though they were well past the typical age for first-time parents in the nineteenth century. They had good reasons for doing what I had considered so strange.

Their story made me wonder how often I fail to consider the circumstances that lie behind the actions of others. I thought of an angry boy in my son Ross's class whom I was quick to dismiss, not realizing his behavior may have been caused by his parents' sudden divorce. I also remembered an acquaintance who'd been mourning a close friend's death for many months and was still uninterested in socializing. I'd criticized her to others, not understanding that her pain was so great she simply needed more time.

My own way of seeing things often looms so large before me it eclipses other possibilities. But if I can push it aside long enough to see things from another's perspective, it's much easier to bridge the chasm between us. I can invite Ross's classmate over to play or call my friend just to talk. So it seems that one of the basics of genealogy, taking the time to find out *why*, serves me well in everyday life, too.

*Lord, whether I'm looking back one hundred years
or across the room at a friend, guide me
to a better understanding, a greater compassion,
and a more loving heart.*

—GINA BRIDGEMAN

OCTOBER 9

Make sure there is no root among you that produces
such bitter poison. —DEUTERONOMY 29:18

The weeds in my rock garden have been especially pesky this year, in spite of my efforts to pluck away at the problem.

"You can't do it that way," a gardener-friend told me as she watched me casually pull a couple of weeds from a bed of bright yellow marigolds. "You've got to dig down deeper and get the whole root system, or that same weed will just keep reappearing year after year." She then rummaged through my basket of garden tools, pulled out a long weed digger, plunged it into the dirt next to a weed, and dug out the weed, along with a clump of dirt. "This is how you get to the root of the problem," she said, sounding like some wise weed philosopher.

Her words got me to thinking about some of the pesky weeds in my life. Take procrastination, for instance. On some days, I have a bad habit of putting off the most important tasks that I must tackle. Finally, I force myself to start the project, but in a couple of days procrastination crops up again. If I stop and dig deeper around the edges of this habit, I find that it is rooted in a fear that I won't do a good job or that I won't adequately meet someone else's expectations. What if I dig out my fear of failure and surrender it to God in prayer?

Thanks to my weed philosopher, my garden is starting to look a little better—and so is my life.

Father, help me get to the roots of my problems
and surrender them to You in prayer.

—CAROL KUYKENDALL

OCTOBER 10

Then Jesus told his disciples a parable to show them
that they should always pray. —LUKE 18:1

*E*ven though it was seven years old, our shiny "new" van was a vast improvement over our battered fourteen-year-old four-wheel-drive utility vehicle. It started, even in cold weather, never stalled when turning, and shifted into reverse without complaint. It never leaked oil or smelled of gasoline. The radio, tape deck, and air conditioner all worked. I could even haul my three children, plus a friend, each in comfort. With its glossy paint and an uncracked windshield, we nicknamed the handsome van Silver Belle.

I had been enjoying Silver Belle for a week or two when I noticed I no longer prayed while I was driving. While I owned the older vehicle, I had invariably started my morning with petitions: *Lord, please let her start! God, don't let me get stuck in the driveway! Lord, let that noise be something harmless and that gas smell be from somewhere else!* After the old vehicle grudgingly sputtered to life on the ninth or tenth attempt, I would mutter a quick prayer of thanksgiving, then head to my substitute-teaching job, continuing to pray about other matters. Now that I drove a vehicle that started, I forgot to pray at all!

I've had to jump-start my prayer life. Instead of asking my heavenly Father for help when I buckle my seat belt, I remember to say, "I thank You, Lord, for a safe vehicle." Most days I can easily think of more blessings to acknowledge: my healthy children; the day's work ; the dramatic Wyoming vistas on the way to school. I still ask God for help when I need it, but I try to remember to say "thank You" even when I don't need to say "please."

Lord, let me always be grateful for answered prayer.
—GAIL THORELL SCHILLING

OCTOBER 11

God has given each of us the ability
to do certain things well. —ROMANS 12:6 (TLB)

*M*y daughter Amy Jo had passed the bar exam, and she and I had driven down to Indianapolis for the swearing-in ceremony. After today, Amy Jo would be licensed to practice law in the state of Indiana—to stand before judges and plead cases, to write briefs and give counsel, to protect people unjustly accused, to "defend the Constitution of the United States against all enemies."

A gavel pounds and the court is called to order. The judges file in—their billowing robes somehow even blacker than the sea of business suits that surrounds them. The soon-to-be lawyers shuffle in, pausing at the microphone to say their names to the judges before whom they will practice. They are nervous, serious, well-groomed. Finally, Amy Jo appears. She's easy to spot: blonde, beautiful, poised—and seven months pregnant. Her black jacket buttons spread neatly across her wide belly. Inside, my grandchild is also a witness to this auspicious event. "Amy Jo Redman," she says confidently into the mike. I smile, remembering the ten-year-old girl who asked one rainy afternoon, "Mom, do you think I'm smart enough to be a lawyer?" My answer:

"Certainly!"

Later, I applaud (perhaps a bit too loudly) along with other proud families. Someday, my grandchild may wonder if he or she is good enough or bright enough or talented enough to follow a dream. When that time comes, I'm sure Amy Jo will know just what to say. She is, after all, pretty smart.

Every good and perfect gift comes from You, Lord.
Thank You for dreams—and for the intelligence
and perseverance to pursue them.

—MARY LOU CARNEY

OCTOBER 12

*Don't you think that God will surely give justice to his people
who plead with him day and night? Yes! He will
answer them quickly!.* —LUKE 18:7, 8 (TLB)

You can tell a lot about a person by looking at the front of his or her refrigerator. My seventy-seven-year-old stepmother Bev has magnets on hers from some of the countries she and my dad have visited over the years. My busy son Michael and his wife Amy have large magnetic alphabet letters at the bottom of their refrigerator for their little ones, Hannah and Zachary, to practice their spelling words. My friend Sharon has hundreds of tiny magnetic words on her refrigerator, so her whole family can create sweet, goofy, or sentimental poems.

My refrigerator is what reminds me to pray a dozen times a day, because the top two-thirds of it is a solid mass of four-by-six-inch photos. Everyone, from 101-year-old Great-Aunt Peggy and ninety-five-year-old Aunt Helen, to my two-year-old granddaughter Riley. My four children, their spouses, my other four grandchildren, my folks, brother, sister, their families, other aunts, uncles, cousins, and assorted friends all hold a place of honor on my refrigerator.

One is a picture of Jane Knapp, a friend I've never met in person.

She interviewed me by telephone on her small radio station years ago, and we struck up an immediate friendship. Jane's e-mails were gut-wrenching updates about her cancer. One day, after months of chemo, I received this note from Jane:

"The doctor called a few minutes ago and told me that the PET scan results showed new cancers in my liver, kidney, and lung. He said usually new cancers do not pop up at the same time, so I'm very discouraged but have to keep believing in the power of prayer."

Jane's photo and all the others on that frequently opened door help keep my loved ones in my mind, heart, and prayers many times a day, every day.

> *Lord, bless, protect, and comfort every person
> whose face is on my refrigerator. And thank You,
> especially, for putting them into my life.*
>
> —PATRICIA LORENZ

OCTOBER 13

And God made the beast of the earth according to its kind,
cattle according to its kind, and everything that creeps
on the earth according to its kind. And God saw
that it was good. —GENESIS 1:25 (NKJV)

The small waiting room at the veterinarian's office was crowded with animals and their humans, including me and my two big dogs, Roscoe and Chaucer. They were getting their nails clipped. The woman next to me held a Schnauzer on her lap. "Routine shots," she said. A balding man with a beard stroked his black mitten-foot cat. "Infected chigger bites," he said. One woman was silent, gently patting the top of a small animal crate, her foot swinging nervously. Finally, the balding man asked, "Is it a cat in there?"

"Yes, she's having kittens," the woman answered. "She's had two, but the third one won't come. She's been in labor all night. She was a stray. She arrived on my doorstep one night, pregnant. I named her Buffy. She's a calico. I'll have her spayed after this, but I'm keeping the kittens."

The room was now silent; all heads turned to the dark interior of the crate that hid Buffy. "She's so sweet and such a good mother to the two already born." The woman stopped and bent her face to the cage door. "Oh, she's had it! Look, here it is!" Carefully opening the door, she held up a wet, mewling little thing, the size of a hairball, its mouth making sucking motions. We clapped, cheered, and beamed at each other. I felt tears on my cheeks.

Why all this emotion? I wondered. *Is it for the woman who took in a homeless feline? For the triumph of the mother cat?* Yes and yes. But a deeper awareness showed itself on each face and in me. Awe. No matter how small the creature, birth is a miracle. As God ordained it so long ago.

Creator God, thank You for the daily miracles
through which You renew Your creation.

—SHARI SMYTH

OCTOBER 14

*Do not conform any longer to the pattern
of this world, but be transformed by the renewing
of your mind.* —ROMANS 12:2

Richard, my oldest grandson, had shown early signs of artistic talent, and since I'm an amateur painter, his mom asked me to give him a weekly art lesson. I let him experiment with pastels, watercolors, and acrylic paints, but he limited himself by making line drawings first, before he'd use any colors.

Finally, one day, I set up a photo of a tiger for a model and said, "Don't draw any lines. Just imagine an invisible tiger on your paper. Color his white throat, his cream chest, his tan sides, his red-brown back and head. Only after coloring his whole shape may you put in his eyes, nose, mouth, and stripes."

Richard worked with pastels until he completed a tiger-colored cloud. Then he added facial features and, lastly, the stripes. On his paper hunkered a truly impressive tiger.

Sometimes I feel that God is an art teacher and I'm the student. My life is my canvas. Like Richard, I try to draw details before I paint any basic design. I pray, "Help me to be more patient," and God says, "Be filled with the Spirit." I want to be a better grandmother, and God says, "Don't be anxious about anything, but trust Me." I pray for a more organized household, and God says, "Forgive your husband." I think I'm beginning to understand. I need to have the shape and color of Christ within me before my Christian stripes will look real.

*Father, help me to be a true artist, as You inspire me
through the Spirit of Christ living in me.*

—ELSIE LARSON

OCTOBER 15

My eyes are ever toward the Lord. —PSALM 25:15 (RSV)

It was a Saturday afternoon in the music-loving city of Salzburg, Austria. Family groups out shopping had paused to listen to a violinist playing in the square in front of the cathedral.

I watched a father hand a schilling to a little boy of perhaps four, then point to the violin case opened at the performer's feet. The youngster stepped shyly forward, dropped the coin into the case, then darted back to the circle of onlookers, searching his father's face. *Did I do it right? Did I do what you wanted?*

The little boy didn't look at the musician to see how his donation was received. He didn't glance around at the audience to see who else had noticed. The child's eyes were only for his father, seeking approval of a task accomplished.

What a model, I thought, *for any act!* The Father has given me a contribution to make. What others do with it, whether the rest of the world applauds, is not my concern...only that I do what He tells me with what He has placed in my hands.

Today, Father, keep my eyes fixed on You.
—ELIZABETH SHERRILL

October 16

My times are in your hands. —Psalm 31:15

My day was overloaded. I was on deadline for two projects, and I was excited and nervous about getting them into final shape. But the bottom of the coffee can glared at me, and there was only white dust in the bottom of the flour canister. Clearly, a trip to the grocery store was mandatory. Worst of all, in doing some last-minute research on the Internet for one of my projects, I ran into a problem telling time. Different websites listed time in different ways.

"Bill, help! What is GMT? What is Zulu Time? How do I know what time it is here?"

"GMT is Greenwich Mean Time. It's the actual time in Greenwich, England, written in Zulu Time. Zulu Time gives every hour of the day its own number. For example, 2:00 a.m. is 0200, but 2:00 p.m. is 1400 (12 plus two hours). To find out what time it is here in Maryland, figure out the hour in England, and, since it is Daylight Savings Time at the moment, subtract four hours. So if the screen says 2215 GMT, then it is 2215 Zulu Time in Greenwich, which means 10:15 p.m. there. Subtract four hours. It's 6:15 p.m. here. Got it?"

Well, not really. And my day was still fragmented into all my tasks clambering to be done. Then Psalm 31:15 popped into my head. I saw it in a new way: My own personal time was really part of GET "God's Eternal Time." And He knew where I was in it. All I had to do was pause and wait prayerfully. Slowly, the chores of the day formed themselves into a doable list. And in all the spaces between, there was time for me to turn and smile and thank Him.

> *Lord, help me remember my times are in Your hand,*
> *hour by hour, day by day, from my imperfect now*
> *until Your perfect forever.*
> —Roberta Rogers

OCTOBER 17

My soul thirsteth after thee, as a thirsty land.
—PSALM 143:6 (KJV)

On an October day, I walked down the road that leads to our family cabin. It had been months since our last visit. And the last few days before we finally loaded the car for the three-hour trip were especially full. A heavy rain had fallen for most of the week, and there was no chance to go on our usual morning walks. My prayer time suffered.

At the lake near our cabin, the water was receding from the shoreline as it does every fall, and the blue herons were keeping their distance. The sky was that vibrant blue that follows a good cleansing rain. Up ahead, the road was littered with fat, ripe persimmons fallen from a tree.

I stopped to take in the day, and a warm longing filled me. Without thinking, I said out loud, "There's a place in the human heart that will always be lonely without You, God." I should know. There have been times in my life when I thought a snazzy car would fill it or really cool clothes or love. Nothing works. We are built thirsty, hungry, lonely—for God.

Weekly worship is an obvious place to begin to satisfy my need for God, but often I never really get around to the worshipping part. There are all those committees and causes and projects and stimulating conversations, and before you know it, it's time to leave. To make my Sundays fruitful, every day should be a day of worship. From scheduled daily prayers to quick pauses to thank God for the moment or to admire His work or just to tell Him that I love Him, I can continually invite God into that space only He can fill.

Father, walk with me, talk with me,
stay with me day and night.
—PAM KIDD

October 18

It is a good thing to give thanks. —Psalm 92:1 (kjv)

As a child, I silently disapproved of my mother's obsession with making me say "thank you." I *had* to say it, even if I wasn't really grateful. One Sunday afternoon Mother took me to visit an elderly neighbor who lived alone. His house was dark and smelled of moth balls. The antique furniture was covered with dust. Mother made polite conversation while I squirmed on the velveteen sofa. The man got up to prepare refreshments. After a few minutes he came back with a crystal plate of broken cookies and glasses of sour lemonade. While he hobbled away to get napkins, I whispered to Mother, "The cookies are stale."

"You will still say 'thank you,'" Mother whispered back. I had to say it three times because he was hard of hearing. As we walked home, she explained that we were expressing gratitude for his efforts, even if we didn't like what he served.

Recently, my two daughters brought their six children over to celebrate my mother's eighty-ninth birthday. I was keenly aware that I didn't have anything really fun for the younger children to do—no elaborate toys or playground equipment. But a few days after their visit I received a note addressed to me in pencil, the handwriting nearly slanting off the envelope. My almost-eight-year-old grandson explained, "I wrote this in the car after we went to your house. We had the best time at your house and eating and swinging on your back porch. Thank you for having us! We all love you! Love, Luke."

> *Lord, teach me always to be grateful*
> *for the kindness people show me.*
> —Marion Bond West

Lord, be thou my helper. —PSALM 30:10 (KJV)

od, help me to cheer up Mrs. Menina." She was the Russian woman I was tutoring in English. I'd already gotten her a plant and some upbeat musical tapes, but she still seemed down lately. The crimson sign of a pet store lured me in; she'd once mentioned admiring some goldfish. I'd buy her a fish!

Once in the pet store, though, I had second thoughts. Never having bought fish, I wasn't sure how expensive they'd be. The clerk said, "We only sell feeder fish."

Not knowing anything about goldfish, this sounded to me like some rare exotic breed. "I haven't got much money on me," I cautioned. "And I'll need two. I wouldn't want them to be lonely." Hoping to get some sympathy for my small purse, I added, "They're for an elderly woman I volunteer with. I want something to make her smile."

An odd look. "How about if I give you two for the price of one?"

I was stunned at his generosity. "God bless you," I said. "That's so kind of you."

He went in the back and eventually came out carrying a plastic bag with two large goldfish. *Uh-oh,* I thought, *they look expensive. I'll have to charge them.* Silently the man handed the bag to me, then punched in a few numbers on the big metal cash register. I handed him my Visa. He looked me in the eye. "That'll be twenty-four cents."

I stared at him and burst out laughing, and after a moment the man joined in. "Twenty-four cents!" I said, gasping with laughter. My prayer had been answered. I now had something to cheer up Mrs. Menina...the story of how I bought her the goldfish!

> *God, when I pray for something, let me trust*
> *that You will answer my prayer—though*
> *not always in the way I expect!*
> —LINDA NEUKRUG

OCTOBER 20

Then will...the mute tongue shout for joy. —ISAIAH 35:6

When my mother moved into a nursing home, I said a pleasant, "Hello. How are you today?" to Mom's new roommate Jeanie, but I got no response. I turned my back and moved on to my visit with Mom.

Over lunch Dad told me, "Jeanie had a stroke and can't talk, but she understands clearly enough."

Feeling a bit ashamed of how I had ignored Jeanie, I decided to make a better effort at conversing with her. As I nervously entered the room, my eyes caught three or four small statues of dachshunds on the bed table. "Did you have a dachshund?" I asked.

Jeanie slowly nodded her head. "Was it a boy?"

She shook her head.

"Was it this big?" I asked, holding my hands apart.

She shook her head and pushed my hands closer together. "Oh, she was a miniature!" I said.

We went on with our yes/no guessing-game conversation, and I discovered that she had a daughter and several grandchildren.

Before my next visit, I found a small dachshund kitchen magnet to take to Jeanie. When she pulled the little gift out of the bag, a small miracle happened. She opened her mouth, and exactly one enthusiastic word came out quite distinctly. "Baby!"

That was all she said, but it was gift enough for both of us. I squeezed her drooping shoulder. "Oh, Jeanie," I said, "how wonderful! I heard you say 'baby' loud and clear."

One of the miracles that always sent shock waves of praise and amazement through the crowds that followed Jesus was when He caused the mute to speak. You, too, can hear a miracle happen if you listen hard enough to the silences beyond the words.

Lord, today, help me to offer my own silences wisely to bring out a word from someone who is struggling to be heard.

—KAREN BARBER

O give thanks unto the Lord; for he is good:
for his mercy endureth forever. —PSALM 106:1 (KJV)

"Please, Lord, help me see the circumstances of this day as gifts from You," I prayed as I sat in a dreary motel room on a drab winter morning, far from home. For the past two days, I'd been at a conference and now it was my husband's birthday, and I just wanted to get home. But because of airline problems, I couldn't get a flight until afternoon, and now it was snowing...hard.

So I packed my bags, caught a shuttle, and got to the airport early.

Upon checking in, I found that all the flights were oversold, and even though I had a ticket, I didn't have a seat. "You're on the waiting list," the ticket agent told me. "I think you'll be fine."

I didn't want to be "fine." I wanted to be on the plane. I wanted to throw a tantrum. I wanted to talk about "being fair." But instead I merely sat down in the waiting area where I watched dozens of people board the flight. At least a dozen more waited, just like me, hoping for seats. Lots of names were called, and people went forward to get their boarding passes, including people who had checked in after I did.

Please, Lord, let me see these circumstances as gifts from You, I repeated, thinking maybe God hadn't heard me the first time.

At last my name was called, and I went up to the gate. "We're out of room in coach," the boarding agent said, "but we've found a seat for you."

An hour later, I was sitting on the plane with a white linen cloth covering my tray table, enjoying an elegant three-course meal, while stretching out to enjoy the extra space (and grace!) of my first-class seat. It seems they had run out of seats in coach and being last had made me first—for first-class.

Lord, even when my circumstances don't include first-class,
may I see them as Your gifts, intended for good.

—CAROL KUYKENDALL

OCTOBER 22

In those days a man will say to his brother,
"You have some extra clothing, so you be our king and
take care of this mess." —ISAIAH 3:6 (TLB)

*O*ne thing about being single and an empty-nester is that you get to fill up all the closets. No sharing; every inch is mine. And what happens over the years is you end up with far too many clothes. I have clothes for every season, every reason, every style, size, and event.

I should take my cue from my stepmother Bev, who, at age seventy-eight, always looks like she just stepped out of a fashion magazine. When it comes to clothes, she's a minimalist. For instance, for summer she has five or six really nice spotless T-shirts; I have about thirty. Some are in the same condition as my dad's shop rags. How can you ever get rid of the T-shirt your daughter painted in high school? Or the one you bought at the Eiffel Tower? Or the one your son bought you for Mother's Day fifteen years ago?

Well, I'm going to try. My goal for this year is to reduce my clothes chaos from three closets, full to perhaps one and a half. I'm going to try to find something that looks really good on me and stick with that style. I'm going to give the rest away to Goodwill or Human Concerns so that others who have little can have more. I'm going to share a few special things with friends who, unlike me and my dreams, have already lost the extra twenty pounds.

Yes, I am going to conquer my closets! My new mantra: less is more. I feel lighter already.

Jesus, thank You for keeping me well clothed.
Help me to be more like You and share my bounty
with others who have less.
—PATRICIA LORENZ

OCTOBER 23

He guides me in paths of righteousness. —PSALM 23:3

*M*y grandmother was dying of cancer. She looked so tiny, so frail as she lay in the hospital bed, so unlike the strong, self-reliant woman I'd seen on so many mornings, sitting at the kitchen table with a steamy cup of coffee.

I spent a few minutes talking with my mother and sister, then offered to stay in the room while they went downstairs for a break. Grandmother had had a restless night, and I knew that they were both exhausted from tending to her.

I pulled a chair close to the bed. Grandmother opened her eyes wide and looked at me, unable to speak. *Does she know who I am?* I wondered. I spoke to her quietly, but my words only seemed to upset her. *Lord*, I prayed, *give me words to calm her*.

I took Grandmother's hand and began to pray out loud the first words that came to me: "The Lord is my shepherd, I shall not want...."

By the end of the psalm, Grandmother was completely relaxed. Her breathing was quiet and even. I gently placed her hand back down on the bed. When my mother and sister returned, they were relieved to find her resting.

"What did you do?" Mom asked.

"Well, I didn't know what to do, so I recited the Twenty-third Psalm," I replied.

My mother looked surprised. "Did you know that the Twenty-third Psalm has always been her favorite Scripture?"

I didn't, but the Lord did.

> *Lord, when I have no words to speak,*
> *thank You for giving me Yours.*
> —MELODY BONNETTE

OCTOBER 24

Give unto the Lord the glory due unto his name;
worship the Lord in the beauty of holiness.
—PSALM 29:2 (KJV)

Remember," our pastor said as he concluded the sermon, "worship is every bit as important to your spiritual well-being as breathing is to your physical health."

While he gave the closing prayer, I checked to see that the music for the postlude was in place and mentally reviewed the introduction to the last hymn. As I played the organ, a familiar feeling of guilt accompanied every note. I had a secret: Although I attended church every Sunday, I didn't worship. I was too busy concentrating on the details of the service.

I hope no one remembers I played the same prelude last month. Will the offertory be long enough? Should I slow down on the last verse of the hymn? I enjoyed the Christian fellowship with my friends and neighbors, was inspired and challenged by the sermons, and missing church left a hole in my week. But I didn't worship.

Finally, I confessed to an older friend who was a professional musician as well as a church organist. Her response was definitely not what I expected.

"Why do you think it's called the worship *service*?" she asked. "Because for many of us—the pastor, the acolytes, the musicians—it's definitely a time to serve. We worship through our work, too, you know. Still, it's important to find times when you're free of responsibility and can give your whole heart to worship."

Her advice helped me relax and let go of the guilt. I began to seek a few nontraditional opportunities for worship: an evangelism event; musical presentations; even an occasional TV service. And a strange thing happened: although most Sunday mornings still find me on the organ bench, and sometimes every head is bowed and every eye closed except mine, there are plenty of times now when heart-worship happens.

Dear Lord, thank You for pastors, musicians, ushers,
nursery workers and all who worship
through service on Sunday.
—PENNEY SCHWAB

OCTOBER 25

Hear my prayer, O Lord, give ear
to my supplications: in thy faithfulness answer me,
and in thy righteousness. —PSALM 143:1 (KJV)

*W*hen my husband Larry and I traveled through Ireland, I lost the habit of spending time each day in prayer. After all, there was so much to see, so much to do!

Then we visited the ruins of Mellifont Abbey, established by Cistercian monks nine hundred years ago. A damp, bitter wind tore at my jacket as the guide led us along the cloister walkway that circled the inner courtyard. The guide explained to us that the Cistercians were an austere order dedicated to silent prayer. The monks had paraded in a line round and round this courtyard, hands folded, eyes down, praying for eight hours every day.

"What about bad weather?" I asked as I clutched my jacket closer. "Well, the walkway had a roof over it then," the guide said. "But, of course, the wind cut right through these open arches."

I envisioned the monks marching past, their robes billowing in the gale. *If those monks could pray for eight hours a day under such conditions*, I thought, *then surely I could pray for fifteen minutes*. And what better place to start than the walkway of a Cistercian abbey?

Father, please give me the strength today to ignore
the distractions that keep me from spending time with You.

—MADGE HARRAH

Listen to your father, who gave you life.
—PROVERBS 23:22

When Dad was getting Mom settled back home after her stroke, I was unsure of how best to assist them. I went nervously to work, clearing the living room of excess furniture to accommodate Mom's wheelchair. I was quite alarmed when Dad said, "We're picking up a new puppy on Monday."

The last thing he needs is a new puppy, I thought, *chewing up every bag in the garage and getting underfoot when Dad is backing the wheelchair through the front door.*

Dad read the look on my face and said meekly, "I've already promised the owner I'd take her."

I immediately added a new task to my list: go to the junk store and buy a playpen to corral a four-footed, yelping cyclone. I didn't find a playpen, and I was upset that I hadn't been able to save Dad from the nuisance of a new, untrained puppy.

The next week when I telephoned Mom, she told me that they'd named the puppy Princess. It had been terribly frustrating trying to communicate with Mom over the phone, but suddenly there was one subject on which Mom could always manage to make sense: Princess and her antics. And the next time I drove up to visit, Mom was sitting in the yard with Princess on her lap. We sat and watched as Princess bounded over the blooming purple thrift and caught a butterfly. I was astounded when Mom laughed out loud, something she hadn't done in years.

I leaned over and gave Princess a pat on her sandy, curly head, thinking I'd learned my first lesson in parenting my parents: I'm sometimes wrong about what's good for them. Just as I do with my own children, I need to trust them— and trust God that they can make good decisions without my dictating what I think is best.

*Lord, give me the grace to support the people I love
in making their own choices and decisions.*
—KAREN BARBER

OCTOBER 27

Therefore I will look unto the Lord...
my God will hear me. —MICAH 7:7 (KJV)

Last year our grandson Andrew attended Monash University in Melbourne, Australia, on the opposite side of the earth from our home in New York. So many miles between us, I thought, places and experiences I couldn't imagine!

So it was a kind of shock—newcomer that I am to the Internet—when an instant message popped up on my computer screen one morning soon after Andrew got there.

"Hi, Gran! I'm loving this place! I've put some photos on my blog." *Blog*? Andrew explained that it's short for "web log," a kind of journal kept on the Internet, and, sure enough, in a moment I was looking at pictures of him and some new friends...the landscape around the school...a car trip just the day before. I didn't have to imagine his new setting, I could see it, share it all with him.

Most wondrous of all to me was that as we instant-messaged back and forth, we were in contact *right then*. How different from my efforts to reach my father and mother from Africa in the early 1960s! I had to find a ham radio operator who would patch a call to someone in Egypt to be relayed to another set, and so on until hours later I'd hear the phone ringing in my parents' house in the United States—on the chance that they were home.

Instant messaging, I thought, as Andrew and I chatted electronically across the globe, is much more like the experience of staying in touch with God. *Right now*, wherever I am in my travels over the Earth and over the years, I can communicate with Him and receive His reply. Unlike phoning between continents in the 1960s, I know that the Father I want to reach is always there. The only requirement: I must remember to go online.

Lord of the journey, what message
do You have for me right now?
—ELIZABETH SHERRILL

OCTOBER 28

*Not one of the good promises which the Lord had made
to the house of Israel failed.* —JOSHUA 21:45 (NASB)

I didn't want to sell the old beige car. I had bought it shortly after I became a widow—the first one I ever bought by myself.

Now my husband Gene thought I should have a newer, safer car. But the old car and I were good friends. Why, I had even driven it when I went to meet Gene for the first time. When I decided to see if I would like working in downtown Atlanta, I bravely and prayerfully drove it for six months through the snarling early-morning traffic. When my son Jeremy was in a terrible accident, my trusty car got me to him in record time. When my daughter Julie's newborn son died at birth, I found sanctuary in that faithful old car as Gene and I drove to the hospital and then to the cemetery the next day. When Julie delivered beautiful, healthy Thomas a few years later, I made the joyful drive to see them in my car. It was crammed full of memories, and its bumpers were covered with stickers that witnessed to the faith that had gotten me through.

In a moment of weakness, I took Gene's advice and bought a new car. But I absolutely refused to leave my old car on the lot, abandoned and unwanted. I drove it home slowly and thoughtfully, while Gene drove the snazzy new car with the sunroof. As I drove, I asked God to send people to buy my car who would love it, be excited over it—and leave my bumper stickers on it. I could hardly believe it when He seemed to say, *Okay.* I parked my car in the yard and we put a FOR SALE sign on it, and I went inside to vacuum and try to work through my feelings.

I turned off the vacuum when Gene came running into the house with a fist full of money and explained, "This is a down payment. A couple stopped just as I parked your car. They've been praying—asking God to show them a car. They don't have a lot of money, but they have a lot of faith. They're in love with your car and, get this, they love your bumper stickers!"

*Father God, help me to learn that when You say
You'll do something, it's as good as done,
no matter how trivial my request.*

—MARION BOND WEST

October 29

I will tell of all your wonders. —PSALM 9:1

My daughter Kendall recently took up painting and immediately became smitten with her new hobby. She watched classes on TV and covered canvas after canvas with mountains and rivers and trees and cloudy blue skies. When she came to visit, she sometimes brought her paints.

"You've got to try it, Mom!" she urged enthusiastically.

"I can't!" I told her just as emphatically.

"Why not?"

"Because...," I sputtered, searching for the right reason, "because a blank canvas scares me!"

A few days later I watched my five-year-old granddaughter sitting at our kitchen counter, a crayon in her hand, gleefully filling blank white pages with stick figures, houses, flowers, and pointy-edged suns. Obviously, blank pages didn't scare her; they represented endless possibilities.

When in the process of growing up did I lose that ability to create without fear of the results? When did self-confidence get replaced by self-consciousness?

Those are questions I can't answer, but this I know: I don't want to grow so far "up" that I get fearful of trying something new, regardless of the results. So the next time Kendall brought over her box of paints and her easel and several blank canvases, I didn't say, "I can't." Instead, I picked up a brush and began dabbing some color onto a blank canvas.

The result? Well, let's just say Grandma Moses would have nothing to worry about from me. But I'm ready to try another painting, and that feels pretty good.

> *Lord, help me to see the possibilities in all*
> *the blank canvases in my life.*
>
> —CAROL KUYKENDALL

OCTOBER 30

Submit yourselves therefore to God. Resist the devil,
and he will flee from you. —JAMES 4:7 (KJV)

*W*e were walking across Manhattan from the library toward Elizabeth's music class. About ten yards from the corner I saw it: an eight-foot-tall monster handing out circulars for Halloween supplies. I pulled nightmare-prone John close to my side, hoping he wouldn't see. Too late. John froze, petrified. I put my arm around him, hid his face in my skirt, and hurried around the corner to the bus stop.

On the bus, John was full of questions. "Why was that monster there, Mommy?" I explained that someone dressed up like that to let people know they could buy costumes at a store nearby.

"But why was he dressed up so scary, Mommy?"

"Because sometimes people like to scare other people, especially around Halloween. Sometimes we like to be just a little bit frightened, because it's exciting that way."

"But why so scary, Mommy?" Good question. I had to think about it.

"Do you remember how scared Elizabeth was when she was learning how to ride her bicycle?" Both children nodded. "After a while, she got used to it. Even though she was afraid of a little hill at first, it would take a very steep hill to frighten her now. The same thing could happen if you listened to scary stories or watched scary videos. After a while, it would take even scarier things to make you frightened. It's like doing something bad so often that you get used to it. What might happen?"

"You might do something worser, because it wouldn't seem that bad!" exclaimed John.

"Exactly. And sometimes we like to do things that seem just a little bit bad, don't we? Because it's kind of exciting that way." The children grinned. "But do you think it's a good idea to do that?"

"No," said John, " 'cause someday it might turn into a monster!"

Lord, no sin is so little that it does not hurt You. Forgive me
for even the small ways in which I depart from Your will.

—JULIA ATTAWAY

OCTOBER 31

When I look at thy heavens, the work
of thy fingers. —PSALM 8:3 (RSV)

*W*hen we first took Rome, my little grandson, to church, he was six weeks old. He was sound asleep in his "chariot"—the name I've given the carrier used by parents these days. Rather than disturb him, my daughter Heather set him (still in his chariot) in the aisle and let me sit next to him. I reached down and wiggled my finger into his tiny fist, and we sat through that first service holding hands. My grandson was unaware of me, but because he was holding on to my finger, whenever he had tummy rumbles and squirmed in pain he instinctively squeezed more tightly to me until the discomfort passed.

I wondered how often I had done the same. Long ago God had tucked His finger into my own hand and, because of that, I had instinctively squeezed more tightly to Him.

What a wonderful picture, I thought, so happy with Rome's wee hand curled around my finger. While I've certainly appreciated the security God's finger has given me over the years, I'd never before understood the idea that the ebb and flow of my own frail humanity might actually give God pleasure.

Dear God, with Your finger You wrote the commandment,
You cast out demons, and You created the stars. You've tucked
that same finger into the curl of my hand.

—BRENDA WILBEE

November

NOVEMBER 1

"Things too wonderful for me to know...." —JOB 42:3

My husband's grandmother turned 102 last year. Her memories of growing up in England are rich and vivid. For example, she still remembers being let out of school when Queen Victoria died! But, of course, she doesn't remember a childhood with automobiles, airplanes, telephones, or television, because they either didn't exist then or hadn't reached her village.

"Maybe you should try living in your grandmother's time," my friend Janine commented as I complained about how slowly traffic was moving as we carpooled one day.

"What do you mean?" I asked.

"If you lived early in this century, for example, you'd be dreaming that one day you'd be fortunate enough to ride in a car just once in your lifetime!"

"Oh, I see," I said. "And here I am—not even a hundred years later—complaining because there's too much traffic, or the line at the tollbooth is too slow."

"Yes, and if you were part of the crowds around Orville and Wilbur Wright," she went on, "you'd be trembling with pleasure at the idea of taking a hundred-foot flight!"

"You're right," I laughed. "And on my last flight what did I do but complain about the bad food and that I'd seen the movie already."

"Look to the future," Janine said. "Maybe someday you'll be chosen to go on a rocket to the moon. Do you want to enjoy the wonder of the ride, or will you be complaining about being weightless?"

God, let me see and enjoy the wonder
of Your inventions today, not their inconveniences.

—LINDA NEUKRUG

How great is the love the Father has lavished on us,
that we should be called the children of God!
—1 JOHN 3:1 (KJV)

*Y*ou know, Mom," my then-seven-year-old daughter Elizabeth declared one afternoon while we were kneading bread together, "sometimes I feel like God is giving me a big hug!"

"You do? Why, that's wonderful!"

Later I found myself wondering, *When have I felt like God was giving me a big hug?* Often I'm so preoccupied talking *to* God, I forget that sometimes I can simply be *with* Him.

Since hearing Elizabeth's comment, I've been trying to put aside all my "grown-up" preoccupations when I pray and picture God enfolding me in His loving presence.

It's hard, though. I squirm out of quiet contemplation just as my two-year-old son Mark wriggles out of my lap when I try to cuddle him these days. He has become so active and independent. I love watching him run, kick balls, and play with trucks, yet I also yearn to hold him and have him nestle close again.

But there is one time Mark will still cuddle on my lap: when we read books before bedtime. How I treasure those moments! Last night after we read his favorite animal and farm and truck books, Mark snuggled a long time and we talked and sang.

Mark has given me an idea. Perhaps reading God's Word is a way I can calm my restlessness and settle down for quiet, receptive prayer. Sinking into my favorite armchair, I read my Bible for a while, then close my eyes and picture myself nestling in for a loving hug....

Abba, Father.
—MARY BROWN

NOVEMBER 3

Hear my cry, O God; attend unto my prayer.
—PSALM 61:1 (KJV)

I t was a bad day. A *really* bad day: tension headache; dirty house; work deadline; a class to teach that night.

With a sinking heart I remembered I'd promised to pick up a manuscript that morning from one of my students, an elderly woman who wanted my advice on a short story she had written for a contest. Begrudging the time it was taking, I drove to Ellen's house, which I had never visited before. It proved to be a homey place filled with her needlework, including an old-fashioned sampler on one wall: WHEN YOUR DAY IS HEMMED WITH PRAYER, IT'S LESS LIKELY TO UNRAVEL.

Following my glance, she said, "That message has gotten me through many a bad day."

So, had I stopped to pray that morning? No, all I'd done was wallow in misery.

I sat back and relaxed while Ellen fixed me a cup of tea. "Lord, take me into Your stillness," I prayed. The tension in my neck and shoulders gradually lessened.

As we sipped tea together, I answered some of Ellen's questions about her story, and in so doing I found the answer to a problem with my own work. By the time I left her house, thirty minutes later, the day had turned into a good one, after all.

Lord, any day is good when I hold You near.
—MADGE HARRAH

November 4

I have learned, in whatsoever state I am,
therewith to be content. —Philippians 4:11 (kjv)

I've been feeling a little restless today. A new house project isn't moving along the way I'd like. My son and his family have moved to Colorado, so I'm missing my grandchildren. And I'm a bit down on myself because a dear friend is depressed and I'd like to be able to take away her pain, but I can't.

Just now, though, I came across this statement in a book I've been reading: "Happiness is the art of making a bouquet of those flowers within reach." Oh, yes! I needed to hear that today! Instead of feeling frustrated about the house project, I can set one small part of it as a goal that I *can* reach today. I can't hold and kiss and play with my grandchildren, but I can bake some cookies to send them. I can't take away my friend's depression, but I can listen, give her a big hug, and pray for her.

Maybe you'll decide to make a bouquet of reachable flowers today, too!

Today, Lord, I'll focus on what I can do
instead of what I can't.
—Marilyn Morgan King

November 5

This is too glorious, too wonderful to believe! I can never
be lost to Your Spirit! —Psalm 139:6–7 (TLB)

I suppose I knew that God cared about me, but I didn't *feel* that He did. That all-important truth of not relying on feelings had somehow escaped me. *Who am I, anyway, that God should really care about me?*

My daughter Julie phoned later that day, and I asked about my grandchildren as usual. "Thomas did something you won't believe," she said. "He's going to be like you about books, I suppose." When I inquired what he'd done, she explained.

"He ran into the house yesterday bellowing for me. He almost ran into me in the kitchen. Out of breath, he gasped, 'Is it true, Mama? Is it really true? Can an eight-year-old boy like me get his own library card?' When I said that he could, he begged me to take him to the library right at that moment. Because it seemed so important to him, I did. He told me to wait in a corner while he walked up to the counter all alone. He was a bit uneasy, but he did it. Mother, he had tears in his eyes when we left! He showed me his library card and couldn't stop smiling! What kind of child do I have?"

I don't remember my answer. There was a message for me in Julie's story, and I listened to the silent voice in my heart. *It's true, Marion. A grandmother like you can have My full attention and care whenever you desire it. Just ask.* After we hung up, I ignored my feelings of fear and doubt and approached the Throne of Grace. I didn't even know what to say.

I've been missing you, child. God reached His loving arms toward me.

Oh, Father, it's true, it's really true!
You know me and love me!
—Marion Bond West

November 6

Casting all your anxiety upon Him. —1 PETER 5:7 (NASB)

The branches of the fir tree scrape against the window pane, needling me to get out of bed. It's a sure sign that a blizzard has blown in very early on this November morning. I look out the window, where the only sign of life is a tardy flicker that missed fall migration. I feel helpless watching that beautiful bird scavenge in vain for berries among the vines. *What do flickers eat, anyway?*

I put on my parka and boots, drop some suet into a mesh bag, and scoop up some birdseed. As I push open the storm door, it scrapes away an arc of snow from the drift on the back step. Sinking deeper and deeper into the drifts, I plunge along to the bird feeder and then retrace my steps.

Stamping the snow off my boots in the back entrance, I worry whether the flicker will be able to withstand the storm. Surely such weather will prompt it to fly south. If not, I hope it will eat the food I've put out for it.

As I turn on the radio, the morning disc jockey is cautioning his listeners to take the storm in stride. "Remember, folks, not everything in life is fixable, so don't sweat it."

He's right, Lord. There's nothing more I can do.

While waiting for the blizzard to blow itself out, I make a big pot of coffee. And then during my quiet time I mentally release that stormbound bird into the hands of God.

> *Lord, I waste so much time worrying over something*
> *I can't help. May I spend that energy*
> *carrying it to You in prayer.*
> —ALMA BARKMAN

November 7

Everlasting joy shall be upon their heads; they shall obtain joy and gladness. —ISAIAH 35:10 (RSV)

One day when my daughter Maria and I were playing on the bed, she suddenly pointed to the fine lines beside my eyes. "What are these?" she asked.

"Wrinkles," I said, thinking, *Oh, great, now my two-year-old has to remind me I'm not getting any younger*.

"Twinkles," she said, pleased with herself.

"No, wrin—" I stopped in mid-correction. "You know, that makes them sound like something good, Maria. Twinkles they are."

That night as I looked in the mirror, I realized that my twinkles do come from smiling and laughing, forming a kind of road map of the great joy with which God has blessed my life. From parents who filled our house with laughter and taught us not to take ourselves too seriously and brothers who are still two of the funniest people I know, I learned the value of a laugh a day. If there's one gift God has given me in abundance, it's joy, and I have the twinkles to prove it.

I'm turning forty in December, and while I haven't been particularly excited about it, or about those subtle lines or my one pesky gray hair that returns each time I snip it off, I'm ready to look at it all in a new way. Mark Twain wrote, "Wrinkles should merely indicate where smiles have been." So, rejoice in the twinkles! They're a sign to the world that God has given us a lot to smile and laugh about.

Joyful Creator, in Your grace continue to fill my life with laughter, joy, and an abundance of twinkles.

—GINA BRIDGEMAN

NOVEMBER 8

"Our Father...deliver us from evil."
—MATTHEW 6:9, 13 (NASB)

*T*he impression was so sharp I actually pulled the car to the side of the road. My husband John, on a business trip to California, needed prayer! I looked at my watch: 4:30 p.m. here in New York, 1:30 in Los Angeles.

Though I had no idea what the emergency was, I'd had too much experience with these nudges to prayer to ignore them. Like the time I'd "known" our granddaughter Sarah was in danger; at the very moment I prayed, I learned later, she'd fallen from the top of a jungle gym—and walked away with only a chipped tooth. Or the letter that came from my elderly friend Barbara Nelson saying she'd prayed for me for hours one day. Barbara had no way of knowing it was the day of my cancer surgery.

So I sat in the car, praying for John's safety. After about forty-five minutes, the urgency left me and I felt a tremendous peace. All evening I wondered what story of averted calamity he would have to tell.

When John phoned around 10:00 p.m., my time, however, it was to report an uneventful day. Where had he been at 1:30? Circling the Farmers' Market, looking for a place to park. No, no particular problems.

I hadn't told John over the phone about my overheated imagination. But when he got home, I mentioned the foolish episode. "I'm glad I was wrong about your being in trouble!"

John shook his head. "I'm not sure you were wrong," he said. "That no calamity happened doesn't mean your prayer was wasted. It means it was answered."

I stared at him in silence. I was thinking about the tens of thousands of miles we drive safely each year, the illnesses we *haven't* had, the plane that *doesn't* crash. The disasters that *don't* happen to John and me, our family, our friends, people everywhere. I thought of the millions of voices joining each day in the Lord's Prayer. *Deliver us from evil*. And I thanked Jesus again for teaching us to pray.

*Our Father, keep me obedient to Your prompting, whether I
see all or only a fragment of Your providence.*
—ELIZABETH SHERRILL

NOVEMBER 9

The Teacher searched to find just the right words, and what
he wrote was upright and true. —ECCLESIASTES 12:10

I was seated in church with my grandson Caleb, age five. He reached for the small pencil and envelope used for recording attendance and giving, and said, "This is so you can write, 'I love You, God.'"

God wrote an entire book saying "I love you" to the human race. But not once did I ever think of scribbling those words on a pew envelope to be offered at the altar in blessing to Him.

My granddaughter Hannah, age seven, once sang me a song she had learned in summer Bible school about following Jesus. She paused mid-sentence to say, "I know how you turn back on the path to God."

"How?" I asked.

"When you read the Bible and pray and obey the commandments...and then you stop."

Her explanation was so stark and pure I felt myself squirm.

I had been experiencing a season of struggle regarding those very issues. I needed a jolt.

I found myself backing away from that abrupt edge, the "stop." I wanted once again to open my Bible and pray and have a heart to obey—to move forward on the holy path. I missed saying, "I love You, God."

> *Jesus, in the pages of my Bible, I find Your reassuring*
> *promises telling me that I can start following*
> *Your path anytime.*
> —CAROL KNAPP

November 10

Love does not demand its own way.
—1 Corinthians 13:5 (TLB)

For thirty-five years my husband Don wanted to take a raft trip down the Colorado River. For thirty-four of those years I came up with excellent excuses: the children were too young; I was starting college; I was too busy at work; it was too expensive. The real reason was that it didn't sound like fun. Sleeping on the ground, bathing in the river, and drying my clothes on rocks was *not* my idea of a good time.

Then one year Don made nonrefundable trip reservations for four (he persuaded my sister Amanda and her husband Tim to go along)—without consulting me. It was a rotten, low-down, underhanded, sneaky, selfish thing to do. I let Don (and everyone else) know it at every opportunity.

Two days before we were scheduled to leave, my daughter Rebecca stopped by my office. "Don't spoil this trip for Dad," she ordered.

"What about me?" I shot back. "This is his dream, not mine."

"Mom, you're an important part of his dream," she said softly. "So promise."

I promised. And keeping that promise wasn't as difficult as I'd thought, because the trip was (I still don't like to admit it) fun! I loved rafting down the rapids, and sleeping on the ground gave us a panoramic view of the night sky. We hiked to the ruins of an ancient Anasazi village, saw petrographs (pictures carved into the rock), and swam in the crystal falls of Havasu Creek. And for the first time in years, my sister and I had uninterrupted time to visit.

Don and I will never have exactly the same tastes in vacations, or even the same ideas about our life together. Sometimes, though, God's richest blessings come through our willingness to be an active part of someone else's dream. I hope I remember and act on that knowledge during the next thirty-five years of married life.

Thank You, Lord, for the special blessing of marriage.
—Penney Schwab

NOVEMBER 11

*In his hand is the life of every creature
and the breath of all mankind.* —JOB 12:10

I was driving home from grocery shopping on a mid-November afternoon; it was drizzling and foggy, and traffic was heavy on the four-lane interstate. *The older I get*, I thought, *the scarier it is to drive in this kind of weather and traffic. Are You there, Lord?*

About a mile from my exit, an eighteen-wheeler cut right in front of me, forcing me into the left lane. By the time my heartbeat returned to semi-normal, I'd crossed a small bridge and caught a split-second glimpse of a black kitten peering into traffic, her mouth open in a cry for help.

I maneuvered back into the right lane. Soon I'd be home—unless I went back for the kitten. *But that would be crazy. How would I find her? What were the chances of her still being there?* Then two bold words flashed into my mind: *Trust God*.

I got off at my exit and back on the interstate, going the other way. I drove to the side of the bridge and pulled onto the right shoulder, putting on my hazard lights. The kitten was right where I'd seen it, perched on the median strip on the edge of traffic. My heart pounded as I crossed the highway. *Trust God*.

I stood on the side of the median strip and called, "Here, kitty, kitty."

She turned her head. Holding my breath, I called again. This time she whipped around and came running to me, wet and bedraggled. I scooped her up and she snuggled into my arms as if she'd been waiting for me.

Today, five years later, as I pet her sleek, black fur, I still see her on that foggy day, by the side of the highway, tiny mouth open in a cry that couldn't possibly be heard, yet was.

*Almighty God, how much more do You hear the cries
of Your children, no matter how weak or small.*

—SHARI SMYTH

The shadow of a great rock
in a thirsty land... —Isaiah 32:2

I love flowers. But when Gary and I built our house in what used to be a wheat field, I faced a dilemma: too much sun. No trees provided the shade I needed for the kinds of annuals I wanted to grow: delicate petunias, salmon-colored impatiens, begonias. Try as I might, I could not get them to grow around my mailbox or in the flowerbeds I put in the backyard. Even with daily watering, the constant, harsh sun proved too much for them.

Then I noticed that the big rock Gary had placed at the end of our driveway—a huge boulder left from the excavation work—provided a patch of shade every afternoon. So I made a new flowerbed around the rock. And— joy!—the flowers that had floundered in the full sun began to blossom here in the shade of the rock.

I'm like those flowers, too. Often I find myself feeling parched and withered. Too many committee meetings, too many projects, too many late-night work sessions. So instead of blooming, I wither under the harsh light of fatigue and overcommitment. That's when I seek the shadow of God's quiet strength, drawing close, becoming still before Him. I read the book of Psalms. I walk in the woods. I set my priorities with prayer. And soon, prompted by His agenda, nestled in His shade, I begin to thrive.

You are my refuge, Father, in a land
of heat and hurry. I want to grow near You!
—Mary Lou Carney

November 13

Pray without ceasing. —1 Thessalonians 5:17 (kjv)

I looked up at the clock on my classroom wall one more time, squinting to see the time through the glare of afternoon sun. It was one o'clock, and still no word from my son Christopher, who was taking his firefighter certification test—a challenging and competitive test that required mental and physical stamina. As a rookie firefighter, Christopher had to pass in order to continue his training. I looked up at the clock again. Only a minute had passed. My students were taking a history test; the room was quiet except for the sound of pencils scribbling furiously and the loud *tick-tick-tick* of the clock.

I prayed silently, as I had all morning: *Lord, bless my students and my son with a clear mind and a steady hand as they take their tests today*.

When the final bell rang to signal the end of the school day, I had still not received word from Christopher. I decided to call.

"Oh, hi, Mom," Christopher said. "Sorry I forgot to call you. I got busy here at the fire station after I found out that I'd passed my test."

I was overjoyed, but also annoyed. I had spent the day in constant prayer while waiting for a phone call that never came. Right before I was about to embark on a "Do you have any idea what my day was like waiting for your call?" lecture, I remembered the advice of a wise friend. "If a problem brings you to prayer, then it has served its purpose," she had calmly stated when offering counsel years ago.

Indeed, I had spent the day in almost continuous dialogue with God simply because I had a problem that led me to prayer. What a blessing!

Gracious and loving God, thank You
for turning my problems into opportunities
to become one with You in prayer.

—Melody Bonnette

NOVEMBER 14

For where your treasure is,
there your heart will be also.
—LUKE 12:34 (KJV)

In my bedroom I have two wooden plaques, a hand mirror, and a small box, all etched with a wood-burning tool and hand-painted by my grandmother in the early 1900s. Minta Pearl Barclay Knapp was a college physics and math professor during a time when most women didn't even finish high school. She died in 1932, long before I was born. In spite of her amazing educational success, it's the objects she crafted in her spare time with her own hands that are her legacy to me.

I, too, have taken up a craft hobby in the past years with the hope that I can pass a bit of my creative self on to my children, grandchildren, and friends. I save glass jars, the kind pickles, olives, bouillon cubes, and mustard come in, and paint them with puffy fabric paint. They're colorful, fun to hold because of the puffy texture, and quite lovely, if I do say so myself. I've filled my puffy paint jars with tea, candy, paper clips, cotton swabs, or loose change, and given more than five hundred of them away to relatives, close friends, and acquaintances.

Friends ask, "Why don't you sell them at craft fairs?"

I answer, "Because I'd never get back the value of my time. Besides, they're meant for people I love...people to whom I want to give the gift of my time and creativity."

Of course, I have to admit that I hope a few of my jars stand the test of time as my grandmother's wooden objects did, so that someday in the 2100s someone will say, "Mommy, where did this colorful jar come from?"

heavenly Father, thank You for the fun of being creative,
but most of all thank You for the loved ones who accept my
simple handmade gifts with such enthusiasm.
—PATRICIA LORENZ

*If a man should cast seed into the ground...the seed should
spring and grow up.... For the earth bringeth forth
fruit of herself.* —MARK 4:26–28 (KJV)

The weather is colder now. When I take my early morning walk, I have to wear a warmer jacket, one with bigger pockets for some of the apples under the tree. Like a mother with arms outspread, it bears more fruit than I can give away—with plenty for the feasting birds and worms and squirrels.

The apples still litter the ground, a curious mixture of sizes and colors: some small, green, and spotty like freckled elves; others large golden globes. I pick my way among them, seeking the fairest and firmest. I wash their dirty faces in the wet grass, wipe them with a paper towel, and fill my pockets.

Munching one on the way, I pause to empty the rest in a basket on my daughter's porch next door. She runs out to greet me and we perch on the steps a minute, eating apples, so crisp and sweet, marveling that such an old tree should be there at all, let alone be so generous.

"I remember when Daddy set it out," Mickie says. "I didn't think it would even grow! But sure enough, when I came home from college, that little tree was loaded!"

"But isn't it strange that apples from the same tree should be so different?" I wondered. "Not only different sizes, but different colors?"

"But why not?" Mickie says. "This is *a family* apple tree, and families are different. Look at us. We're not all the same size, and we don't all look alike. Thank goodness!"

Laughing, she pats my knee. "What I love about our tree is that it didn't go away just because we did. It kept right on blooming and giving fruit, almost as if it knew we'd be back someday. And now that we are closer, we can enjoy it together. There are plenty of apples for everybody—and best of all, even more to give away!"

*Dear Father, how grateful we are for the example of that
faithful tree. Let us all continue growing
and bearing good fruit for others.*

—MARJORIE HOLMES

*Let your requests be made known
unto God.* —Philippians 4:6 (kjv)

When we four kids were young, we were always losing things: a mitten, a schoolbook, a favorite toy. We'd whine to Mom, hoping she'd help us find it. Instead, with her hands busy in the biscuit dough or with a basket of laundry in her arms, she'd ask, "Have you prayed?" Off we'd go, talking to God about what had happened, asking Him to show us where the lost item could be found. We'd start searching again, and invariably we would locate what we needed.

Years later, when our sons lost some valuable binoculars, I heard Mom ask them, "Have you prayed?" Off they went, just as I used to, while questions raced through my "grown-up" mind: *Will this lead to irresponsibility on their part? Are they going to see God as a celestial errand boy? If the boys don't find the binoculars, will they lose faith in prayer?* It seemed to be a rather risky experiment.

I needn't have worried. Less than fifteen minutes later, they burst noisily into the kitchen, waving the binoculars. Their faces were radiant with gratitude.

How about you? Is it a lost friendship? Lost self-esteem? Lost peace? Have you prayed about it? Talk it over with God, then set about following Him. He really cares, and He will help if you'll ask.

Thank You, Lord, for Your care about the details of my life.

—Vicki Shad

NOVEMBER 17

Hold unfailing your love for one another, since love
covers a multitude of sins. —1 PETER 4:8 (RSV)

Kendall, you forgot to turn off the horses' water!" I yelled, looking out our bedroom window at the river of water overflowing the trough and gushing down the hillside.

"Sorry, Mom," eleven-year-old Kendall apologized, as she ran out the front door to turn it off. "It was a mistake," she yelled back over her shoulder.

"A *silly*, *wasteful* mistake," I corrected her. "You need to be more careful."

She came back inside a few moments later and I gave her one of my "guaranteed-to-produce-guilt" looks.

"Gol, Mom, don't you ever make a mistake?" she asked timidly, heading down the hall to her room. "I'm not a saint," I heard her mutter to herself as she closed the door.

I chose not to answer her question about making mistakes. Besides, the buzzer on the dryer called me. When I opened the door, I saw that the load of white socks and underwear was tinged a slight pink. And then I saw the culprit: one bright red sock thrown in by mistake.

Later, I apologized to Kendall as I handed her a pile of pinkish socks and underwear. "Will you forgive me?" She looked puzzled, so I sat down on her bed to tell her about saints: As God's children, we all are considered "saints." But as human saints, we all make mistakes, and my biggest mistake was acting as if I were perfect.

Lord, thank You for the "colorful" reminder that I make
silly mistakes. And because You forgive me,
I forgive others—swiftly and surely.

—CAROL KUYKENDALL

November 18

*"Just as a hen gathers her brood
under her wings."* —LUKE 13:34 (NASB)

I remember my mother slipping some duck eggs under a hen one summer. The hen never surmised that she had hatched ducklings until the day her mottled babies took to the river.

Eventually, there was only one duckling left, but the old hen was determined to mother that one duckling as long as possible. Despite its protests, she tried to sit on it to protect it long after it was a fully grown duck, and farmyard visitors often chuckled over that "two-story bird."

As my own family matured, letting go of our three sons was hard enough, but parting with our only daughter Gae was even worse. I tried to influence her as long as possible, but one day when I took exception to the music she enjoyed and then turned around and criticized her style of clothes, she reacted to my nagging by exclaiming, "Mom, would you just quit sitting on me all the time!"

Her words brought back memories of that overprotective old hen. Acknowledging that Gae was developing into an independent young woman with tastes very different from my own, I had to learn to *mother* her, not *smother* her.

The nest has been empty ever since my "bird of a different feather" found her wings, but in letting her go, we came closer together.

Father, help me to nurture—not nag—those I love.

—ALMA BARKMAN

NOVEMBER 19

*But solid food is for the mature, for those who have
their faculties trained by practice.* —HEBREWS 5:14 (RSV)

"Mom, let's take cooking lessons." That suggestion from a twenty-four-year-old guy more likely to be listening to rap than spending time in the kitchen came as quite a shock.

"Why would you want to do that, lovey?" I asked.

"Well," he answered bluntly, "you can't cook and neither can I, so Dad cooks for you, and I just eat expensive junk food. We should both give it a try."

So we did, taking an eight-week course in basic cooking techniques. I was definitely the oldest student, and my son was the only male among bright, energetic young women. I was skeptical at first, but Daniel loved every minute of it, energetically carving up a raw chicken with a vicious eight-inch chef's knife. The only part he didn't like was chopping garlic cloves, until the teacher told him lemon juice would remove the pungent aroma from his hands. I enjoyed learning about different foods and listening to the witty and talented teacher. But even more I enjoyed watching my son.

After about half the classes were over, Daniel actually cooked dinner for some of his friends and invited me. As he brought the platter of chicken Marsala out of the kitchen to the astonishment of the assembled youth, there was such a look of pride on his face that tears suddenly stung my eyes. My troubled, angry, disaffected teenager had turned into a self-confident young man who was proud of his achievements and actually enjoyed his mother's company.

"We had fun, didn't we, Mom?" he said as he set the platter down. "And, by the way, I'll make the pies for Thanksgiving—and the pastry."

*Thank You, Lord, for young people
who bring light and laughter into my world.*
—BRIGITTE WEEKS

For you have been born again...through the living
and enduring word of God. —1 PETER 1:23 (KJV)

*O*nce a week, I stop by Mom's house for a cup of coffee and "Granny Hour," when we read the letters my great-grandmother wrote to her family in the early twentieth century.

At first, I wasn't really eager to spend an hour reading yellowed letters in a difficult handwriting. I'd already heard stories about my colorful Great-Granny; that was enough. Besides, I had other things to do. But I went for Mom's sake, so we could pare down her closet clutter and save only the important things.

As we read the letters to each other, I began to appreciate my great-grandmother's humor, struggles, shortcomings, wisdom, creativity, and faith as she labored through some of life's most difficult circumstances.

The stories I'd heard really hadn't told me much about her. Yet by reading her letters, her words to her children, she became real to me.

I find my Granny Hour has reinforced something I know in my heart but often fail to practice: I can hear stories about God, and I can read devotions and books about Him. But until I get into His Word, His letters written to us, His children, I can't really know Him.

Father, as I read Your Word, reveal Yourself to me,
so I can know You better and love You more.

—MARJORIE PARKER

NOVEMBER 21

"Do not destroy it, for there is a
blessing in it." —Isaiah 65:8 (rsv)

I spilled some coffee on the kitchen counter this morning. I grabbed the sponge to wipe it up, then looked closer. The stain was shaped like a sassafras leaf! I stood for a moment, enjoying the pattern—and remembering an art exhibit.

I've always admired the work of the sculptor Henry Moore, whose giant creations enhance public spaces around the world. So I was lucky to be in Texas two years ago when the Dallas Museum of Art held a Moore retrospective. Room after room, his genius unfolded—huge, sensual, curving shapes, compelling and memorable.

Leaving the exhibit, I noticed a glass display case holding what looked like an array of rubbish awaiting the dustbin. Pebbles, broken shells, splinters of wood, bits of bone, scraps of rusting metal. Why in the world would an art museum put such worthless stuff on view?

I bent down and read the label. The objects in the case, it stated, came from Moore's studio, where they had been for him "a constant source of inspiration." All his life, the label continued, Moore had picked up such random debris, drawing from the shape and texture of the smallest, most insignificant objects, ideas for his monumental sculptures.

Worthless stuff? Not to the discerning eye of the artist. I thought of Leonardo da Vinci's famous remark that he could be inspired by "the mottled stains on an old wall." I'll never have the perception of a Moore or a da Vinci, but since that visit to Dallas I've often been aware of pattern, color, surprise harmonies, in the untidiness of daily life.

Spilled coffee—a small mess or a small blessing?

Give me an artist's eye, Lord, to see in the accidental
a display case for Your wonders.
—Elizabeth Sherrill

He does great things beyond our understanding. —JOB 37:5

*M*y husband Whitney and I were waiting in line to board a crowded flight from Portland, Oregon, to Dallas, Texas. Outside it was gray and raining. Inside, on the chilled ramp leading to the plane, the line had stopped. We waited, human islands of dull silence. Ahead of me was a tall young man with a ponytail, wearing a denim jacket. Through the crook of his elbows, I saw a glass box cupped in his big hands like a treasure.

"Butterflies!" I gasped.

He turned around grinning. Inside the cage, five brilliant orange and black monarchs fluttered like exquisite jewels. Excited murmurs surged through the line. A packed circle gathered round, *oohing* and *aahing*. "They're from my cousin's biology class," the man said. "They hatched from their cocoons too late to migrate safely to Mexico, so I promised the class I'd give them a lift to Dallas. From there, they'll make it."

"I'd forgotten they fly that far," said a man in a suit, carrying a briefcase. "Isn't it amazing?"

A child traced a finger on the glass. "Pretty," she said.

Someone else said, "You know, their brains are the size of a pin head. Yet they know the way to Mexico. Can you believe it?"

"And those colors, the design so perfect on each wing," a woman added. Then the line began to move. We stepped back into formation, now bonded together by reverence, wonder, joy.

> *Oh, Master Artist, Your handiwork on even*
> *the smallest of canvases brings praise to our lips.*
> —SHARI SMYTH

NOVEMBER 23

And he said to them, "Follow me."
—MATTHEW 4:19 (RSV)

Almost thirty years ago I faced a decision. Should I quit my salaried job at a magazine to help my husband launch a new business? On one side, a regular income in the family, work I enjoyed. On the other, challenge, risk, the excitement of pioneering together.

"When I have a choice to make," our minister advised me, "I simply go to the Bible."

Simple for him, maybe—he knew the Bible inside out. But where would I even begin looking? I remembered a friend telling about getting a Bible verse over the phone when he had to make a choice. "The caller couldn't possibly have known my situation, yet the verse he gave me was my answer!"

No such phone call came for me.

"I pray for guidance," another friend said, "then just let the Bible fall open." I tried this. I closed my eyes, put my finger on a page and read, "Ozias begat Joatham; and Joatham begat Achaz; and Achaz..." (Matthew 1:9 KJV).

When I laughed about this with a neighbor, Co Holby, she nodded. "That time my husband was so ill, I did just what you did, opened the Bible at random looking for guidance." Instead, Co found herself staring at the blank page between the Old Testament and the New. "The only words there were 'The Gospel.'"

We started to laugh again—then realized what she'd said. *The Gospel*! That's where Co and I and every Christian would find direction. Asking God for a specific verse for a particular situation, after all, is asking for a miniature miracle—wonderful when it happens, but not something I can summon on demand. My husband and I began a daily reading of the Gospels in terms of my decision, finding our fears, our egos, our hidden motives exposed to the light of Jesus' life and teaching. In the end I quit my job, but what came out of that time was something more important: a pattern for bringing every decision before Him who followed His Father's will without fail.

Show me Your Son today, Father, as I read Your Word.
—ELIZABETH SHERRILL

November 24

Out of them shall come songs of thanksgiving, and the voices of those who make merry. —Jeremiah 30:19 (RSV)

Sweet potato casserole has long been a favorite dish at Thanksgiving dinners in the South. Mine is a traditional part of our family's meal as we gather at my daughter Emily's house to celebrate.

My casserole tastes best straight out of the oven, so I like to prepare it at Emily's house. To make sure I have everything I need, I measure and package all the ingredients before I leave home and put them in Emily's refrigerator when we arrive. Then at cooking time, I mix them, pour the mixture into a baking dish, and pop it into the oven.

Last Thanksgiving, however, something went amiss. I carefully rechecked the containers I'd brought. "Oh no," I moaned. "I forgot the sweet potatoes!"

Emily turned from basting the turkey. "Are you sure?"

"They were in a round red container," I recalled. "I cooked, peeled, and mashed them and put them in a bowl. I must have left it sitting on the kitchen counter."

Emily stood silent before the yawning oven. Granddaughter Christy, a stalk of celery in one hand, a paring knife in the other, looked up from her salad making. My husband Bob and our grandson Bob came into the kitchen from the living room with quizzical looks on their faces.

Young Bob tossed his head back and roared a wonderfully happy, youthful laugh. "Grandmom," he taunted, "you can't make sweet potato casserole without sweet potatoes!" He threw his arms around me and hugged me. His glee broke the tension in the room, and everybody, including me, began to laugh.

At the dinner table, Christy's place was full, except for one round spot. "That," she announced, "is where my sweet potatoes were to go."

We all laughed at her gentle teasing. And joy and love prevailed in that house, and my heart overflowed with thanksgiving.

Father, accept our thanks today for Your many blessings,
especially for family, for love, and for the ability
to laugh at ourselves.
—Drue Duke

NOVEMBER 25

On this mountain, the Lord Almighty will prepare a feast of
rich food for all peoples. —ISAIAH 25:6

The cornerstone of our Thanksgiving feast in Hawaii was potato dressing. The recipe had entered our family via my *tai kung* or great-grandfather, an immigrant from Canton, China, who had learned it from the New England missionary family for whom he had cooked at the turn of the century.

The family recipe went with me when I moved to New York. For years, the dressing graced our Thanksgiving table, enjoyed by my husband, myself, and our growing family, which now included our small son Tim, my brother Jerry, and his wife Donna.

When Jerry and Donna moved to Oregon (taking the recipe along), I grumbled to a girlfriend about the futility of making turkey and dressing for three.

"Could I join you?" my friend asked, and kept coming for six Thanksgivings. By the time she moved to Wisconsin with my recipe and her two babies, I had gained an appreciation for the dressing's miraculous ability to change strangers into participants in an ongoing Thanksgiving tradition that had, over the course of a century, traveled from continent to continent, culture to culture, and family to family.

This year, new friends will join our family at the table. The Bertrands will bring Haitian rice and a cousin or three; the Gaspariks a Southern-style pecan pie; Una will cook up Shanghai noodles; my brother's son Brian, visiting from college, will bring his two hungry roommates. And at the center of the feast will be my tai kung's potato dressing, still feeding and binding our family across the years and the miles in marvelous ways.

You who fed the multitude, we come
to Your table with thanks this day, one family
strengthened and renewed by Your grace.
—LINDA CHING SLEDGE

November 26

"Seven years of great abundance are coming."
—Genesis 41:29

I've always thought that people who had more than one cat were a little odd. I thought one cat made a nice pet, but two or more were... excessive. That was before I went to the ASPCA to look for a new cat. "If you're thinking about getting a cat," the lady there said, "get two. Two will be easier than one."

I smiled but thought, *She works for the ASPCA! So her job is to get cats adopted. Next, she'll tell me that six are easier than two!*

But God seemed to nudge me to take both cats. So I ended up with Stripe and Biscuit.

I frequently see Stripe and Biscuit tussling, and I enjoy the way they coexist at their food and water bowls. (Though they're not so generous-spirited when it comes to playing with their shared catnip toy!) Sometimes we may think we know what's best for us, but God gives us more than we want. And sometimes that turns out to be *just* what we wanted.

My friend Yvette confessed, "When I first heard that I was expecting twins, I was overwhelmed. But now that they're here—well," she said with a laugh, "I'm *still* overwhelmed, but I can't imagine life without both of them."

Dear God, today, let me accept all the unexpected
abundance that You want me to have.

—Linda Neukrug

NOVEMBER 27

You shall love your neighbor as yourself.
— LEVITICUS 19:18 (NKJV)

*E*arly on a Saturday morning, my husband and I woke up in a lovely, old-fashioned bed-and-breakfast room. We were due at a prayer breakfast in what seemed a very short time. I jumped out of bed and ran over to the window. There was snow—lots of it—and our car, parked beneath the window, looked like an igloo. "Edward, get up," I urged. "We don't even have a scraper."

We began to get ready in disgruntled haste, not at all the right frame of mind for gathering to pray. And I was responsible for the opening words.

Suddenly, I heard an odd rhythmic noise, like a distant lawn mower. Hairbrush in hand, I walked over to the window. There below me was the hooded figure of a fellow guest whose acquaintance we had made only briefly the night before. As quietly as he could, he was cleaning the snow off our car windows. He had already finished his own car parked next to ours.

I drew a deep breath as I let the curtain fall into place. Someone, almost a stranger, without fuss was smoothing our path that early morning. Scraper in hand, he was loving his neighbor in practical fashion. Clearly he planned to drive off unseen. I had no difficulty with that day's opening prayer, entitled, as it happened, "For Others."

Dear God, bless those who care for others
in so many ways and ask for no reward.
—BRIGITTE WEEKS

NOVEMBER 28

David and the whole house of Israel were celebrating
with all their might before the Lord. —2 SAMUEL 6:5

As a family, we believe that too much of a good thing is never enough. We celebrate everything and anything. Most of all we celebrate birthdays, especially the big ones: ten, twenty, thirty, forty, fifty.... For these we try to plan something hilariously outrageous, wickedly generous, and passionately memorable.

When our neighbor turned forty, her husband hid forty small gifts in tuck-away places around the house and yard: her favorite perfume; a glitzy pen; a new pair of gardening gloves; a book on her "want to read" list; and on and on. Each was tied to an alarm clock or timer, preset to buzz one after the other every fifteen minutes. She had a frantic, fun-filled day, especially as the gifts were so well hidden that before she found one another was buzzing.

We loved this idea, so on my husband's fiftieth birthday we scoured the stores for fifty different candy bars, especially those he fondly remembered from his Canadian childhood. We hid these around the house, not with buzzers, but with a paper trail of clues, one leading to the other. The final clue took him to a card with reservations for dinner at his favorite restaurant.

Life is the gift of God's superlative imagination! Fill it with love and have fun living it.

Thank You, Father, for all Your good gifts.

—FAY ANGUS

Freely you have received, freely give. —MATTHEW 10:8

*M*y friend Barbara stopped by today to finish up some pillows we've been designing. As I walked her to her van, I stopped by the mailbox under the arbor. Inside was the newest issue of Mary Engelbreit's *Home Companion*. One look at the red and green cover promising EASY WAYS TO MAKE A HOME FOR THE HOLIDAYS and TASTY TREATS TO MAKE AND GIVE, and I was secretly planning my escape. There's nothing I look forward to more than sitting down with a cup of coffee and the latest issue of *Home Companion*.

"Is this the magazine by that greeting-card artist?" Barbara asked. "I went to the grocery store to get the Christmas issue and they were out. The bookstore too."

My mind traveled back forty years. My grandmother had just retrieved the holiday issue of *Good Housekeeping* from her mailbox. I grabbed it from her ottoman as soon as I spotted the cover announcing an article on making gingerbread houses. A few minutes later when Mother came to pick me up, Mamaw handed me the magazine. "You take it, honey. I can look at it later," she said. I murmured a brief thank-you and slid it under my arm, even though I could see the yearning in Mamaw's eyes and remembered the cup of coffee waiting for her on the kitchen table.

All afternoon, I kept thinking about that look in Mamaw's eyes. She ran a little alterations shop from her dining room, and there wasn't much money for extras. Her favorite magazine was her only extravagance, but she had let me enjoy it first.

I handed my new *Home Companion* to Barbara. Sometimes the best way to say a second thank-you for a long-ago deed is simply to repeat it.

> *heavenly Father, thank You for Mamaw*
> *and all the models of unselfishness who've taught me*
> *the importance of giving.*
> —ROBERTA MESSNER

November 30

Accept one another. —Romans 15:7 (NASB)

Lovey, our golden retriever/Labrador, wags her tail at everything that moves—squirrels, butterflies, strangers, even cars whizzing by. Most of the time, they don't respond. But that doesn't faze Lovey. She keeps wagging her tail as if the whole world loved her. Maybe dogs don't worry about being rejected, but I do. I'm afraid to make friends because I'm afraid I'll lose them. Whether it's a gradual cooling of friendly feelings, a change in circumstances that forces someone to move away, or the forces of life over which we have no control, like sickness and death, something will happen to take my friend away from me.

As we walk, Lovey pulls hard on the leash and begins to wag her tail furiously. A neighbor we hardly know is approaching her mailbox. She bends down to give Lovey a pat. Lovey looks back at me, panting with wild delight, as if to say, "See, she accepts me. I am loved!" Then I remember that this neighbor is going through a family crisis. Reluctant to get involved, I say a polite "hi," planning to move on quickly. But Lovey drags me to within inches of the woman. I can see the agony in her face. I'm startled, shocked. "Are you okay?" I ask her.

She starts to cry right there by the mailbox. Not neat little tears, from the corners of her eyes—the kind you can dab away—but deep, racking sobs. Even as she cries, her gentle eyes hold mine.

"Listen, let me put the dog in the house and I'll be right back, okay?"

She nods and stands there and waits for me at the mailbox. I hurry.

Father, help me overcome my fear of rejection
and get on with the things You have for me to do.
—Marion Bond West

December

December 1

Again, the kingdom of heaven is like unto a merchant man,
seeking goodly pearls. —Matthew 13:45 (KJV)

*M*y grandson Daniel is two, with round cheeks and a smile that nearly runs out of room and a welcoming heart. When I come to visit, he is waiting at the door with shining eyes and that amazing smile. When he wakes in the morning, he comes looking for me with that same irrepressible delight. Wherever Daniel appears, he makes me feel as if I'm the sunrise on his horizon.

David, Daniel's younger brother, just turned one. Although we don't really know him yet, he has my grandmother's dimple in his chin. She and I giggled a lot. I have high hopes for David.

Another grandson, Joshua, almost four, I call "moonchild."

He and I both like the moon. One wintry evening when I was visiting him in Alaska, I carried him outdoors in bare feet and pajamas to admire its brightness. Later that night the moon glow through his bedroom window cast its luminous purity across his sleeping face.

These encounters with my grandchildren have become perfect pearls, strung together in love. For me, they're the "pearly gates" swinging wide on heavenly joys right here, right now!

Jesus, jewel of God, lead me to my true pearls.

—Carol Knapp

December 2

*We have different gifts, according
to the grace given us.* —Romans 12:6

While my boys were in college, they struggled with what to buy their grandparents for Christmas. They wanted my mom and dad to know how much they loved them, but finding a gift within their price range became more of a challenge each year.

Then one Thanksgiving, my father casually mentioned how much he had loved decorating the house with lights every Christmas. He couldn't any longer and that saddened him.

Shortly afterward, Ted and Dale came to me with an idea. As their Christmas gift to their grandparents, they wanted to make the three-hour drive to their house and decorate it for Christmas.

I pitched in and purchased the necessary supplies, and the boys spent two days stringing up lights and boughs all around the outside of the house. Every bush, plant, and tree trunk was wrapped in lights. My dad beamed with pride that his house was the most brilliantly lit home in the neighborhood.

Ted and Dale had such a good time with my parents, and each other, that they returned every couple of months and completed necessary tasks around the house that my father could no longer manage. My parents treasured this special gift more than anything the boys could have purchased.

I learned something valuable from my sons that year: An extra toy under the tree for the grandchildren won't mean half as much as playing a game with them or holding a special tea party complete with fancy hats and gloves. The gift of my time will be remembered long after they have outgrown their toys.

*Lord Jesus, at the first Christmas You gave us the gift
of Yourself. Help me to make myself a gift to others.*
—Debbie Macomber

December 3

*The purpose of tithing is to teach you always
to put God first in your lives.* —Deuteronomy 14:23 (TLB)

When my mother died a few years ago, Dad gave me a box of papers from her desk. Included were her down-to-the-penny household statements for each month during my childhood years.

Every month she paid eleven bills by check: house payments, taxes, insurance, utilities, groceries, etc. The rest of the family income was placed in ten separate envelopes labeled CHURCH, SCHOOL EXPENSES, CLOTHES, GIFTS, REPAIR AND IMPROVEMENT, DUES AND LICENSES, DOCTOR-DENTIST, DAD'S ALLOWANCE, MOM'S ALLOWANCE, and SAVINGS.

The June 3, 1960, ledger states that she wrote $274 in checks. The cash in the envelopes totaled $130. Our family of five was living on $404 a month. In spite of the tight budget, Mother and Dad were giving more to the church than they were keeping for themselves. Mom kept $10, Dad kept $10...and $24 went to the church.

Have I followed in my parents' footsteps? Hardly. The excuses come too easily. Four children to put through college. A big mortgage. An emergency that might come up. The vacation fund.

As a child I never had the slightest notion that my parents inched their way through on such a tight budget. Yet every month they gave no thought to doing any less for the church than the absolute maximum that their tiny budget could stand. Maybe that's why I felt so rich as a kid.

*Lord, give me the courage to tithe and then
to trust my budget concerns to You.*
—Patricia Lorenz

DECEMBER 4

Suffer the little children to come unto me...for of such
is the kingdom of God. —MARK 10:14 (KJV)

I was feeling resentful and frazzled as I entered the little family restaurant for a quick bite. I had come from one meeting in White Plains, New York, and was soon to rush to another in Tarrytown. No time to go home, no time to catch my breath. I wolfed down a sandwich and was gulping my coffee and making some notes when a little, rosy-cheeked fellow came in with his parents and marched right up to my table.

"Boons!" he cried ecstatically. "Boons!" he said again when I didn't understand. He pulled my sleeve and insisted that I share his joy.

Lifted out of my self-absorption, I smiled at his enthusiasm. My eyes followed the little hands pointing to the wall above me. I hadn't noticed it at all, but there, perched gaily over my table, was a picture of a rocking horse with brightly colored balloons tied to its saddle. At last, I joined in the child's laughter. "Yes," I agreed, "balloons! Beautiful balloons!"

We smiled at each other as I left the restaurant. *Amazing*, I thought, *how much lighter I feel*. In fact, I practically floated out the door. Only later, quite by accident, I found the word *boon* in the dictionary. It's defined as a favor or blessing, and it comes from the Old English word *ben*, which means prayer.

Dear Father, thank You for the many ways
in which I may lift my heart and spirit through prayer.

—SUSAN SCHEFFLEIN

DECEMBER 5

Remember the wonderful works that he has done.
—1 CHRONICLES 16:12 (RSV)

After reading about the world's fourth-best bird-watcher, Peter Kaestner of Lansing, Michigan, who has seen almost seven thousand bird species, my husband Alex and I were inspired to start a list of our own sightings over the years.

As we reminisced, delighting again in scarlet rosellas right on our balcony in Australia and pretty pine grosbeaks that visited our feeder here in Michigan one winter, I thought of other sightings I wished I'd recorded over the years: glimpses of God's presence. I told Alex about God's miraculous protection when camping with my college friend Joann in the Porcupine Mountains. Two drunken men started unzipping our tent—we prayed very hard, and they suddenly fled.

Then Alex mentioned our rescue in a blizzard in Wisconsin. "Remember that state trooper who followed us on the shoulder and guided us to an exit?"

I found another notebook, and we began recording our sightings: God's bringing Alex and me together, and helping us through our long, dark tunnel of infertility, wondrously answering our prayers for children; His leading us to a loving church family; shining a light of guidance on when and where to go for Alex's sabbatical; providing a renter for our house two weeks before we left; hearing Him in the laughter of our children....

We want to keep recording our "sightings" for grandchildren to read someday, but also for those dark times when we feel God has flown, so that we may recall glimpses of His golden wings.

Lord, help us recall special sightings of the past,
and grant us eyes to see Your wondrous presence today.
—MARY BROWN

DECEMBER 6

I waited patiently for the Lord; and he inclined unto me,
and heard my cry. —PSALM 40:1 (KJV)

W henever my husband Norman and I traveled around the country for his speaking engagements, we met people who gave us new insights about prayer. One of the most unusual came from a woman in Atlanta.

She'd been worried about her son Dan, who lived far away from her. He had three young children and a demanding job that he felt locked into. He commuted to work by bus, and when he finally returned home in the evening, he often dropped into a bar before heading home to his family. He developed a serious drinking problem, and his marriage had worn pretty thin because of it.

"If only I could ride the bus with Dan and get him home safely to his family each night," the woman thought. Then she got an idea: "Why *not* ride the bus with him?"

So the next morning she got on the bus with Dan—in her prayers.

She rode alongside him, sometimes reminiscing about things that happened when he was a boy and sometimes silent—just loving him and praying that he would ask for God's help. That night, when he caught the bus for the ride home, she again boarded with him, riding beside him, loving him, praying for him. Twice a day from then on, she'd remind herself, "Now's the time to ride with Dan."

Some months later, visiting her son at Christmas, she learned that Dan wasn't drinking anymore.

"You know, I have a long bus ride back and forth to work," he told his mother. "Somehow, day after day, I thought about my drinking while I was riding the bus. Finally, I made the decision to stop, and once I did, even the bar on the way home didn't tempt me."

This woman reminded me that prayer is a perfect vehicle—for commuting *and* communing. Prayer, indeed, can get you where you want to be.

Thank You, Lord, that "more things are wrought by prayer
than this world dreams of" (Alfred, Lord Tennyson).

—RUTH STAFFORD PEALE

DECEMBER 7

But I have calmed and quieted my soul.
—PSALM 131:2 (RSV)

Twenty-five kindergartners make a lot of noise. On the mornings when I helped out at our son Scott's school, I'd notice my voice rising louder and louder over the din. That wasn't the teacher's way! A veteran of thirty years' experience, Mrs. Dietz would step to the front of the room and make her announcements in a whisper.

"If we're not very, very quiet," the soft voice would begin, "we won't hear what Mrs. Dietz is saying, will we?"

Near her, a few children, straining to hear, would shush others, shouters would be poked, and a wondrous hush would descend on the room as Mrs. Dietz whispered the names of the orange juice captains or the words of a new song. Because she spoke so quietly, the children's listening had a special quality. An alert, breathless attentiveness lest the barely audible message be missed.

When, years later, I began praying for guidance, I thought of Mrs. Dietz and that boisterous classroom. God will not raise His voice to be heard above the racket of my life. He wants me to shut off the TV, lay down the newspaper, let the phone ring. He calls me to a room alone, then waits for the inner commotion, too, to subside. He will not shout down my preoccupations, the conversations in my head. Like Mrs. Dietz, He speaks more softly than them all, until one by one they cease their chatter.

Then, quiet without, quiet within, I listen for the still, small voice that spoke the world into being.

Help me carve a quiet time from this active day, Father,
when I can listen for the whispers of Your love.
—ELIZABETH SHERRILL

DECEMBER 8

*And do not neglect doing good and sharing, for with
such sacrifices God is pleased.* —HEBREWS 13:16 (NASB)

When our daughter Gae and son Glen were preschoolers, they were given an Advent calendar. Behind each little door marking off the days until Christmas was a tiny picture depicting some aspect of Christ's nativity. Every morning Gae and Glen jostled for the chance to open the day's door and tell me how the picture behind it fit into the Christmas story:

"That's the star that led the wise guys to Baby Jesus." "That's the angel who singed to the shepherds." "That's Jesus' mommy. She wears a scarf over her head because it's cold in the barn."

While their innocent explanations were delightful, their daily squabble about who should open the door often carried over into playtime.

"It's my turn!" "No it's not!" "Yes it is!"

I issued an ultimatum. "From now until Christmas, neither of you opens the Advent door if you bicker about it. Not only that, but if you misbehave during the day, you also lose your turn."

Interesting remarks soon started filtering out of the playroom. "We've only got a few days left, Glen. I'll share my toys."

"Not many days left, Gae. You can have my cookie."

This year when I opened the door on December, I thought back to Gae and Glen's Advent calendar, only now I was the one who didn't want to share. "I know it'll soon be Christmas, Lord, but I just don't feel like baking for shut-ins this year, or sewing stocking stuffers for singles, or taking the elderly shopping. Can't You find somebody else to do it?"

That's not how my Son responded, God seemed to say.

A few minutes later my husband Leo came in from outside, where he had been clearing a neighbor's driveway with the snowblower. "Mmmm, what's that I smell?"

"Christmas cookies for Vera and Betty," I replied. "Not many days left."

*Father God, remind me of the ways You've given me
to share Your love with others.*

—ALMA BARKMAN

December 9

I want to know Christ and the power of his resurrection.
—Philippians 3:10

Family Christmas cards matter to me—the kind with a photo and personal message. That's a legacy from my parents, who used to take a picture of us kids every year, standing in a snowbank or playing musical instruments or wearing sheets and old bathrobes, looking at a doll in a wooden box filled with straw. Then they wrote a caption that said it all.

Ever since Lynn and I got married, I've been making picture cards with a short message that sums up our family highlights for the year. "We're hanging a new stocking" (to announce Kendall's birth); "We've had a MOVING experience" (showing the kids lined up in front of our new house).

I'm working on this year's card. In preparation, I spread out all our past cards and noticed how they not only tell the story of a growing family, from births to graduations to weddings, but they also tell the story of a family's growing faith in Jesus. As years pass, the cards contain a more meaningful message about the gift of Jesus in our lives.

This year's message will be a challenge because we've had so many life-changing experiences—the deaths of both Lynn's parents, the move back to Colorado for two of our children, the birth of our first grandchild, and the marriage of our daughter Lindsay. In the midst of all this mostly good news, I want our friends and extended family to know what matters most.

Finally, I decided on this message: "Life changes...but our Greatest Gift remains the same." In smaller print, underneath some pictures, I'll describe these changes in our family, and end with the message that God's greatest gift is Jesus, because no matter what changes, He does not. And that matters most of all.

Father, the gift of Your Son Jesus matters
most of all—at Christmas and throughout the year.
—Carol Kuykendall

DECEMBER 10

Then our mouth was filled with laughter.
—PSALM 126:2 (NKJV)

*M*innie, our cat, adores a soft, fluffy white blanket of ours. Anytime we bring it out, she eyes it from afar, then slowly makes her way to it, trying to appear casual. If no one scolds her, she's soon curled up on the blanket as though it were her very own. Minnie isn't the only one who enjoys that blanket; it's also a favorite of my mother's.

Today, it took Mother ever so long to inch her way with the walker from the car to her recliner in our living room. I'd taken her to the doctor, and the trip had required great effort. Each step resulted in tremendous pain. She forced a determined smile onto her drawn face. I moved ahead of her, propping pillows on the comfortable chair and then laying out the white blanket.

When Minnie saw Mother coming, she deliberately beat her to the blanket in the chair. Mother's pain seemed to precede her and fill the entire room. It was intense and had wearied both of us. Suddenly, Mother spoke in a sharp, commanding voice that startled Minnie and me. "*Is that cat on my blanket again?*"

I laughed, softly at first. Then my snickering turned into rippling, uncontrollable hee-haws. I laughed hysterically until I hurt. Mother paused with her walker and, to my amazement, also began to laugh. Minnie watched, wide-eyed. Mother bent over the walker as laughter overtook her. We both laughed helplessly and loudly until we could hardly speak. Occasional bursts of laughter continued to escape from us, like an important P.S. on a letter.

Gradually, the laughter ceased. But it had done an extraordinary thing. I felt better. I enjoyed preparing supper. Mother and I both smiled more during the meal. Things didn't seem so difficult. Loading the dishwasher was almost fun.

Lord, send laughter to rescue me more often.
—MARION BOND WEST

And pray in the Spirit on all occasions with all kinds of prayers and requests. —EPHESIANS 6:18

I love windows, so when my husband Gary and I built our house twenty years ago, we put in lots of them. And every Christmas, I put an electric candle in each one—all twenty-one of them! I love the way it looks from the road, all those soft white lights brightening each window. What I don't love is going around every morning to turn them all off. And every afternoon to turn them all on. *Tromp, tromp. Click, click.*

I began to dread this twice-a-day ritual that lasts for the whole month between Thanksgiving and Christmas. Then my friend Charlene gave me an idea. "Why not 'name' each candle and then pray for that person as you click it off and on?"

So I did. Now twenty-one of my family and friends receive an extra holiday gift from me: daily prayers. And my twice-a-day ritual has become one of my favorite parts of the day.

Keep me alert, Father, to any bright idea
that will enable me to pray for my loved ones.

—MARY LOU CARNEY

Then said Jesus unto him, Go, and do thou likewise.
—LUKE 10:37 (KJV)

I placed an order for a small Coke at the fast-food drive-through. "No ice," I emphasized. I had a terrible toothache and was afraid that ice would really set it off. But at the window, the cashier shoved a Coke overflowing with ice at me. "I need this without ice," I repeated, fixing my eyes on the plastic holiday wreath to avoid her glare.

The cashier twisted her face into a scowl and, to the astonishment of the customers lined up at the counter inside, threw the Coke toward the coffeemaker, screaming a string of expletives. "I wish you'd take your hateful self and go home!" another cashier snapped at her as she dodged the sticky puddle on the floor.

I'll take this up with the manager, I decided, silently preparing my speech. But something stopped me. That something was a sea of faces, those who have lived out the attributes of Jesus before me.

These folks have been like Jesus to me when I needed it most and deserved it least. *Help me, Lord, to see this cashier through Your eyes*, I prayed. *Who is she? A single mother up all night with a croupy baby? Worried about a car that doesn't run half the time and no extra money for Christmas? The target of endless impatient customers? Could I have been the last straw?*

Oddly, when she returned with my replacement drink, I found I wasn't irritated at all. "I'm sorry I made things harder for you," I said. "You don't know how much I appreciate this drink with no ice." I pointed to my mouth. "It's this awful toothache."

Bless her, Lord. Really touch her life, I silently prayed, smiling up at her from my car window.

"Let me get you a napkin," she said, a smile tugging at the thin line that had been a scowl. "I hope that toothache gets better."

Thank You, Lord, for those who
tirelessly teach me to follow in Your steps.
—ROBERTA MESSNER

*We give thanks to the God and Father of our Lord Jesus
Christ, praying always for you.* —COLOSSIANS 1:3 (NKJV)

E very year my husband Rick and I argue about the same thing: how to decorate for Christmas. I'm the get-it-done-quickly type, and he's a man of detail. I love simplicity, using things from nature, while Rick likes figurines, sparkly ornaments, and a train that toots and whistles its way around the Christmas tree.

So when he announced another new idea, I wasn't too thrilled. "Why don't we buy ornaments and write the names of family and friends on them?"

"Think how expensive that will be," I said. "And can you imagine the time it's going to take to do it?"

"Just go to the store and pick out plenty of silver balls," Rick said.

"Get green, blue, and gold markers. I'll help you write."

To avoid another Christmas argument, I went along with him. I found the decorating items the next day.

"Let's get started," he said, breaking open the packages.

"Can I ask you one question?" I said. "Why are we doing this? Who's going to notice? All these people won't be visiting us this Christmas."

Carefully, Rick began writing names on the ornaments: *Marion, Jennifer, Jon, Jeremy, Gene*—my mother, my sister, my brothers, and my stepfather. Then he answered me. "We're going to pray for every person on our tree this year."

After writing all our family names, we began with our friends, our pastor, and even the country's president. And every night during the Christmas season, instead of watching the endless holiday TV shows, we stood together by the tree and prayed.

Father, thank You. As we pray, Your glory shines around us.

—JULIE GARMON

December 14

*Behold what manner of love the Father hath
bestowed upon us.* —1 John 3:1 (kjv)

The day I walked into that upscale Chattanooga, Tennessee, store, I was eighteen, fresh from my first semester in college, and appropriately worldly. My father and I were there to choose a Christmas gift for my mother.

"Something in cashmere," I was saying to the saleslady as the door to the shop swung open and a waft of cold air introduced a ragged child.

Everyone in the store stopped in mid-sentence. The silence was icy. The little boy, thin even in his too-small sweater, was carrying a box of paper flowers, tied together with cheap ribbon. They looked like corsages. The child was an intrusion. His presence sliced through our shopping comfort like a sharp knife. In the hush, a clerk recovered her bearing and moved toward the boy to shoo him from the store. I swallowed hard, no longer feeling the least bit sophisticated. I didn't think I could bear the little guy's coming humiliation.

And then, my father saved us all.

All six foot, four inches of Daddy were striding toward the boy, his deep, booming voice filling the store. "What have you got there, lad? My, what pretty flowers. I don't guess you'd let me buy one of those for my girl? You would? Well, thanks, son. Thanks, and merry Christmas!"

The store let out its breath, the boy left with a full pocket and a smile, and I walked proudly down a Chattanooga street arm-in-arm with Daddy—wearing the tackiest purple flower you ever saw.

That flower, now carefully framed, hangs on our wall each holiday season. It brings back that wonderful day when my father reached out past proprieties and gave me the real Christmas. And it reminds me that Christmas still waits to be found again in unexpected places.

*Father, You offer us Your best gift,
wrapped in swaddling clothes. Thank You
for loving us this much.*
—Pam Kidd

DECEMBER 15

The Lord is able to give thee much more
than this. —2 CHRONICLES 25:9 (KJV)

We live a four-hour plane ride from most of our family. But neither distance nor time can stop two grandmothers' love. You should see the Christmas gifts waiting for my three-year-old son. Piles of brightly wrapped boxes of every imaginable shape and size tower above him.

One morning another package arrived at our door. I started to complain to my husband. "Don't you think this is a little much?"

Jacob just looked at me and smiled. "What did you say you were thinking of making for breakfast?"

"Hotcakes," I replied, pulling a glow-in-the-dark frog and a toy car from the box with a sigh.

"*Mmm*...," Jacob said, pouring coffee.

As I got out the big metal mixing bowl, the flour, eggs, sifter, and buttermilk, my mind began to drift. My mom was a single parent for a while when I was growing up, and I ended up spending a lot of time with my grandparents. I played all sorts of wonderful games with my grandfather. He possessed a mind and a heart full of stories. He taught me to embrace my imagination. My grandmother had wonderful recipes. She shared with me the basics of cooking that I relied on when I was married. To this day, whenever I make hotcakes, I think of my grandmother lovingly guiding and instructing me. I remember feeling so proud the day she asked if I would make the hotcakes while she set the table. Jacob's simple question reminded me that glow-in-the-dark frogs, stories, toy cars, piles of presents, and hotcakes are all ways for grandparents to say the same thing: "I love you."

Lord, help me to remember that love is a gift.
—AMANDA BOROZINSKI

And the evening and the morning were
the first day. —GENESIS 1:5 (KJV)

My grandmother was a grown woman before she saw her first automobile. That seemed remarkable to me as a child, but what seems more so to me now is that in the six decades that followed that first astonished encounter, she never got over the marvel of the internal combustion engine. "So quiet!" she would exclaim when she was in her eighties. "So fast! Just a little pressure on the pedal and off we go!"

My father kept a sense of wonder, too. For him it was oranges. I would come into the kitchen and see him holding one, unopened, in his hand. He would stroke the textured skin, sniff the tangy rind:

"Marvelous!"

At Christmastime, as the pile of presents grew beneath our tree, he liked to tell about the year when he was nine and drew from his stocking his sole gift—a single orange. "It was the first one I ever had, and I've never forgotten the thrill." By the time I myself was nine, Daddy was buying oranges by the bagful; there was always a bowl of them on the kitchen table. Yet to him they remained an ever-new delight.

As I remember Grandmother and Daddy, I reflect that with everything that touches our lives, there had to be a very first time. Our first pair of shoes. Our first snowfall. The first time we read a book all by ourselves. What if the thrill of first discovery stayed with us? What if we added a new one each day? What if every day we drew a never-before-tasted orange from the toe of our Christmas stocking?

Give me grace in the years ahead always to see
Your world with newly opened eyes.

—ELIZABETH SHERRILL

I will remember the works of the Lord: surely I will remember thy wonders of old. —PSALM 77:11 (KJV)

I don't care what you say," my daughter Anne sighed, placing another ornament on the Christmas tree, "it just doesn't seem like Christmas when the temperature's in the eighties, everyone's running around barefoot, and the garden is full of gardenias and palm trees."

She did have a point. As far as tradition goes, we were in short supply. There were no sleigh bells ringing in glistening, snow-filled lanes, Frosty didn't have a prayer, and I heard something about Santa arriving on a surfboard later in the week. Christmas in Hawaii certainly wasn't your typical winter wonderland. But then I looked around our home and pointed out to my disappointed daughter that we had an opportunity to make some new traditions.

Though she was initially apprehensive, it wasn't long before she was excitedly suggesting some Hawaiian twists to our holiday preparations. We found some dolphin and palm tree cookie cutters, and supplemented our gingerbread stars and wreaths with these island shapes. We gathered ferns to place around the manger scene and made garlands from *kukui* nuts to hang on the tree. Stockings bearing Hawaiian quilt block designs adorned the windowsills, swaying as the trade winds brushed against them. And in place of our old "Merry Christmas" banner, we stretched a new one over the doorway that declared: "*Mele Kalikimaka.*"

When the decorating was completed, we sat by candlelight one evening and listened to Christmas carols recorded by a local choir in the beautiful and ancient language of Hawaii.

"It really does seem like Christmas after all, doesn't it, Mom?" Anne whispered. I nodded and closed my eyes, letting the haunting words and music of "Silent Night" float around me, glad that the beauty and wonder of God's love for us at Christmas knows no boundaries of time or place or language.

Thank You, Lord, for the universal message of love in the gift of Your Son.
—PAMELA KENNEDY

Christ Jesus...being in the form of God...
made himself of no reputation, and took upon him the
form of a servant, and was made in the likeness
of men. —PHILIPPIANS 2:5–7 (KJV)

We are halfway through Week Three of the flu at our house. This week Mary has it, while John recovers and Elizabeth is getting her first coughs. I have had so little sleep lately that the few thoughts that make their way across my weary synapses are mostly about how sleep deprivation is a form of torture.

Last night my feverish baby was unable to sleep except in my arms. Even then, she awoke frequently, crying, "Mama! Mama!" with the high-pitched whine of a toy doll. I held her and rocked her and whispered to her. Sometime in the blur of the early morning hours, I asked God to give me something good to think about.

Nothing dramatic happened. I stroked my baby's hot, smooth skin and idly wondered if Baby Jesus ever had the flu. Surely He must have been sick sometime. Surely His mother nursed Him, held Him, comforted Him. Perhaps she stroked His back to ease the aches. My hand lingered on my own baby's back as I paused to think about Jesus with the delicious, smooth skin of a baby. It seemed amazing. God with baby skin. God you could touch. God you could hold tenderly in your arms. God who is...human.

Mary moved restlessly in my arms. Jesus once weighed twenty-five pounds, too. Odd, isn't it, how in some ways it's harder to understand the smallness of God-made-man than the greatness of His heavenly Father?

Infant Jesus, help me hold You in my heart
as surely as I hold my baby in my arms.

—JULIA ATTAWAY

DECEMBER 19

The God of love and peace will be with you.
—2 CORINTHIANS 13:11 (RSV)

*T*his year, instead of outlining my picture window with Christmas lights, I strung them across it, forming the word *LOVE*. If Jesus' message could be summed up in one word, it would be that one, and I liked knowing that my Christmas lights were passing on His love to neighbors and to all who drove by. But there was one problem. From the inside of the house, the letters were backward! And I wanted, most of all, for my family and friends to experience Christmas love *within* my home.

I thought of taking down the lights and going back to the old outlined window, but I was tired from a day of shopping and errand running in Nebraska winter weather. I was also frustrated and upset with one of my sons, so I just gave up, turned off all but the backward *LOVE* lights, curled up in my recliner with Mother's afghan, and listened to a tape of Christmas carols. When the music ended, I just sat in the silence, sensing Christ's presence, feeling thankful for this prayerful quiet time. And I noticed that, reflected on the glass door of my china hutch, were the lighted letters from my window turned around right!

How subtle is my God to remind me in this beautiful way that, when I bring my frustrations and upsets to Him in prayerful reflection, His love will turn them right again. Then a bonus! John walked in and said, "Hey, Mom! LOVE in the window—cool!"

"But it's *backward* from the inside."

"No it isn't!" John pointed to the mirror opposite the front entry, and there was LOVE again, turned around right. And, you know, I couldn't for the life of me remember why I'd been upset with my son.

Lord Christ, thank You for the transforming grace
of quiet time with You, a grace that can soften my heart
and right my distortions.
—MARILYN MORGAN KING

*We are bound to thank God always for you...and the charity
of every one of you.* —2 THESSALONIANS 1:3 (KJV)

Aunt Minnie, my mother's sister, had been divorced for many years. She earned her living as a salesclerk in a ladies' clothing store. Sometimes sales would be very slow, and the store would have to temporarily lay off some of its employees. When Aunt Minnie was among them, she often lived with us because she had no income. She was a jolly person who loved my two sisters and me, and we were devoted to her, too.

At Christmas, Aunt Minnie always had a gift under the tree for each of us. When she was working, it would be a nice scarf or blouse. In her lean times, the gift was much less expensive, but something would be there.

Today, I have among my table six silver little fruit spoons, which I cherish. A set of these was Aunt Minnie's gift to each of us on the last Christmas of her life. I know how she must have saved carefully for a long time to pay for them. Now each time my family uses them, I wash, dry, and put them away carefully to make certain I never lose one of them—but, more importantly, so I'll always remember the love that made them mine.

*Dear God, how thankful I am for the many ways
in which love can be expressed.*
—DRUE DUKE

*There are different kinds of gifts,
but the same Spirit.* —1 CORINTHIANS 12:4

My family never had a real Christmas tree, though I asked for one every year. "Too many pine needles in the carpet," Dad would say. "The sap will get everywhere. The tree will turn brown and the cats will go crazy," my mother would add. As a result, we've had many unusual Christmas trees through the years.

One of my favorites was Grandma Ellen's antique aluminum tree, with its rotating colored spotlight. Our holiday guests would comment on the shiny silver tree, looking rather puzzled, and ask Mom where she found it. The year we moved, there wasn't room to set up a tree amid all the boxes, so we decorated my dollhouse's Christmas tree. But every year, no matter what the tree looked like, we would gather around it and sing and celebrate Christ's birth.

This Christmas was the first on my own, and I vowed I would have a real tree—a normal tree. My roommate and I piled into her family's station wagon and went to look for the perfect tree. She, a wise and experienced tree-huntress, found it immediately. Once we had it decorated, I sat back and inhaled the pine scent. *At last*! *A real Christmas tree*, I thought. I enjoyed finally having a living room that looked just like a Christmas card. But something was missing. Without my family there to celebrate, it also *felt* like a Christmas card—flat.

Then I visited my parents' home for the holidays, and my Christmas spirit was renewed. Their tree this year? My brother's seven-and-a-half-foot-tall contrabass saxophone strung with twinkle lights and festooned with candy canes and Christmas cards. My brother played carols on the Christmas tree, Dad and I worked on the lights, and Mom fed us cookies and found more ornaments. It might have looked strange from the window, but it was our family tradition, and it was good to be home.

*Father in heaven, thank You for reminding me that,
under any circumstances, celebrating Your Son
always creates a picture-perfect scene.*
—KJERSTIN WILLIAMS

*Not a word failed of any good thing which the Lord
had spoken to the house of Israel. All came
to pass.* —JOSHUA 21:45 (NKJV)

*P*rayer sometimes worries me. Don't get me wrong; I do it every day. It's just that sometimes I wonder about whether I'm doing it right. For example, people tell me all the time that "God told me" to do something. This information is usually communicated with a great deal of delight and confidence. For years, I'd be happy for them, but I couldn't help but wonder how they *knew* God was talking to them. I wanted to believe God actually talked to me, giving me clear-cut direction in my life. But all God's answers to me sounded suspiciously like my own words. Then a Christmas sermon for children gave me a new perspective on the problem.

There was once a farmyard full of geese. The geese constantly fought with each other about one thing or another, and the farmyard was in chaos. God decided to do something about it: He sent a goose from heaven to the farmyard. The goose from heaven explained that the geese must stop fighting and learn to live in peace. They listened and changed, because the goose from heaven spoke in goose words, so they could understand. So when God wanted to teach us, He sent His Son, a little baby who grew up to speak in people-language so we could all understand.

The children were delighted, but they weren't the only ones who learned an important lesson. Why was I so suspicious when God answered me in words I could understand? How else would I get the message?

*Lord, thank You for speaking to me in a language
simple enough for me to comprehend.*
—MARCI ALBORGHETTI

December 23

And the glory of the Lord shone around them. —Luke 2:9

*O*ut on the cold, rocky hillside, the shepherds hadn't a clue. Same old, same old for them—tending somebody else's sheep. They were hirelings, just above the bottom rung of society's ladder. So their wildest dreams couldn't have prepared them for the one-of-a-kind gift about to be hand-delivered to them. Imagine the fearful, wonderful shock of it: the blaze of angelic glory and the news that they were important to God.

It was Christmas Eve. I was ten years old and in my customary place in the front pew. The church was packed and beautiful with draped greenery, poinsettias, and a lighted tree. The program pictured shepherds on the hillside, their faces lifted radiantly to a lighted, angelic sky.

Franklin Groff was first. He was going to sing "O Little Town of Bethlehem." His mother shuffled him to the front. Franklin was about forty years old. His big head towered over a small body. His short legs ended in little feet that seemed to go every which way in their specially made shoes. In addition to his other disabilities, Franklin was blind.

Mrs. Groff sat down, beaming with pride. I wondered why she wasn't ashamed of him. Franklin, his face filled with a happiness I couldn't grasp, said, "Before I sing, I'd like to say that I'm crippled and blind. But I can see the glory of God. It fills me with love."

My literal child's mind spun. To me, the glory of God was the picture of the lighted, angelic sky on my program. Franklin said it was love. Then I looked at Mrs. Groff looking at Franklin and saw the light in her eyes.

Lord, help me to see with Your eyes, the eyes of love.
—Shari Smyth

DECEMBER 24

Know how to give good gifts. —MATTHEW 7:11

This past year, when scattered children and grandchildren came home, my oldest son produced a special treat: our old movies of Christmases past, all of which he'd transferred to videotape.

Then, when the show was over, they all began to discuss other Christmases. "Remember the years we adopted some poor family? How everybody got busy making or buying presents. You and Daddy let us pick out the turkey, and we were so proud, but one time Mallory dropped it in the mud. Sure wish we had a shot of that!"

"Me, too," his sister spoke up. "But what I remember most are those Raggedy Anns and Andys we made. I helped Mother sew them, you younger kids did the stuffing, and she took you along to deliver them. Boy, were you excited!"

"I was selfish," Melanie confessed. "I wanted to keep my Andy. But I was never so thrilled as when I handed him over!"

On and on they went, recalling things I'd almost forgotten. And listening, I suddenly noticed: Not once did they mention anything they got. Not even a first bicycle or special doll. Instead, to my surprise, the memories they treasured most were the fun they had in giving.

"Oh, Mother," Melanie was laughing, "doing things like that was the best part of Christmas."

"It sure was," the others agreed, expressing only one regret: how nice it would be now to see movies of those times, too.

Then several of them expressed it: Yes, but we didn't need them. We were doing something more important. The pictures were already engraved on our hearts.

> *Dear Lord, we weren't perfect parents.*
> *You know how often we failed our children,*
> *but now my heart overflows with thanksgiving.*
> *To realize we did give them something*
> *money couldn't buy or any camera record*
> *—the sheer wonder and joy of giving!*
>
> —MARJORIE HOLMES

December 25

Therefore if any man be in Christ,
he is a new creature. —2 Corinthians 5:17

As a civil engineer with a specialty in water conservation, erosion, and related problems, my husband has spent a lifetime taming the mountain ranges along our California coastline. Building dams, run-off channels, and rainwater catch basins, John is used to kicking a rattlesnake off the trail or clearing out an access with a hatchet.

He is a rugged man. Strong. Silent. Honorable. Given to hard work and a clear, rational response to life that leaves no room for error: "It's either right or wrong. So what's the problem?" But human relations are not that simple or logical, and in the family, John's matter-of-fact manner frequently left a trail of misunderstanding and hurt feelings.

So you can imagine my surprise when John tenderly took our first grandchild Brandon into his arms, sitting down (this face-anything, fearless man) "to have a safer hold." He looked into the baby's small, scrunched-up, just-born face and then turned his eyes to the hills.

"This little fellow has given me a whole *new beginning*," he said quietly in a voice choked in emotion. "He has never seen me angry. Never seen me lose my temper. Never seen me impatient or frustrated. Never seen me walk out of a room saying, 'I don't have to listen to this!' Never seen me slam a door with irritation...and I hope he never will!"

New beginnings from a newborn babe.

Lord Jesus, You came as a newborn Babe to give us all
a new beginning. Thank You that with Your help I, too, can
change, to become more the person You'd like me to be.

—Fay Angus

DECEMBER 26

Christmas day had dawned near perfect. The night before, we had celebrated with my mother and my stepfather Herb. A lovely candlelight communion at our church, a warm supper of vegetable soup, turkey sandwiches, and boiled custard (all prepared in advance by me), then presents and family fun.

The next morning I was up early pulling big pans of cheese grill and sausage casserole and sweetbreads out of the refrigerator. By the time an assortment of guests arrived for our traditional Christmas morning breakfast, the grits were bubbling and the smell of spicy wassail was wafting through the house. Later, as the breakfast wound down, I sat in the living room amid carols and laughter and thought: *Perfect. Now all I have to do is round up the family for a visit to Frances, then come home, set the table, pop dinner in the oven, put the music on, rewarm the wassail...and the day will have been a masterpiece of organization.*

"Mama, can I talk to you?" my daughter Keri beckoned from the hallway. "Charlie"—one of our breakfast guests, recently divorced—"is going over to the Salvation Army to help with the dinner for the homeless. I wish I could go."

"Now, Keri, our day is planned. First Frances, then Herb's family for dinner. I need you here."

A few minutes later I saw Keri standing at the window. A single tear rolled down her cheek. She was watching Charlie walk alone to his car. It didn't take me half a second to toss aside my plans. What difference would a couple of hours make to Frances, our dinner guests, or to me, the perfect planner? "Wait, Charlie!" I called as I ran out the front door. "Wait for Keri!"

Later, when we finally got around to dinner, Keri confided, "You should have seen how happy we made those homeless people, Mama. It was my best Christmas ever."

I had a lot I wanted to tell Keri, but just then there was a lump in my throat about as big as a partridge in a pear tree.

Father, in this season, and all year through,
keep me open to Your invitations.
—PAM KIDD

His work is perfect. —DEUTERONOMY 32:4 (KJV)

I pride myself on having a very clear awareness of my failings. I keep a mental list under the heading "Fix These." I also know what I'm good at, and this much smaller list falls under the heading "Acceptable Behavior." I've filed "Good Organizer" in the "Acceptable Behavior" column, and I use my almost-daily walking time to hone this skill.

This past Sunday my husband Charlie accompanied me on my walk. At six feet, four inches tall, he's got quite a leg-span advantage over me, but he had to pay attention to match my determined stride. Where he might have meandered, I sped along, dragging him with me. As we passed ice-covered inlets, snow-brushed marshes, deserted winter beaches, and warmly lit houses, I plunged ahead with my agenda, talking nonstop about our budget. How much will our vacation cost? Will we have enough saved by then? Do we have enough frequent-flyer miles for a free ticket? What about two free tickets? Has he made the reservations yet?

Suddenly, Charlie interrupted me. "Marc, look at the Canada geese on the ice!"

Without even glancing to where he was gesturing, I snapped, "Are you even listening to me?"

Charlie gently took me by the shoulders and turned me toward the cove. I gasped in surprise: there were more than a hundred Canada geese waddling around on top of the ice as if waiting for the sun to melt it and restore order in their lives.

I put my arms around Charlie. When we got home, I would have to make a few changes to my "Acceptable Behavior" list.

Lord, You've given us so much!
Open my senses to Your many gifts.
—MARCI ALBORGHETTI

DECEMBER 28

Pray for one another that ye may be healed.
—JAMES 5:16 (KJV)

*I*n January, as I was sorting through the Christmas cards I'd received, I found myself with a dilemma I have each year: what to do with the snapshots of families, friends' children and grandchildren, and other loved ones tucked inside the cards. I delight in receiving the photos, but after the holidays I don't know what to do with them.

This year, I had an inspiration for keeping the gift alive. I decided to use them as bookmarks. In addition to marking my stopping place, I also use the pictures to mark special pages I want to come back to later. Each evening before I start to read, I look at the picture that is marking my place and pray special blessings upon that person. After finishing the book, I go back and pray again for all those people whose photos are marking special passages. Then I leave them in the book, to be found sometime later.

During the past week I've been rereading a book I first read in February, so I've prayed another time for my nephew David and his family, for the cute little granddaughters of my high school friend Jeri, even for "Poor George," the fluffy white dog of Janelle in California. I feel a special bonding now with friends' children I've never met, a renewed closeness to old friends I haven't seen in years, a personal relationship with readers I may never meet. It has enriched my prayer life in a deep way, and it's going to become a tradition with me!

Thank You, God, for new ways to pray
for lives that touch mine.
—MARILYN MORGAN KING

December 29

*Give me time to tell this new generation
(and their children too) about all your mighty miracles.*
—Psalm 71:18 (TLB)

*W*hen my dad, brother, sister, and I bought a small vacation condo in Florida, I met many of the residents in the community, mostly snowbirds from the North, at the complex's large outdoor swimming pool. I discovered that many of them define their lives by their children's and grandchildren's accomplishments, and that many of them are wrapped up in their aches and pains.

After my first visit to the condo, I went home to Wisconsin determined to grow older with gusto. I even mentioned it to my women's group, SWILL (the Southeastern Wisconsin Interesting Ladies League). "When we go around the room to discuss whatever is on our minds, let's try not to focus so much on our children, grandchildren, or health problems," I suggested.

Rosemary, a delightful woman in her seventies, giggled. "You'd love my FOSSILS group, Pat," she beamed. "FOSSILS stands for Friends over Seventy Seasoned in Life Society. Just like SWILL, our FOSSILS group has no dues, agenda, committees, minutes, rules, food worries, dress code, or bylaws. We just have stimulating discussions. And we've agreed to avoid talking about our husbands, children, grandchildren, aches, pains, and doctors."

Rosemary said her FOSSILS discussions have included how the older generation can help stop child abuse; how World War II compares with the war on terrorism; and why we provide so many activities for children these days instead of letting them have time just to goof off and use their own imaginations to find creative play.

Thanks to Rosemary, as I get closer to my sixties, I'm inspired to keep finding new, interesting topics of conversation with my old tried-and-true friends up North, as well as my new, somewhat older ones in Florida.

*heavenly Father, thank You for the books, classes,
workshops, and groups of friends that help keep my mind
active and my life punctuated with pizzazz.*
—Patricia Lorenz

*Though our bodies are dying, our inner strength in the Lord
is growing every day.* —2 CORINTHIANS 4:16 (TLB)

I have a fear of growing old and becoming so set in my ways that I no longer hear God's continuing call to change and grow. So when I see an older person still responding to His nudges, I tuck away the memory in my treasure chest of "Examples to Grow Toward." Recently, I included this one from Eva, my eighty-three-year-old mother-in-law.

As we prepared to leave her house for the hour-long drive home a few Sundays ago, she began packing some little jars of homemade jelly into a box for us.

"Mamma, do you have any more of your bread-and-butter pickles?" my twenty-year-old daughter Lindsay asked hopefully.

Mamma hesitated a moment, and then answered kind of slowly. "No...I guess I'll just have to make more of them next year."

We went on our way, but a few days later, a package arrived in the mail, neatly addressed to Lindsay. Inside, this little note was wrapped around a jar of pickles:

Dear Lindsay,

Upon reflection, I realize I flubbed. I had a jar of pickles left when I told you I didn't. So dear Lindsay, and dear Lord, please forgive me.

Your ever loving Mamma

Lindsay had tears in her eyes as she showed me the note. As I read it, I pictured the possible scenario: Eva was down to her last jar of pickles on the shelf. Maybe she planned to share it with friends or maybe because she lived through the Depression the last jar of *anything* symbolized security. The details hardly mattered, but the pattern mattered greatly. Upon reflection, Eva went to the trouble of boxing and wrapping this jar and getting it to the post office.

She gave her granddaughter something more precious than a jar of pickles. She gave her an example to grow toward. And she gave me one, too.

*Father, thank You for the example of older people
who aren't afraid to admit mistakes
or to make changes in their lives.*
—CAROL KUYKENDALL

DECEMBER 31

I can do all things through Christ.
—PHILIPPIANS 4:13 (KJV)

I have an idea for a new creative project that I've been thinking about for months. "I'm going to try it one of these days," I keep telling myself. But it doesn't get done. In fact, it doesn't even get started! Lying in bed last night, in the silence that's filled with the mystery of God, I asked why. Immediately, one word flashed through my mind. *Fear*. Of course! Fear of failure. How many of my best ideas are buried beneath that canopy!

This morning, some words in an article I was reading suddenly sprouted wings. They were spoken by that wonderfully creative singer, dancer, poet, writer, and storyteller Maya Angelou. She said, "I know that there is no place that God is not. And by knowing that, I can dare things. I can dare to succeed because I can dare to fail."

Oh! I'm going to place those words over my desk, on my bathroom mirror, refrigerator door, on my pillow, wherever I'll see them many times a day. This morning, as soon as these thoughts are printed out, I will begin my new creative project. If I fail, I fall only into the arms of the Spirit of infinite creativity, ready for a new beginning!

> *With Your great creative Spirit, Lord, I can risk, I can dare,*
> *I can become all You would have me be!*
> —MARILYN MORGAN KING

A Note from the Editors

Guideposts, a nonprofit organization, touches millions of lives every day through products and services that inspire, encourage, and uplift. Our magazines, books, prayer network, and outreach programs help people connect their faith-filled values to their daily lives. To learn more, visit Guideposts.org or GuidepostsFoundation.org.